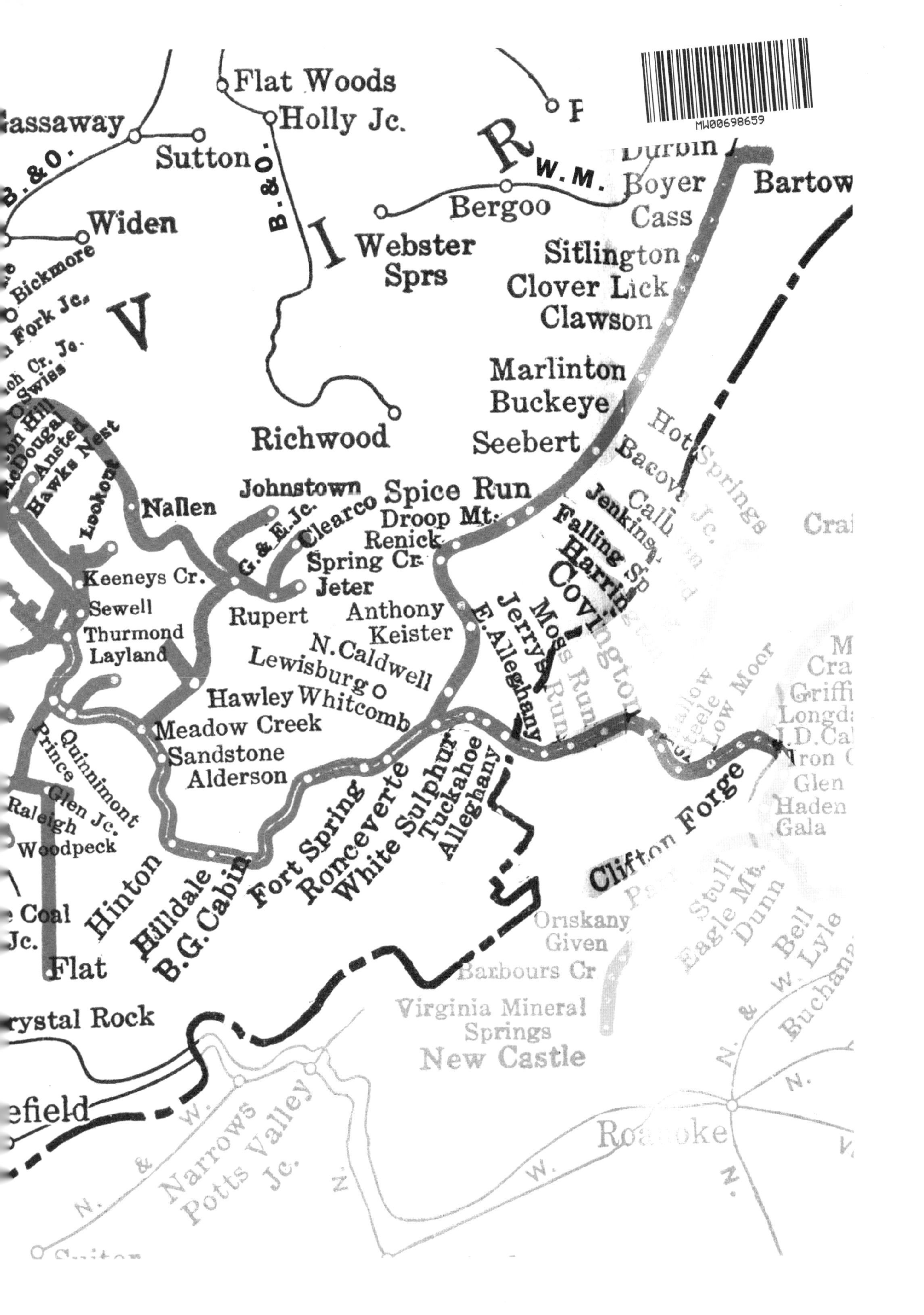

Flat Woods
Holly Jc.
Sutton
B.&O.
B.&O.
Widen
Bickmore
V
I
R
W.M.
Durbin
Boyer
Bartow
Cass
Bergoo
Webster
Sprs
Sitlington
Clover Lick
Clawson
Marlinton
Buckeye
Seebert
Richwood
Hot Springs
Johnstown
Spice Run
Droop Mt.
Clearco
G.&E.Jc.
Renick
Spring Cr.
Jeter
Nallen
Lookout
Hawks Nest
Ansted
Keeneys Cr.
Sewell
Thurmond
Layland
Rupert
Anthony
Keister
N.Caldwell
Lewisburg
Hawley
Whitcomb
Meadow Creek
Sandstone
Alderson
Jenkins
Covington
Jerrys Run
E.Alleghany
Quinnimont
Prince
Glen Jc.
Raleigh
Woodpeck
Hinton
Hilldale
B.G.Cabin
Fort Spring
Ronceverte
White Sulphur
Tuckahoe
Alleghany
Clifton Forge
Low Moor
Steele
Glen
Haden
Gala
Oriskany
Given
Barbours Cr
Stull
Eagle Mt.
Dunn
Bell
Lyle
Virginia Mineral
Springs
New Castle
Flat
Coal
Narrows
Potts Valley
Jc.
N. & W.

West Virginia Railroads
Volume 2: Chesapeake & Ohio

Thomas W. Dixon, Jr.

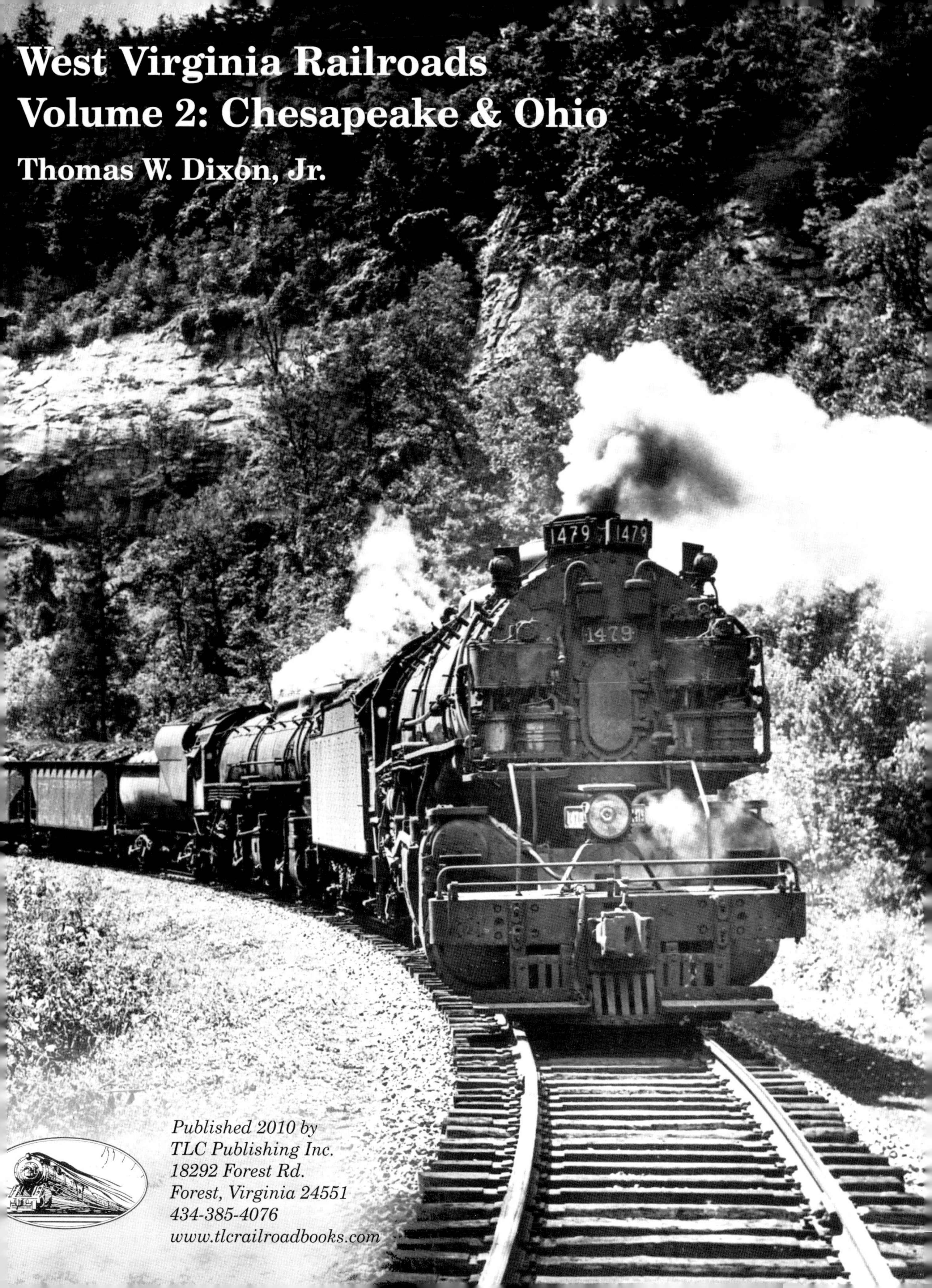

Published 2010 by
TLC Publishing Inc.
18292 Forest Rd.
Forest, Virginia 24551
434-385-4076
www.tlcrailroadbooks.com

© Copyrignt 2010 TLC Publishing, Inc.
All Rights Reserved
No part of this book may be reproduced without
written permission of the publisher, except for
breif excertps used in reviews, etc.

ISBN 9780939487950

Library of Congress Control Number 2010930021

Digital Photo Production, Design, and Layout
by
Karen Parker

Printed in the U.S.A. by
Walsworth Printing Company, Marceline, Mo.

Front Cover: H-8 No. 1643 exiting Big Bend Tunnel with an eastbound coal train at Talcott, W.Va. in September, 1949. (photo by and courtesy of Charles H. Kerrigan, colorized by Karen Parker)

Title Page: In October, 1945 H-6 2-6-6-2 No. 1479 doubleheading with an H-4 2-6-6-2 leads a coal train down the Piney Creek Sub-Division to the junction with the main line at Prince and the marshalling yard at Quinnimont, from where its loads of coal will be sent either east to Newport News or west toward Russell, Ky. (C&O Railway photo, C&OHS Collection, Image No. CSPR-304)

Facing Page: H-5 2-6-6-2 Nos. 1527 and 1520 simmer on a cold winter day in 1946 at the engine terminal at Peach Creek, W.Va. Both will soon be dispatched on mine runs up the many branches radiating from this major coal assembly point. (C&O Railway photo, C&OHS Collection, Image No. CSPR-231)

Back Cover Top: RSD-12s No. 6704 and 6701 are passing FD Cabin at Logan, W.Va. in January, 1961. (Gene Huddleston photo, C&OHS Collection)

Back Cover Center: C&O Train No. 3, the Fast Flying Virginian*, pauses at Kenova, W. Va. Union Station in 1962 with E8 No. 4007 in the lead. (Gene Huddleston photo, C&OHS Collection)*

Back Cover Bottom: K-4 Kanawha (2-8-4) type No. 2709 running light, with a caboose, passes the depot at Hinton, W.Va. in the early 1950s. (Bob's Photo Collection)

Table of Contents

Foreword

This is the second in a series of books that details the major railroads that operated in the state of West Virginia. The book *West Virginia Railroads - Railroading in the Mountain State*, published in 2009, was an overview and introduction to the railroads that operated in West Virginia, with a short historic, photographic, and map treatment of each. Follow-on books such as this build from that basic overview with more photos, maps, and details.

This treatment of the C&O is just one in a fairly long line of books that cover C&O operations in West Virginia, which include the following:

Chesapeake & Ohio in the Coal Fields (Dixon, C&O Hist. Society, 1999),

Chesapeake & Ohio in the Coal Fields of West Virginia and Kentucky (Dixon, C&OHS, 2006),

Cheaspeake & Ohio Coal and Color (Huddleston, Joseph, and Young, C&OHS, 1997)

Chesapeake & Ohio in West Virginia, Photos 1940-1960 (Dixon, C&OHS, 2005),

Chesapeake and Ohio Main Lines and Mine Runs in West Virginia (Dixon, Carstens Publications, 1988),

Chesapeake & Ohio Alleghany Subdivision (Dixon - C&OHS, 1986),

Riding That New River Train (E. L. Huddleston, C&OHS, 1989),

Chesapeake & Ohio Huntington Division (Sprakmon, C&OHS, 1983).

The three books on the coal fields cover the coal-specific operations fairly thoroughly, with a sampling of many branches, tipples, yards, coal camp towns, motive power, etc. The photo book is an east-to-west tour of the line photographically. The *Alleghany Subdivision* and *Riding That New River Train* give detailed historical and operational background on two of the three major mainline subdivisions that constitute the C&O in West Virginia, while the *Huntington Division* is more of a pamphlet with some general information and photos on the mainline Kanawha Subdivision and some of the coal branches from it. *Main Lines and Mine Runs* is another photo album with extended captions.

With this much coverage, what is now needed in addition to a detailed book on the Kanawha Subdivision (mainline and branches west of Handley)? With this question in mind, the present book was formulated as a general historical background piece fully illustrated with good photos from all areas of the C&O in West Virginia. But also, it has an emphasis on maps, yard and track diagrams, plats, station lists, and statistical data that are aimed at making it more of a "Gazetteer," to which the reader may refer for specific information. It is also hoped that it will be a readable book that will explain how C&O operated in West Virginia, especially in the era from World War II to the early diesel era, a period in which there is much interest.

The interest in the 1945-1965 era because it was time of transition, when the railways stopped being the dominant intercity carriers, yielding ever more to highway and air travel and competition from barges on navigable rivers. It was also the era when steam locomotives reached the pinnacle of their development and then suddenly were wiped away by diesel-electric technology. It was the time when passenger trains, and all that they meant to ordinary people, reached a high state of efficiency and then quickly declined. Concomitant with these changes were the elimination and consolidation of stations, yards, and facilities, the abandonment of no longer profitable branches, and the shift of railroads from common carriage to bulk-materials transport. This was especially so in West Virginia, where coal was (and is) the major commodity that railroads transported then and now.

This book would not have been possible without the close cooperation of the C&O Historical Society, its directors, officers, and staff, as well as others who helped materially. The design and layout work by Karen Parker was also key in bringing the book to successful conclusion, as was the expert advice, photography, and memories of Gene Huddleston.

This author has studied the C&O as a life's hobby and business since 1966, founded the C&O Historical Society in 1969, and has written numerous books and articles about the C&O including several of those cited above that deal with West Virginia subjects.

Thomas W. Dixon, Jr.
Lynchburg, Virginia
Summer, 2010

The Chesapeake & Ohio (C&O) traces its lineage from the Louisa Railroad, chartered in 1836 to build a line in Louisa County, Virginia, to take farm products to market. It expanded so that by 1850 it had reached Richmond to the southeast and Charlottesville to the northwest of its original line. With designs on further expansion, its name was changed to "Virginia Central" in that year.

By 1854 the line had crossed the Blue Ridge (with help from the Commonwealth of Virginia through the state-financed Blue Ridge Railroad) and Shenandoah ranges and had reached the foot of the Alleghany range. Meanwhile, the Virginia General Assembly had incorporated anther state-backed line to build from the Virginia Central's endpoint at Covington on to the Ohio River, under the name Covington & Ohio Railroad. Work was commenced, but soon halted because of the War Between the States. After the war and West Virginia's statehood, the Virginia Central and the Covington & Ohio (the latter contained mainly within the new state), were combined under the new name Chesapeake & Ohio. The C&O attracted financial backing from Collis P. Huntington, who was at the time (1869) just finishing his work on the Central Pacific portion of the Transcontinental Railroad. His intent was to use C&O as an eastern link to a "true transcontinental" under the control of one company or person (him).

In the summer of 1869 the C&O built across Alleghany (spelled with an "a" in this region) summit and reached White Sulphur Springs, West Virginia, which had been an important destination for passengers since the stage-coach days of the 1820s. From then onward White Sulphur Springs would be an important factor in C&O passenger service, and in later days, passengers were brought in from the great Northeastern cities so that they could "take the waters," in the European spa style. As late as the 1960s passenger traffic, particularly from the Northeastern cities, to White Sulphur Springs' Greenbrier Hotel (owned by C&O after 1910) was a very important element in C&O's passenger operations.

From 1869 through the spring of 1873, C&O's line was built across the state, reaching the Ohio River at the new city of Huntington, established by and named for C. P. Huntington. In the 1870s C&O began shipping coal eastward to Richmond and points east, and set a pattern that it would follow down to the present day. Because it had no good railroad connection at Huntington, its traffic on to Cincinnati was by steamboat. By 1881 a connection through railroads in Kentucky also controlled by Mr. Huntington helped it reach Louisville and Cincinnati as well, in a round-about way. Finally, in 1888 the line down the south (Kentucky) side of the Ohio River was built and an impressive bridge took C&O into the Queen City.

Huntington held control of the C&O throughout this period and for a couple of years actually achieved his true transcontinental with C&O as its eastern link, but in 1889 C&O fell into hands of the Vanderbilts. Under its new leadership C&O was completely rebuilt and upgraded through the 1890s, at the very time that coal was becoming its most important traffic. It also started up an important and highly advertised through passenger service. Its trains originated in New York and traveled over the Pennsylvania Railroad to Washington, over the predecessor of the Southern Railway line to Charlottesville and thence over the C&O through Virginia, West Virginia, and Kentucky, to Cincinnati where through connections were available over the Vanderbilt's Big Four Railroad to St. Louis, Indianapolis, and Chicago.

While using its passenger service to publicize itself, C&O's management worked hard to provide for the real wealth of the line by building lines to serve the coal mines that were opening throughout the southern West Virginia and eastern Kentucky coal fields. With a good grade over the Alleghany range, and a water-level down-grade line to the sea at Newport News (opposite Norfolk on Hampton Roads Harbor), which it acquired in 1890, C&O coal could be shipped by water to the northeastern cities at rates that competed with coal produced in Pennsylvania.

C&O's first coal came from mines located on or near its early mainline through the New River gorge west of Hinton and along the Kanawha River. In fact, coal had been mined in the Kanawha Valley since the 1790s, and that region of what would become West Virginia was developed because of the salt that could be recovered from saline wells along the river. The salt brine had to be boiled so as to produce the "alum salt" that was a key in those days to the preservation of food. Coal was used in the salt furnaces after wood became scarce, but before long it was also transported by boat or barge down the Kanawha and the Ohio to Cincinnati. Therefore, by the time that C&O arrived in the valley the coal industry was already established.

Coal was recognized to exist in good quantities along the New River gorge as well, and the first mines were opened near the station of Quinnimont. Soon after the C&O was opened to traffic a large iron furnace was established at Quinnimont so as to take advantage of the nearby coal reserves for making coke to be used in the iron-making process. The ore was brought in from western Virginia by the C&O and the finished product taken out by rail. Although the iron industry did not continue to develop, the coking of coal for use in steel making became more important in the following decades as it was shipped to the great industrial centers.

All this built a foundation for the coal business on the C&O, and by the early 1890s the first branch lines were being built away from the mainline to reach the vast reserves of coal lying under the nearby countryside.

The first ceremonial train across the C&O between Huntington and Richmond in 1873 arrived at the latter city with a car of West Virginia coal. It was the first of a flood that was soon enough released. Through the rest of 1873 C&O handled 22,813 tons of West Virginia coal, and over 34,000 the following year. By 1880 this had reached 333,829 tons and over a million by 1887. This again doubled by 1895 and as new branches made many more rich seams available for mining in the following two decades, the quantities multiplied exponentially. Most C&O coal was from

The C&O Mainline in West Virginia. This map was prepared as part of the Congressionally mandated valuation of the railroads in 1916. The Valuation data was used by C&O as the basis of all its engineering work from that time forward to the present. As can be seen the main line consisted of 206.6 miles from Tuckahoe on the east to the Big Sandy Bridge on the west. (TLC Collection)

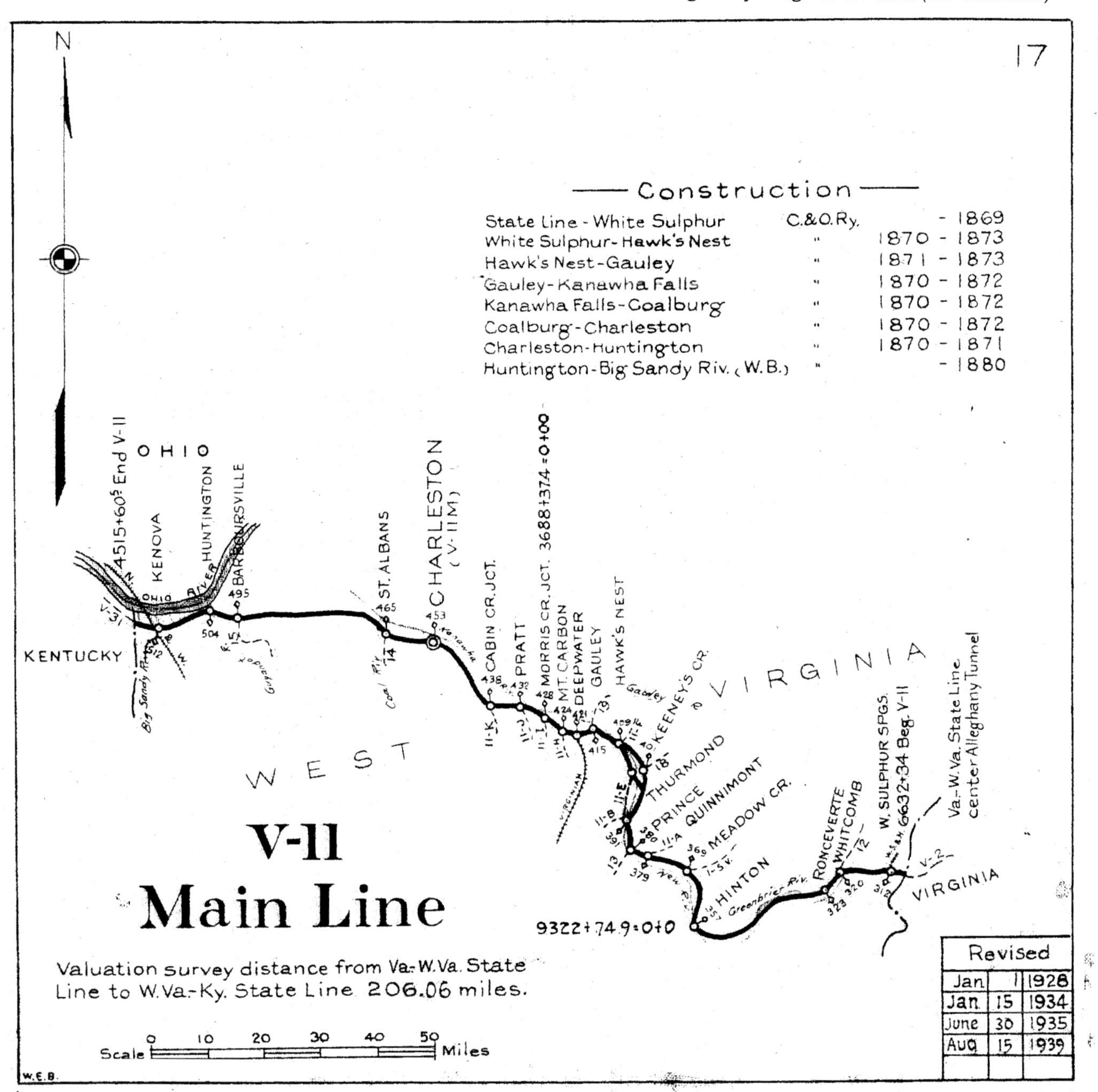

West Virginia until just after 1900, when the rich Big Sandy field in eastern Kentucky came into production.

During the era 1895-1920 C&O built scores of coal branches in West Virginia and eastern Kentucky. Since after 1910 C&O had a line available to the west via the Hocking Valley Railway of Ohio (which it controlled), it began to ship as much coal west as east. Norfolk & Western entered the southern West Virginia coal fields about a decade after C&O, and in this same era was doing the same thing as C&O, building coal branches that were providing a flood of coal east to Hampton Roads (Norfolk) and west to Great Lakes shipping. C&O and N&W became and remained actual competitors in the coal markets. The competition eastward was further complicated by the arrival of the Virginian Railway in 1909, taking coal from the same region to Norfolk as well.

C&O's principal coal districts in West Virginia began just west of Hinton. At Meadow Creek the Nicholas, Fayette & Greenbrier Railroad (NF&G) joined the main line. It was jointly owned and operated by the C&O and the New York Central (NYC). C&O extracted coal from mines closest to its line while NYC served mines more westerly along the line connecting with its Gauley Branch out of Gauley Bridge. NYC itself entered the state at Point Pleasant from its Ohio lines, and extended a line up the Kanawha River to Charleston and Gauley Bridge. C&O served 24 mines on the NF&G in the Greenbrier field (in Greenbrier, Nicholas, and Fayette counties) according to its 1950 coal mine directory. C&O also served the giant Meadow River Lumber Company sawmill at Rainelle (where the NF&G headquarters, engine terminal and marshalling yard were located). Predecessors of the NF&G were logging roads built by Meadow River Lumber Company and later purchased by C&O, then consolidated with other lines to form the joint NF&G Railroad in the late 1920-early 1930s. Meadow River log trains headed for the woods were run over NF&G tracks to get to their various logging branches.

The New River coal field was accessed by branches connecting with the C&O main line at Prince and Thurmond, and comprised numerous branches that served (in 1950) 41 active mines of various capacities. Attached to the field, but separated by C&O in its accounting was the Winding Gulf Field, which had 14 active mines in 1954, of which several were joint mines served by both C&O and Virginian. Further west along the C&O main line were the Coal River and Kanawha Fields. Branches serving the Kanawha Field connected with the main line at Mt. Carbon, Morris Creek, Pratt, and Cabin Creek Junction. There were (in 1950) 22 active mines in this field.

West of Charleston, along the Kanawha, was the rich Coal River Field, connecting with the main line at St. Albans, and serving 27 active mines. The westernmost C&O coal region in West Virginia was the Logan Field, which connected with the mainline at Barboursville, just a few miles east of Huntington. It had 47 active mines in 1950. C&O also served coal fields in Kentucky and in Ohio after the 1930 merger of the Hocking Valley. C&O had more mines and produced more coal from its West Virginia branches than from its other operations

In the early 1920s C&O came within the control of the Van Sweringen brothers, financial wizards who assembled a huge railroad empire in the 1920s based in Cleveland and originally centered on their first property, the Nickel Plate Road (New York, Chicago & St. Louis Railroad). C&O soon became the keystone of their empire which included Erie, Pere Marquette, Hocking Valley, C&O, and Nickel Plate as well as part ownership in several other railroads. This is why some of C&O's highest executive offices were moved from Richmond to Cleveland, a city not even on a C&O line. However, this association with the other lines did improve C&O's traffic position, especially in the Midwest.

By the 1940s C&O was the largest originator of bituminous coal in the United States (and the world), followed closely by N&W, while B&O and Virginian ran third and fourth in coal transported from West Virginia.

C&O used its prodigious income from coal to rebuild and upgrade its physical plant over the years, so that by the 1930s it had one of the most solidly built and best maintained railroads in the country, operating with the largest and most modern of locomotives and cars.

It used some of the largest and most powerful locomotives in service anywhere for hauling its heavy coal trains, using the Mallet compound articulated type extensively, as well as modern "Super Power" locomotives not only for its coal trains but for its best passenger trains and through freights. C&O had a wide variety of steam locomotive types, many of which were restricted to particular regions of the railway. West Virginia, of course, was the home of many of the biggest and strongest of C&O's locomotives. Hauling its eastbound coal C&O had a distinct advantage over the other lines because its eastbound crossing of the Alleghany range was the easiest. Because of this it could haul heavier loads with less motive power than the other lines, all of which suffered grades three-to-four times steeper.

C&O was late to dieselize, not wanting to change from coal as fuel since it was actively engaged in trying to convince customers that they should stick with coal instead of going to oil or natural gas. As late as 1949 it was receiving new steam locomotives, and in fact its ten H-6 class 2-6-6-2 type delivered in September 1949 comprised the very last steam locomotives built commercially for an American railroad. Only N&W had later locomotives, which it built at its own Roanoke Shops through mid-1952.

When C&O finally decided that the economics of the diesel were just too great ignore, it dieselized rapidly. Getting its first diesels in 1949 it was 80% diesel-operated by 1954, and after a brief respite in 1955-56 when some steam was recalled because of increased traffic, all steam was gone by late August 1956. A few miles to the south, N&W remained all steam until 1955 and kept some of its most powerful steam locomotives operating in the West Virginia coal fields until 1960, the last Class I American railroad to fully dieselize.

C&O's coal business remained strong and in 1958 when it went looking for a merger partner, it began discussions with B&O. This resulted in C&O's control through stock ownership of B&O in 1963. In the following decade the two lines gradually amalgamated their operations and they essentially merged in 1972 into Chessie System Railroads, which Western Maryland joined in 1975. Therefore, by this time the largest railroad operator in West Virginia was C&O/B&O (later Chessie System and now CSX).

C&O also had its major locomotive repair shop in West Virginia at Huntington, which was at about the center of its system. The huge facility was gradually upgraded and expanded so that it became one of the largest steam locomotive repair facilities in the eastern U. S. This shop was later converted to diesel repair and remains today as one of three shop facilities on the huge CSX system. The railroad's coal department and finance department were also headquartered at Huntington in the 1920-1960s era, as well as its engineering department from 1960 until the mid-1980s. It was the only one of West Virginia's major railroads to have a large part of its operational headquarters and maintenance shops within the state's borders.

The city of Huntington itself owes its existence to the coming of the C&O in the early 1870s when C&O president C. P. Huntington bought the land on which the city is situated, and sold it off to help finance his railroad venture. Because of its good location on railroads and waterways, Huntington became an industrial center of considerable importance and one of West Virginia's largest cities. C&O's presence was always the key to the city's development.

C&O also had major divisional terminals at Hinton and Handley, and many smaller yards and engine servicing facilities in the coal fields.

A great tradition of folk themes centered on the C&O, which included the John Henry legend from big Bend Tunnel, near Hinton.

As noted before, White Sulphur Springs was a center for much of C&O's most lucrative passenger business. When M. E. Ingalls became president of the C&O in 1889, he wanted to buy the hotel because it appealed to him, but it was not available, therefore he moved on to Virginia's Hot Springs, where he built the fabulous Homestead Hotel. Later, in 1910, C&O management was able to acquire the White Sulphur Springs property and built the new Greenbrier Hotel. With its heritage, it became one of the great resorts of the eastern U.S. The bulk of its clientele came from the great Eastern cities, and they came via C&O's trains. Regular Pullman sleeping car lines were established which delivered and picked up cars at White Sulphur Springs on a regular basis, and throughout the years, but most especially in the era 1920-1969, large numbers of special movements of cars came to and from the hotel from both east and west, sometimes added to regular trains, and sometimes as a special or even groups of special trains. There was no other location in West Virginia that had the passenger attraction of the Greenbrier, and C&O used it not only to generate that extra business, but as part of its publicity about itself. The Greenbrier was C&O's "crown jewel." CSX retained the hotel until 2008.

The Chesapeake & Ohio entered West Virginia from Virginia mid-way through Alleghany* Tunnel, the bore which took C&O's mainline Alleghany Subdivision under the mountain ridge of that name, which also serves as the Virginia/West Virginia border.

Since railways don't usually conform to political boundaries, they are not always neatly compartmentalized as we are doing in this book, so a little background is necessary at the outset.

From reading the overall background history in the introduction you'll understand the geographical context of the whole C&O and the key role that West Virginia played in it, both from the standpoint of historical development, and from the point of view that West Virginia always supplied the C&O's strength because of its coal. However, we don't want to say simply that the C&O came into West Virginia through Alleghany Tunnel and drop it at that. Where was the line coming from?

The answer is that the east-west mainline entering West Virginia originated at the large yard, terminal point, and shop area at Clifton Forge, Virginia, about 30 miles east of the Alleghany summit. Clifton Forge was the junction point for three major segments of the C&O's line. The first of these was the C&O's original 1850s mainline, called the Mountain Subdivision by the railway. This line came across the Blue Ridge and North Mountain regions from Charlottesville. The second line from the east which entered Clifton Forge came from Richmond following the James River through Lynchburg. It was this line, acquired in 1890, that C&O used (and CSX uses today) for transport of coal to Tidewater shipping. The third line was, of course, the line that came in from the west via the Alleghany crossing.

In 1889 C&O installed a major shop complex here and Clifton Forge served as C&O's second most important shop, subordinate only in size and work to the Huntington, West Virginia, shops.

When coal came out of West Virginia bound for the Northeastern U. S. or foreign export, it was consolidated and classified at Clifton Forge, so Clifton Forge really was the gateway for West Virginia coal in the east. West of Clifton Forge the Alleghany subdivision ran 29 miles to the town of Alleghany at the top of the steep grade, thence through the tunnel and on to Hinton, the next major mainline division point and yard 47 miles west. Thus the total length of the Alleghany Subdivision was 77.8 miles, of which 47.8 were in West Virginia. The management of this line was out of Clifton Forge, whereas the manage-

* - Alleghany is spelled with an "a" instead of the more common "e" in this region of Virginia. The town, county, and mountain are all so spelled, and C&O spelled its subdivision name this way as well. When the 2-6-6-6 locomotives were developed in 1941 largely for use here, the name of the type was spelled "Allegheny," apparently an error by the Advisory Mechanical Committee in Cleveland.

A condensed profile of the Alleghany Subdivision well illustrates the topography over which the line operated. Eastbound was the important grade since that is the direction that all West Virginia coal had to move in the direction of Tidewater. As can be seen, the grade ascends steadily out of Hinton, with the most important portion east of Ronceverte. The top of the grade was actually in Virginia just east of the portals of Alleghany Tunnel. The average of 0.56 % grade was the easiest of any major railroad crossing the Appalachian chain and markedly better than the other West Virginia coal haulers (B&O, WM, N&W and Virginian). (From C&O condensed profile drawing).

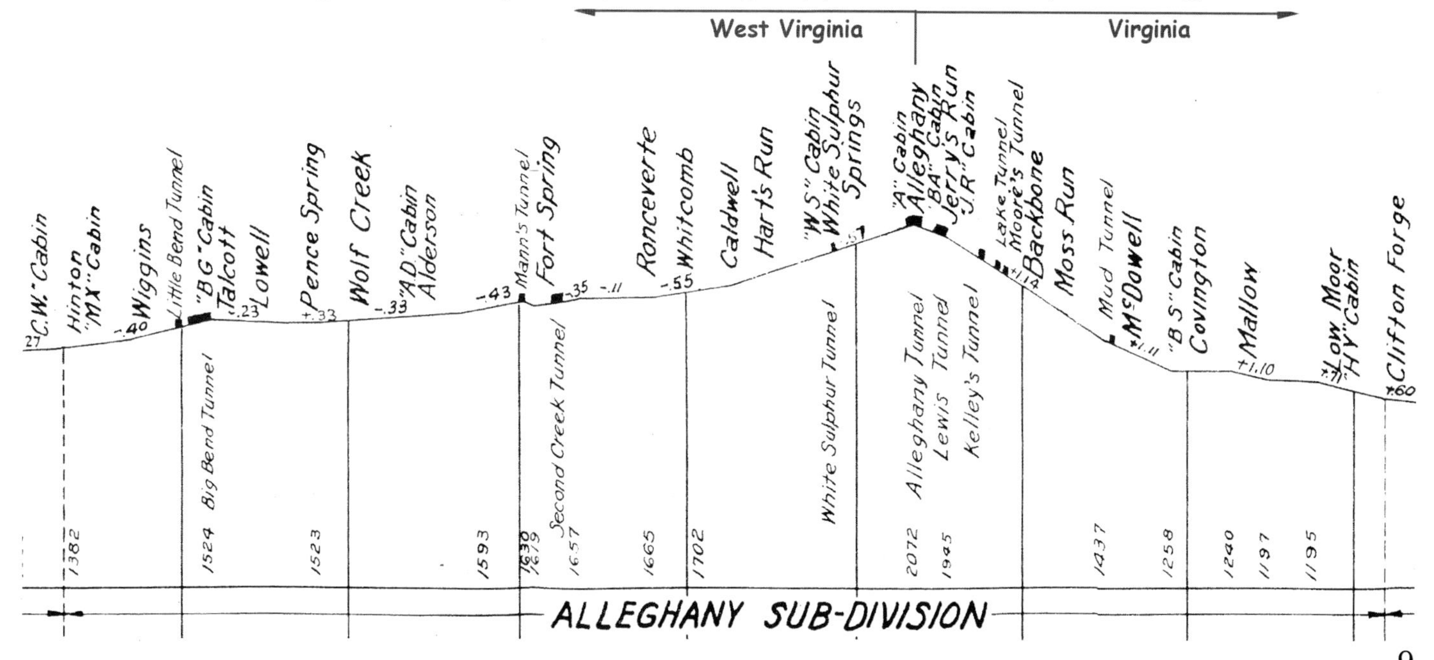

Dist. from Ft. Monroe	Tel. Calls	Station No.	Code No.	STATIONS
277.5	*F	277	0577	④**Clifton Forge**----Va
278.1		278		†H. Y. Cabin------Va
281.2		281	0730	Low Moor--------Va
286.6		287	0734	†Mallow----------Va
289.7	CD	290	0738	②④**Covington**-----Va
291.2	*BS	291		††B. S. Cabin-----Va
292.1		292	0782	‡Boys Home------Va
293.4		293	0784	McDowell--------Va
295.3		295	0786	Callaghan--------Va
297.7		298	0788	Moss Run--------Va
300.2		300	0790	Backbone--------Va
304.2		304	0792	Jerry's Run------Va
306.4	*A	306	0797	④**Alleghany**-------Va
308.0		308	1000	Tuckahoe-----W Va
311.9	*WS	312	1002	④**White Sulphur Springs**------W Va
			1003	" Hotel-----------
315.5		315	1008	Hart's Run----W Va
317.3		317	1010	Caldwell------W Va
319.8		320	1012	②†Whitcomb---W Va
322.8	*RV	323	1014	④**Ronceverte**---W Va
326.5		326	1018	†Rockland-----W Va
329.0		329	1022	④**Fort Spring**---W Va
330.1		330	1024	†Snow Flake----W Va
330.8		331	1026	‡Frazier--------W Va
335.8		336	1030	④**Alderson**-----W Va
336.4	*AD	336½		††A D. Cabin---W Va
337.4		337	1032	†Glenray-------W Va
339.4		339	1034	Wolf Creek----W Va
341.5		341	1036	†Riffe----------W Va
343.4		343	1038	Pence Spring--W Va
345.8		345	1040	Lowell--------W Va
347.2		347	1042	Talcott--------W Va
349.5	*MW	350	1046	Hilldale-------W Va
352.6		353	1049	Wiggins-------W Va
355.3	*MX	355		M. X. Cabin--W Va

This listing of stations shows the Alleghany Subdivision between Clifton Forge, Virginia, and Hinton, West Virginia, Milepost 277.5 to Milepost 355.3, at the west end of Hinton yard, a total of 77.8 miles, of which 47.3 miles are in West Virginia (between Tuckahoe and MX Cabin). The list shows the milepost, the station telegraphic call letters and station number as well as indication of special situations at each station. This was taken from the C&O Agents, Officers, Stations, Etc. list of August 1948.

ment of the lines west of Hinton was from that point.

The makeup of C&O's operating divisions changed fairly frequently over time, however the subdivisions (originally called "districts"), hardly ever changed. They were occasionally shifted from one division to another, but the names and composition remain the basic constant within the C&O's operational system. To today's CSX most remaining C&O subdivisions still retain their names.

Leaving Clifton Forge the main line ascends Alleghany Mountain. The steepest part of the ascent begins just west of Covington, Virginia, and the summit is reached just east of Alleghany tunnel. The steepest gradient on this line westbound is 1.14%. Because the heavy coal traffic was westbound, the eastbound traffic was largely empty coal cars, so though heavier grades were encountered, they presented a far less daunting challenge than that encountered by their eastbound loaded counterparts.

As the C&O mainline exited Alleghany Tunnel into West Virginia at a station called Tuckahoe, it was already west of the summit. From this point onward the line passed over successive ridges formed from the Appalachian plateau. The C&O gradually descends from here into the Ohio Valley via several important rivers flowing in the same direction. The continental divide, separating waters flowing east to the Atlantic or west to the Gulf of Mexico occurs right at Alleghany Tunnel.

From Tuckahoe the mainline descends the valley of Dry Creek, and encounters the Greenbrier River (which rises to the north in Pocahontas County), and follows that stream to its confluence with the New River (rising in the south in North Carolina and flowing northwestward through a portion of West Virginia). The C&O then follows New River to its junction with Gauley River (rising in the central area of the state). The Gauley-New River confluence results in the Kanawha River which then flows to the Ohio at Point Pleasant. The C&O follows the Kanawha as far as St. Albans, and then takes a more direct westerly path, while the river flows to the northwest for its junction with the Ohio.

As stated before, the Alleghany Subdivision ended at Hinton. West of that point the C&O mainline consisted of the New River Subdivision as far as Handley, W. Va., and then the Kanawha Subdivision on through Huntington, and ten miles beyond the West Virginia border, terminating at Russell, Kentucky.

Hinton was the point at which coal trains were assembled before their dispatch eastward. The ruling grade from Hinton to Alleghany summit was about 0.56%, or a rise of about ½-foot for every 100 feet for horizontal distance. The steepest portion was between Ronceverte and Alleghany (about 15 miles) at about 0.56%, whereas the rise between Hinton and Ronceverte ranged between 0.11% and 0.33%. This was the easiest eastbound crossing of the Appalachians of any railroad that operated east-west across the region, including Norfolk & Western, Virginian, Baltimore Ohio, and Pennsylvania. This was a great advantage to the C&O in its ability to transport a larger amount of coal eastward at far less cost in infrastructure and motive power utilization than the other railroads.

Motive Power

In the 1890s, as C&O began to develop rapidly as a coal carrier, the company began to use pushers to increase the weight of eastbound coal that could be handled. At first the small 2-8-0 Consolidation type locomotives were standard in this service, and C&O continually developed them over the years up to 1909, when its G-9 class was a very large and powerful locomotive, the final development of the 2-8-0 type on the C&O. Other railroads had heavier and more powerful Consolidation types, and ones built much later, including the Western Maryland in northern West Virginia, but C&O's G-9s were exceptionally large for their era.

However, in 1910, many railroads in the country began to adopt or experiment with the new Mallet Compound** locomotives, which were introduced in 1904 on the Baltimore & Ohio. C&O purchased a single 2-6-6-2 type in 1910 as its H-1 class. This locomotive was tested so successfully that C&O adopted the 2-6-6-2 compound articulated design for its heavy coal train service and built them extensively through 1923. It loaned one of its early 2-6-6-2s to neighbor N&W which also adopted the design and made 150 copies before it settled on the 2-8-8-2 compound.

C&O was very pleased with the performance of the 2-6-6-2s on the Alleghany grade from Hinton to Clifton Forge because they increased the tonnage that could be hauled by about 30%. Pushers of either 2-8-0 or 2-6-6-2 types were still used out of Ronceverte to Alleghany, as had been the pattern since the early 1890s. The new Mallets were also used on manifest freight trains, enabling them to be increased in size as well. This allowed C&O to increase its merchandise freight business, which it really considered to be anything it hauled except coal. In later years of big steam after the late-1920s the pushers ran all the way from Hinton to the summit at Alleghany.

Passenger trains also needed new power over time, having been handled on all lines by 4-4-0s and 4-6-0s, C&O adopted the 4-4-2 and 4-6-2 types

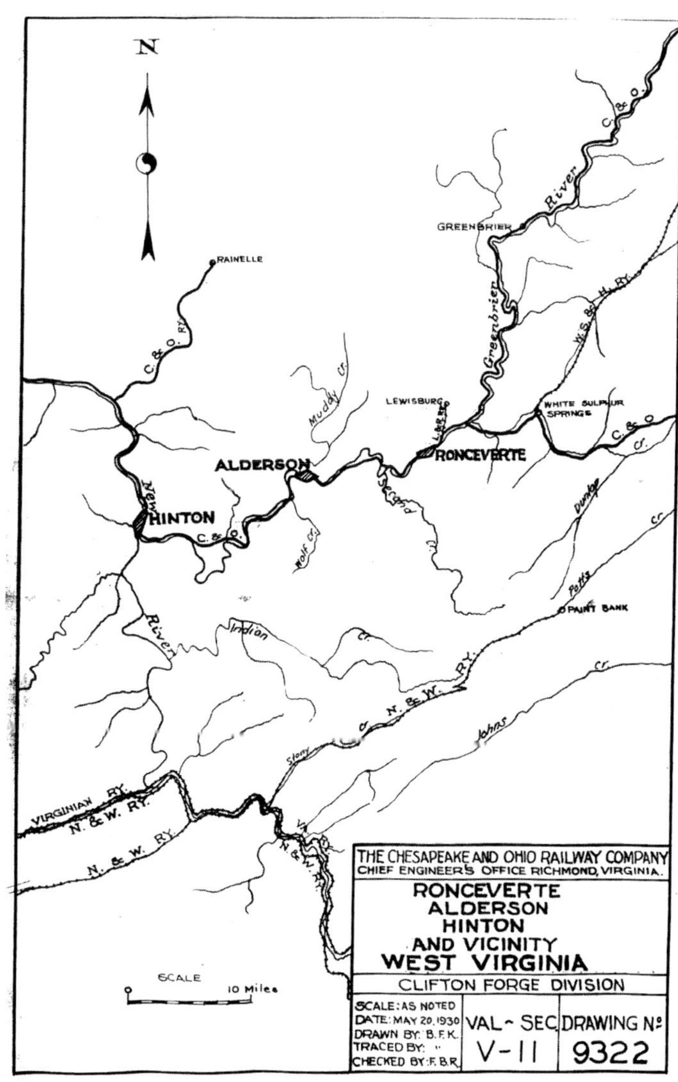

This general map shows the C&O mainline from just west of the Virginia border on beyond Hinton illustrates how the Alleghany Subdivision in West Virginia was situated in regard to the rivers and creeks in the area. N&W and Virginian mainlines are at the bottom of the map in Virginia. The White Sulphur & Huntersville Railroad is shown on this 1930 map. It was a short line operating out of White Sulphur as far as Neola (beginning about 1902). Its service was abandoned by the late 1920s. The L&R (Lewisburg & Ronceverte) is shown from Ronceverte. This was a 4-mile line that connected C&O with Lewisburg beginning in 1907. It was abandoned in 1929, after a good highway was available between the two points. It first operated with Shay geared locomotives and later was electrified. (C&O Drawing 9322, C&OHS Collection).

in 1902. These locomotives most often saw their initial work on the heavier grades from Charlottesville to Clifton Forge and from Clifton Forge to Hinton. The Pacific type (4-6-2) soon became the standard for trains over the Alleghany Subdivision with either a Pacific or an Atlantic west of Hinton. Certainly by 1910 the 4-4-0s and 4-6-0s were largely gone from the West Virginia portions of the mainline, except for use on local trains with only a few cars.

After World War I, C&O's motive power department went to work on further locomotive development, and

** This type of locomotive was invented by Anatole Mallet, a Swiss mechanical engineer in the 1880s It used two sets of cylinders and two sets of driving wheels. The rear cylinders/drivers were affixed rigidly to the boiler, while the front set swiveled under the boiler. The rear set used steam taken directly from the boiler while the front set used exhaust team from the rear cylinders. In this way steam was used twice, and the rigid wheel-base shortened. Two sets of cylinders and driving wheels under one boiler was termed articulation, while the double use of steam was called "compound" use.

The west portals of Alleghany Tunnel are the first location on the C&O in West Virginia on its eastern border. Here local passenger train No. 13, powered by F-15 class Pacific type No. 436 is emerging from the new bore on August 3, 1946. The old bore to the right was double-tracked in 1904, but as equipment got bigger it became too small, and the new tunnel was completed in 1932, allowing the old tunnel to become single tracked again. (J. I. Kelly photo, D. W. Johnson Collection).

the Alleghany grade out of Hinton played its usual important part in these considerations. The result was a series of very heavy and well designed 2-8-2 Mikados. The 2-8-2 had been on the C&O roster since 1911 and had proven its worth both on the other areas of the system and in the mountains. The new K-2, K-3, and K-3a Mikado classes came from C&O's favorite hometown builder, American Locomotive Works' Richmond Locomotive plant, between 1924 and 1926.

Also in 1923 C&O purchased from Alco's Schenectady Works a new concept, a big simple articulated, the H-7 class 2-8-8-2. Instead of using the steam twice as in all previous articulated designs (compound), this locomotive was designed with enough steaming capacity (furnace area and boiler size) to supply high pressure steam to all four cylinders, thus giving it more power. The 25 new locomotives went into service on the coal trains out of Hinton and were so successful C&O ordered 20 more (this time from Baldwin), in 1926. The H-7s were kings of the coal trains between Hinton and Clifton Forge for the next fifteen years. They were used as road engines with 2-6-6-2 pushers, and also in combination with an H-7 road engine and H-7 pusher. This new leap in technology again increased the amount of coal that C&O could handle per train and thus improved its bottom line as far as costs. The H-7s were the first series of successful simple articulateds and established the dominance of the simple articulated over the compound design for American railroads. Only a few such experiments had been tried before. After the H-7s only a few Mallets were built. Almost all new articulated designs were simple, with the single exception of Norfolk & Western which built its magnificent Y-class series compounds up until 1952!

While this was happening in coal and freight train motive power, the 4-8-2 type was developed first by C&O (in 1911) to handle the increasingly heavy passenger trains consisting of the new design all-steel cars over the heavy grades, including the Alleghany Subdivision between Clifton Forge and Hinton.

Through the boom years of the 1920s and the leaner times of the 1930s, C&O continued operations basically as they were constituted in the mid-1920s. Mikados often handled freight trains over the line and were in charge of local freights as well. The compound 2-6-6-2s remained in service, but the coal trains were almost

The easternmost station in West Virginia is Tuckahoe, seen here hosting a eastbound coal train in January 1942. The sweeping curve here was ideal for photography but is now grown up with trees. This photo was taken by C&O to show the new Allegheny type 2-6-6-6 Super Power locomotives which had just arrived from Lima Locomotive Works in December. Some points to note are: razor edge ballast preparation, heavy rail, the monster locomotive itself, and the heavy train. This is on the 0.56% grade, the ruling grade over which C&O had to lift its coal eastbound. Just behind the photographer by about ¼ mile are western portals of the twin Alleghany Tunnels. (C&O Ry. Photo, C&OHS Collection, Image No. CSPR-810.031)

exclusively the domain of the sturdy and powerful H-7 class 2-8-8-2 simple articulateds. For passengers, the heavy Pacifics still handled many of the trains over the line, along with the Mountain types (4-8-2). The 4-8-4 Greenbrier types arrived in 1935, with the greatest power yet for a C&O passenger locomotive. They mostly handled trains from Charlottesville to Clifton Forge, and from Clifton Forge to Hinton, sometimes running through without change at Clifton Forge.

During this period as well the coal business expanded, and though there was some contraction during the Depression, it remained basically strong, thus C&O remained strong. It was during this time that a great physical plant upgrade occurred, during which weight of rail was increased, bridges replaced or strengthened, and large grade and tunnel work done.

On the eve of World War II C&O had already decided that the H-7 design was outmoded and the H-7s themselves were worn out. The Advisory Mechanical Committee of the Van Sweringen railroads (of which C&O was a member after 1923), designed the fabulous H-8 2-6-6-6 simple articulated. Much has been written about this superb locomotive, and many consider it the pinnacle of steam locomotive development. Coming from Lima Locomotive Works, the foremost practioner of the "Super Power" concept for modern steam, these monstrous locomotives went into service starting in December 1941. Their number increased to 60 by 1948. During this period they took over completely from the H-7s in the coal train and manifest freight train business on the Alleghany line.

During this time new 2-8-4 types also arrived (starting 1943), and soon became the standard multi-purpose locomotive. Though much more common west of Hinton, and especially west of Handley, they did work on the Alleghany Subdivision from pushers on coal trains, to manifest freights, and even passenger trains.

In the final years of steam, the C&O experimented with a Steam-Turbine-Electric locomotive of monumental proportions. It was intended for *The Chessie* streamliner, which was cancelled and never put into service. For about a year, the three locomotives of this unusual type handled many of the mainline trains between Cincinnati and Washington. Specially designed coaling stations were erected at Hinton and Clifton Forge to fuel these

A few years later in the summer of 1957, and just a hundred yards east of the previous photo, the eastbound coal train, crawling to the summit at 8 mph, now is powered by the GP9s which supplanted big steam on the C&O, while an Alco S-4 switcher sits on the center siding with a ditcher/spreader work train. Throughout West Virginia on C&O mainlines and some branches the cantilever signal tower was a standard. Note that the blast plates are still in place on this one. They were needed to protect the structure from the effects of the heavy blast of exhaust from steam locomotives. (Gene Huddleston Photo, C&OHS Collection, Image No. COHS-1022)

One of C&O's J-3A class 4-8-4 Greenbrier type locomotives is seen here in 1950 powering Train No. 3, the westbound Fast Flying Virginian at Tuckahoe. Note the center siding between the mainlines, and the side track to the right. (B. F. Cutler photo, TLC Collection)

monsters, and they stood until the early 1960s.

As dieselization occurred, the Alleghany Subdivision began to get diesels as new GP7 types arrived from General Motors' Electro Motive Division in 1952-53. For a while one could see a couple of GP7s on the head of an eastbound train leaving Hinton's Avis yard, with an H-8 or even a 4-8-4 Greenbrier (displaced from passenger work) pushing. By 1954 steam was essentially gone on this line, and the GP7s and GP9s dominated for the next 15 years. Some F7s occasionally traveled over the line on manifest freights, but they usually kept in the western regions of the C&O (Ohio and Indiana).

In the mid-1960s new diesels were ordered, and for a while SD18 types and U-25Bs (from General Electric) were used on the Alleghany Subdivision, but they didn't prove successful as compared with the sturdy GP7s and 9s. But by the late 1960s newer diesels were coming into the fleet and by the mid-1970s had displaced most of the GP7s and 9s on the line. These consisted of the earlier mentioned GE U-25Bs, as well as EMD SD35s and SD40s. By the early 1970s as well the motive power fleets of C&O and its partner B&O were integrated and B&O locomotives were often seen on the line.

Passenger trains were dieselized in late 1951 and early 1952 by EMD E8 locomotives, which re-

An aerial view shows the big curve at Tuckahoe as the C&O mainline exits Alleghany Tunnel at left. (T. W. Dixon, Jr. Photo)

The engineer waves as H-8 class 2-6-6-6 No. 1640 is seen here as the road engine on an eastbound coal train between White Sulphur Springs and Tuckahoe as the train ascends the steepest portion of the grade, in June 1951. (Gene Huddleston Photo, C&OHS Collection, Image No. COHS-1186)

The track chart of the Alleghany Subdivision mainline Tuckahoe to Whitcomb shows a straight-line diagram which indicates grade, curvature, type of rail, ballast, bridges, tunnels, road crossings.

Stone
Other
Cinder
Chips
E.B. Tunnel
W.B. Tunnel (New)
E.B. Alleghany Tunnel 4743
W.B. Alleghany Tunnel 4751
Tuckahoe
Watch Box
White Sulphur Springs
Tunnel 300'
Pop. 2093
McPherson
Harts Run
Caldwell
Watch Box
To Barton
Whitcomb
Jct. Greenbrier Sub-Div.
307 308 309 310 311 312 313 314 315 316 317 318 319 320

No. 1641, another of the gargantuan 2-6-6-6s, is pushing a coal train east between White Sulphur and Tuckahoe in September 1952, as the steam era was drawing to a close. (Jeremy Taylor Photo, TLC Collection)

E8 No. 4010 leads Train No. 4, The Sportsman. *through the short, curved White Sulphur Tunnel, after leaving the station about half a mile to the west, in 1957. C&O dieselized its mainline passenger trains in late 1951 and early 1952. (Gene Huddleston Photo, C&O Hist. Soc. Coll., Image No. 1054)*

mained until the late 1960s when some B&O E8s and E9s infiltrated the area. In May 1971 Amtrak took over the remaining C&O passenger service and used inherited E-units from C&O, B&O and other roads, until it began to buy its own units.

The era of Chessie System and today's CSX is beyond the scope of this book, but motive power gradually became larger and more reliable. Today's CSX's giant wide-cab 4400 hp AC4400 models dominate on the Alleghany Subdivision.

Stations

The Alleghany Subdivision's first important station west of the state line is White Sulphur Springs. It was here that the old Sulphur Spring resort hotel was a major attraction in Virginia since before the War Between the States. C&O actually bought the property in 1910 and turned it into today's Greenbrier Resort Hotel. It was always an important passenger stop on C&O, and grew in importance through the years. In the 20th Century, C&O installed special sidings to accommodate Pullman sleeping cars that routinely came to the hotel carrying both regular pas-

In the era of this book, the years from 1940 until 1954 saw almost exclusive use of the 2-6-6-6s on the Alleghany Subdivision trains. Here No. 1604 is powering an east-bound manifest freight train past the White Sulphur Springs station platform in April 1947. (Ray Tobey photo, TLC Collection)

One of the showplaces of the C&O, the crisp white station at White Sulphur Springs served as gateway to the fabulous Greenbrier resort hotel, playground of the rich and powerful from the eastern cities, who reached it in the speed and comfort of trains such as The Sportsman. In an era of transition, just before the whole structure of passenger service collapsed, the shining E8 diesels, led by 4019 have a train of about 15 cars stretching out of sight. (C&O Ry. Photo, C&OHS Collection, Image No. CSPR-4689)

The station at White Sulphur Springs was equipped with a pull-through track behind the station building, four park tracks, and a "pocket track," all arranged so as to leave sleeping cars from both regular and special trains for arriving and departing hotel guests. In this 1956 photo the C&O office car Chessie-29 is on a park track at left, while a string of sleepers is in the pull-around track behind the depot. (Frank Schaeffer photo TLC Collection)

One of the more scenic locales on the Alleghany Subdivision is the area of Harts Run, just west of White Sulphur Springs. In this 1964 photo four of the brand new SD18 diesels are powering an eastbound train up the grade. After about a year these second-generation diesels were withdrawn in favor of the GP7 and GP9 models which had been in use since 1952. This location was the ruling grade for eastbound coal because of heavy reverse curves. (C&O Ry. Photo, C&OHS Collection, Image CSPR-5033)

sengers and many special parties. Many mainline passenger trains had regular sleepers which were dropped at White Sulphur so that the passengers could occupy them until a normal hour in the morning. There were tracks, however, to accommodate many extra cars that came in either special trains or as special cars on regular trains. C&O also operated seasonally scheduled "Resort Special" trains during the "springs seasons," to accommodate people going east back to New York. Most of the business for the Greenbrier came from the eastern cities, with some, though a much smaller volume, from the west.

In 1930 C&O replaced the old frame depot here with a very attractive white brick station and a long covered platform. The station uses many architectural attributes reminiscent of Colonial Virginia, a theme the railway was using in all its advertisements and promotions in the era. It is still standing and at this writing is used by the Greenbrier Hotel company as a Christmas store. The platform is still used for Amtrak passengers. During World War II, the hotel property was sold to the U. S. government and used as a residence for interned Axis diplomats until they could be repatriated and then as Ashford General Hospital, to treat wounded soldiers. After the war Robert R. Young, C&O's board chairman, had C&O buy it back. The company spent a large sum to completely redecorate and refurbish the hotel, and it has remained as one of America's premier

At Whitcomb C&O crossed the Greenbrier River for the first of three times. The Greenbrier branch joined at this point and the interesting depot/tower combination structure was used by the agent/operator, but by the time of our post-war era it was long gone as automatic signals had eliminated the need for an operator here. (From a postcard view, TLC Collection)

Ronceverte, about four miles west of Whitcomb, served as the yard for the Greenbrier Branch and has this imposing two story brick depot with covered platform. Built in 1917, it still stands of this writing. (C&O Ry. Photo, C&OHS Collection, Image No. 10393.130)

resorts. In 2009 the Greenbrier was sold by CSX.

At Whitcomb, eight miles west of White Sulphur, the Greenbrier Branch connects with the mainline. Just four miles farther is Ronceverte, where C&O installed a small yard that initially was used as the terminal yard for the Greenbrier branch. Ronceverte was also the station for Lewisburg, the Greenbrier County seat.

Ronceverte's yard was relatively small, but had a two-stall engine house, 100-ft. turntable, small 75-ton coaling station, as well as watering facilities. Ronceverte itself also had a large lumber mill for many years.

From Ronceverte the line follows the Greenbrier River's north bank closely, plunges through Second Creek Tunnel, crosses the river, goes through Fort Spring Tunnel, and the small town of Fort Spring, then through Mann's Tunnel.

At Snow Flake, just beyond the Fort Spring station, at Milepost 330.1, was the large Acme Limestone Company rock quarry which has produced a huge amount of limestone for various purposes since the turn of the 20th Century. Just behind it was the C&O-owned Frazier quarry which supplied ballast stone for C&O for many decades.

At Milepost 336, was Alderson, a town of a little over a thousand people, but one that always figured large in the freight and passenger traffic on the Alleghany subdivision because of the wide and fertile farming region that was tributary to it. C&O had a large frame passenger station here as well as a sizable freight station, and wood yards were operated here both for shipment of lumber logs (especially ve-

The small yard at Ronceverte accommodated the needs of the commercial activities there (which served Lewisburg, the county seat), and the Greenbrier Branch, which was built in 1901. This drawing shows the small engine house, and turntable, the station and other fatalities which made Ronceverte a small but busy little terminal. Between 1907 and 1929 the Lewisburg & Ronceverte short line railroad connected at Ronceverte and ran a little over four miles to Lewisburg. (C&O Drawing 9284 (extract), C&OHS Collection)

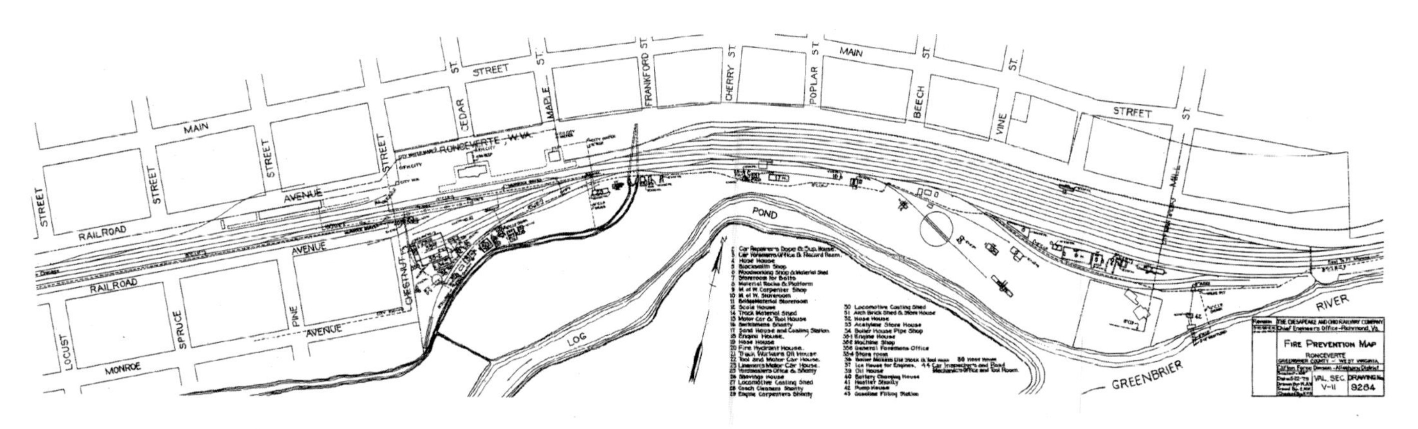

The small 75-ton concrete coaling station at Ronceverte was one of the smallest of the C&O, and was used simply for refueling locomotives used in the yard and headed up the Greenbrier branch. The late 1940s-era photo shows hoppers of coal stationed and ready to recharge the tower as the fuel was dispensed to locomotive tenders. (TLC Collection)

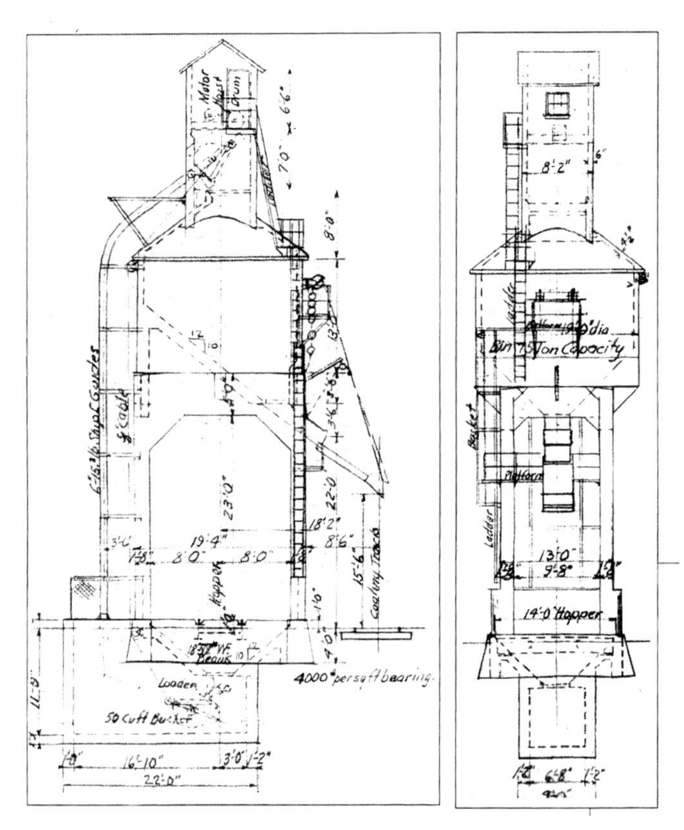

Drawings show the arrangement for the Ronceverte coaling station, which was built by Ogle Construction Company in 1935, replacing a wooden structure at this point. This was the only coaling station available on the Alleghany Subdivision, because very large locomotives with huge capacity tenders were used and only emergency refueling would be needed. (TLC Collection)

Track chart for main line near Whitcomb to Ft. Spring.

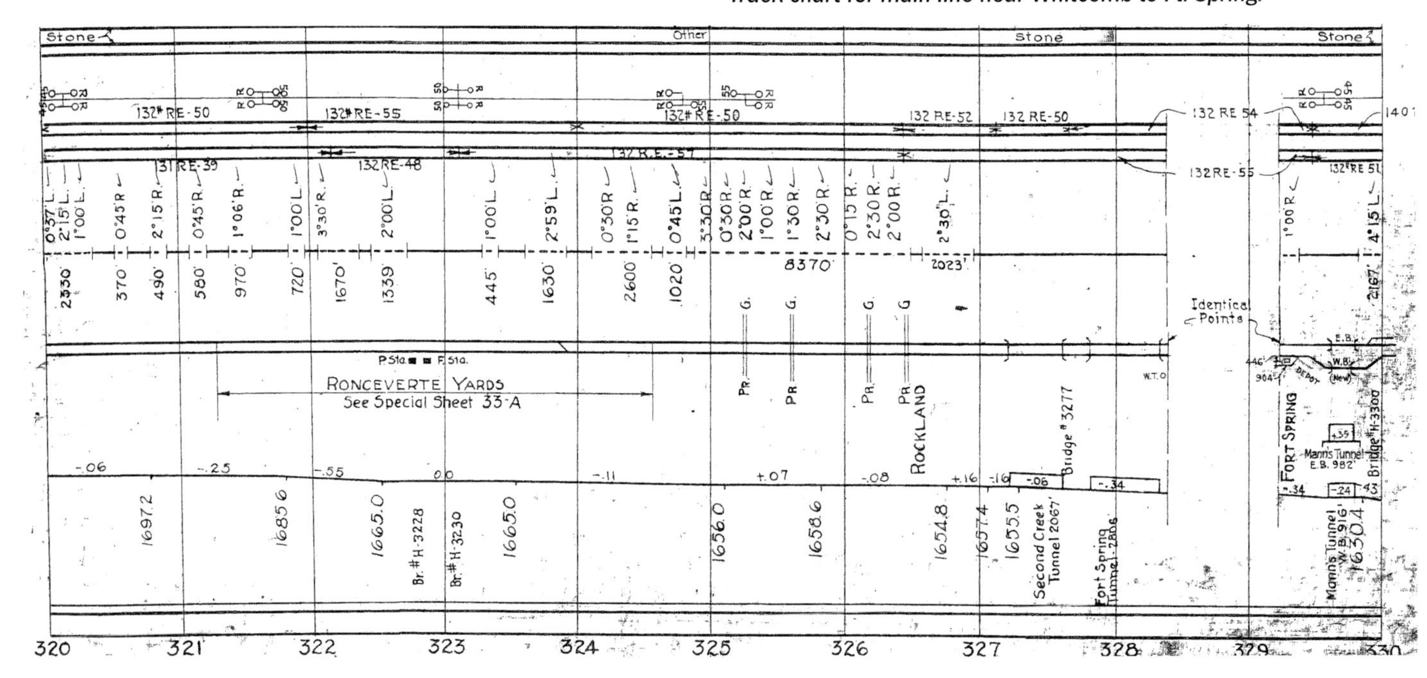

C&O gas-electric car No. 9051 and a trailing combine are seen here in 1949 parked beside the Ronceverte engine house, as a 2-6-6-2 H-4 No. 1359 awaits assignment. After 1930 passenger service on the Greenbrier branch was handled by two gas-electrics with trailer cars. The last two runs were finally discontinued in 1957. (T. L. Wise photo, TLC Collection)

When the new 1947 line was built, C&O had to erect a new station at Ft. Spring, and built this non-descript frame structure sided with shingles. Looking through Fort Spring Tunnel, you can just barely see Second Creek Tunnel. Turning around behind the photographer, one would be looking at the double portals of Mann's Tunnel. Standing here you can see three tunnels. (TLC Collection)

West of Ronceverte the C&O hugs the left (south) bank of the Greenbrier, then passes through Second Creek Tunnel, crosses the river again and goes through the new Fort Spring Tunnel. Bored in 1946-47 it was built to eliminate a sharp curve following the river at this point. It is the newest of the mainline tunnels, and sported this interesting Art Deco portal. Here GP-9 No. 5996 leads three sisters on a coal train out of the east portal of the tunnel. (Gene Huddleston photo, C&OHS Collection, Image No. COHS-1053)

neer wood), and pulpwood headed east to Covington. In late years as regular passenger business declined the Alderson ticket business was bolstered by the transport of prisoners and visitors to and from the Federal Reformatory for Women, the large federal women's prison established there in the mid-1930s.

Beyond Alderson, only small villages were located along the line,.

Pence Springs (MP 343.4) had a sulphur spring and from the early 1900s to the 1940s boasted a medium-sized resort hotel, and generated considerable passenger business. However, its decline was steep and early. Lowell was at MP 345.3. It had a large frame station dedicated to shipments of farm products, and just beyond it was Talcott, made famous for the John Henry legend, as the east portal of Big Bend Tunnel was located here.

West of Big Bend there was nothing of consequence until Avis, which was the east end of the Hinton terminal yard complex.

The Alleghany Subdivision terminated at the Avis yard limits. Hinton was part of the New River Subdivision.

From Fort Spring the mainline hugged the Greenbrier River very closely as it passed through a fairly short gorge, emerging at Alderson. The town's business was generated by the bluegrass farming and cattle raising area surrounding in Monroe, Greenbrier, and Summers counties, near whose junction the town was situated. The passenger station, shown here, was erected in 1896 and enlarged in 1917, and is still standing, completely restored to its original appearance and used both as an Amtrak station, and for other purposes. This 1935 photo is looking east. The structure just beyond it is the freight station, and the town's main street is at right. (William Monypeny photo, C&OHS Collection, Image No. COHS-3027)

The large Alderson freight station is seen here as it appeared in the mid-1950s. The building was originally the combined depot for the town, built in 1875, but when the new passenger station (left) was erected in 1896 it was converted for exclusive use for LCL freight. It was demolished about 1962. (W. Richard Ford photo, TLC Collection)

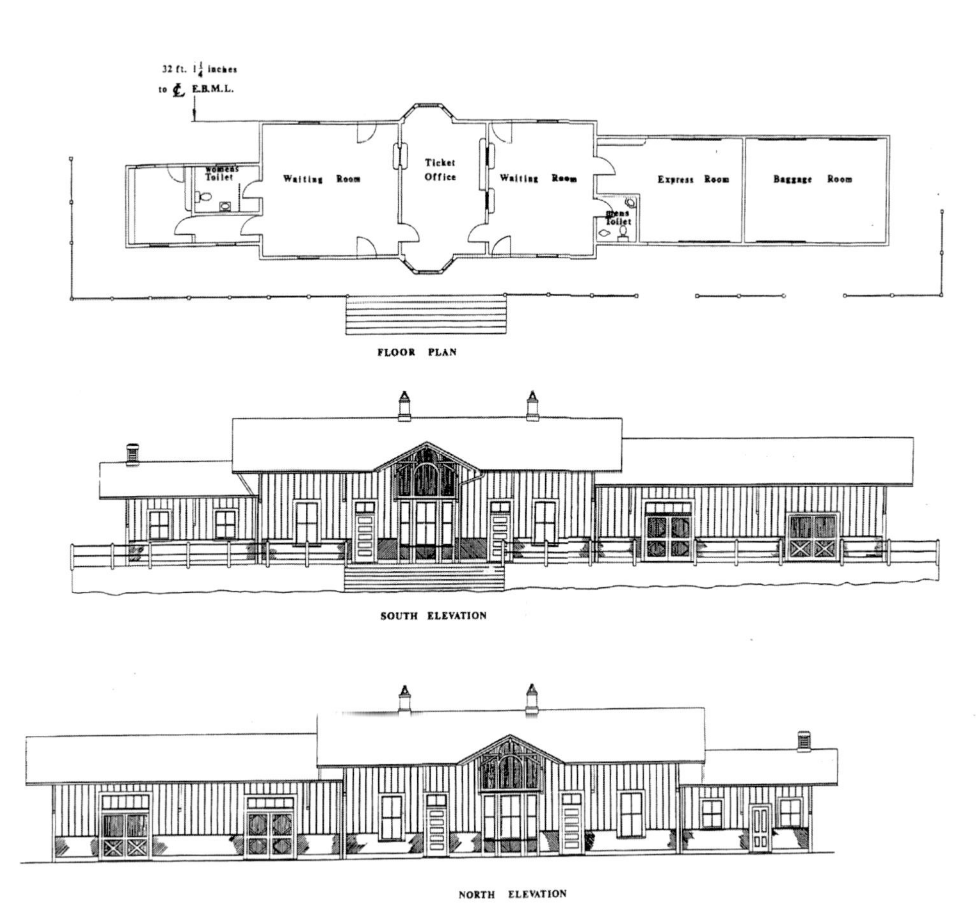

These drawings show the Alderson depot as it appeared in the late 1960s. It was one of only two of the standard structures that also had a bay window on the street side. The design itself was adopted by C&O in about 1890 and was built in scores of locations up until 1908 when a more simplified standard was adopted. (Ron Piskor Drawing - not to scale)

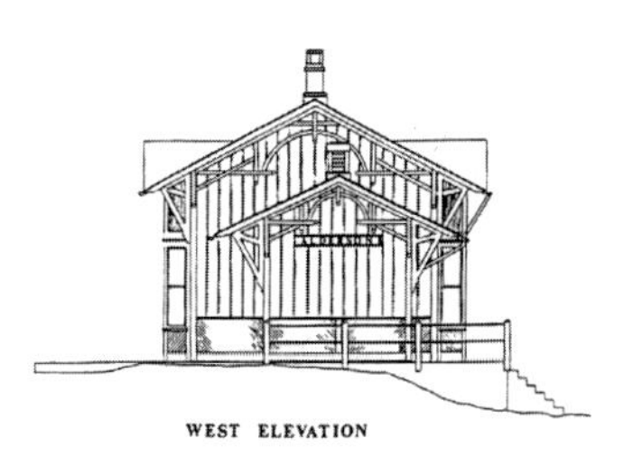

AD Cabin was located about ½ mile west of the Alderson depot and was in service until about 1962 when Centralized Traffic Control eliminated the need for operators on the Alleghany Subdivision. It was a non-standard design, having been rebuilt from an earlier standard building. C&O called its telegraph operator/signal towers "cabins," stemming from some ancient usage, perhaps the only railroad to do so. (W. Richard Ford photo, TLC Collection)

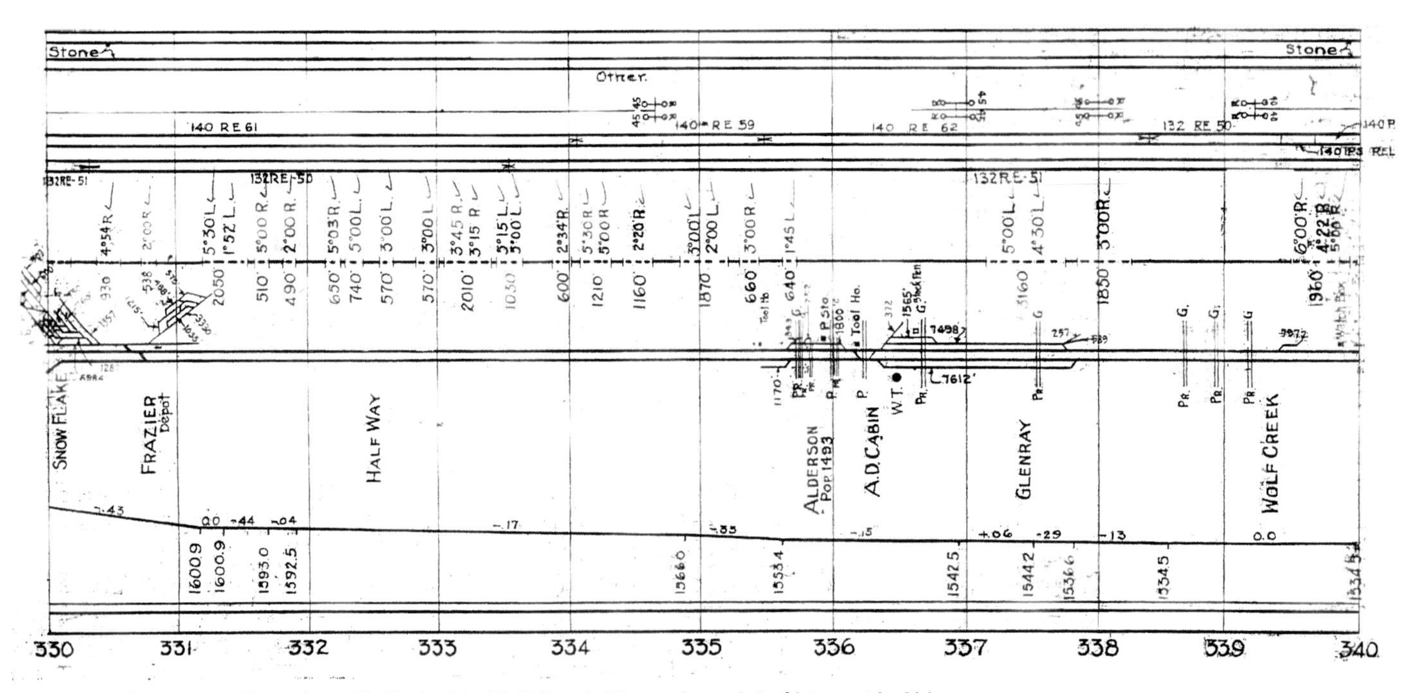

Track chart from Snow Flake (near Ft. Spring) to Wolf Creek. The major point of interest is Alderson.

A westbound manifest freight train is rounding the curve at Wolf Creek, a few miles west of Alderson, where the Greenbrier Valley is wide and afforded much land for farming and livestock raising. An H-7 2-8-8-2 powers the train, so the photo was taken before 1943. (TLC Collection)

The longest tangent track on the Alleghany Subdivision is almost 2 miles long at Riffe, seen here from the overlooking bluff. The gentle Greenbrier which is at left created this flood plain through the long ages. (TLC Collection)

Pence Springs station, one of the C&O standard types (it originally had a tower on top) is seen here in 1935 still doing a brisk business with the local passenger train. The station was originally called Stock Yards and was the point at which C&O rested and watered livestock until that operation was moved to Hinton in the early 1900s. The station remained important for passengers coming to and from the sulphur spring resort hotel here. One of the lesser "Springs of the Virginias," it attracted a substantial summer clientele until the 1930s. (William Monypeny photo, C&OHS Collection, Image COHS-3029)

Talcott was the station located in the small settlement at the eastern portal of Great Bend/Big Bend Tunnel. The building shown here was one of a fairly standard design erected in the mid-1870s soon after the line was built. It originally had a porch on the passenger end. (William Monypeny photo, C&OHS Collection, COHS-3030)

Right-of-Way

The principal feature of the Alleghany Subdivision in West Virginia is its tunnels. It enters, as stated, via Alleghany Tunnel under the ridge that separates the states. Just east of White Sulphur Springs the line passes through the very short (300-feet) double tracked White Sulphur Tunnel. At Milepost 327 west of Ronceverte the mainline again passes through the double tracked Second Creek Tunnel (2,067-feet). This is a new tunnel, bored in the 1930s on a new alignment to replace an older one. Immediately after the line emerges from this tunnel it crosses the Greenbrier River on a heavy girder bridge, and goes directly into Fort Spring Tunnel (2,806-feet). This is the newest C&O mainline tunnel, bored in 1947-48 during a major realignment project to eliminate a broad curve following the river at this point. West of this tunnel was the Fort Spring depot, and within a few hundred yards the lines separate and pass through the twin bores of Mann's Tunnel (two bores, both 330 feet). The older of the two once accommodated two tracks, but a new tunnel was bored in 19___ to allow the older one to be single tracked and thus helping with clearance problems. It is interesting that one can stand at the old location of the Fort Spring station and see the portals of Mann's Tunnels, Fort Spring Tunnel, and looking through Fort Spring Tunnel, Second Creek Tunnel is visible.

There are no more tunnels until Talcott is reached, where Great Bend and Big Bend Tunnels are located. The old bore (Great Bend) was 6,500 feet, while the new one (Big Bend) is 6,168 feet. This is one of the most famous spots on the C&O because of the John Henry legend. As the C&O line was being built westward in the early 1870s, the decision was made to use a long tunnel through the spur of Big Bend Mountain in order to eliminate a much longer line following the Greenbrier River around the mountain. The resultant tunnel work was very difficult given the variety of rock types encountered, including unstable shale. According to the folk story, John Henry, one of the African-American drillers at the tunnel, challenged a steam drill to a race and did better than the new machine. This would is entirely plausible, because the Burleigh Steam Drill, a new device, had problems in that its drill tended to choke with rock dust in the hole causing the bit to break. This was not the case with a human driller because he had a "shaker" who raise the drill and shook it between blows, which kept the hole fairly clean of debris.

At least four scholarly books have been written about the incident, two in the 1920s when there were still people at Talcott who remembered the tunnel work. Another one is about the folk story and many songs variations, and a recent one postulates that this was not to location of John Henry's tunnel work

During World War II, watchmen's guard shanties were placed at strategic locations. Here, in 1942, one can be seen just to the left of Extra 1604 east at Talcott. Note the smoke emerging from Big Bend Tunnel in the background. The new tunnel did not have a ventilation system, although the old one did, because of its close clearances. (TLC Collection)

H-8 2-6-6-6 No. 1600 is seen here at Talcott, about to enter Great Bend Tunnel westbound with a manifest freight train in September 1949. The giant 2-6-6-6s were standard power between Hinton and Clifton Forge for both coal and fast freight. They were replaced with 4 or 5-unit GP7/GP9 diesel sets by 1954. (Charles H. Kerrigan photo)

at all, but rather that he worked at Lewis Tunnel on Alleghany Mountain just over the border in Virginia.

Regardless of the truth, the legend gave rise to a myriad of versions of the John Henry folksong, which placed him not only on the C&O but even in New Orleans and Jamaica! He become the great black hero of the age, and in many ways is still.

This tunnel was called "Great Bend Tunnel" and continued to be important in the operations of C&O in the early days. It was gradually brick lined to eliminate continual problems with rock falls in the 1880s and 1890s. In the 1890s-early 1900s it was the location of a number of deaths of crewmen from asphyxiation when a train stalled in the tunnel and the locomotive exhaust created bad air. In the 1917 a large fan was installed at the west portal which blew the smoke ahead of the train as it passed through, and this helped greatly. However, the tunnel remained a bottleneck as traffic increased on the mainline, but this was finally eliminated when a new tunnel was bored in 1930-31. It was exactly parallel to the old tunnel but was lettered with the name "Big Bend" instead the older name of "Great Bend," as the local terminology had changed.

Less than a half a mile west of Big Bend was another tunnel called "Little Bend," which was only 692 feet long. It was a double tracked tunnel and was ultimately completely eliminated by a large cut beside it in 1972.

Other engineering features of importance were the three bridges crossing the Greenbrier River, one at Whitcomb (Milepost 319.8), the second between Second Creek and Ft. Spring Tunnels (Milepost 329), and the third at Lowell, (Milepost 345.3) not far from Talcott. Today, all these bridges are heavy steel girder types capable of supporting the heaviest trains. The Lowell bridge is on a newer alignment from 1947 as several areas of the C&O mainline through western Virginia and West Virginia were given a new alignment to eliminate or straighten curvature and thus make it easier for faster operations. The new Fort Spring Tunnel resulted from the before mentioned realignment at that location.

The only important changes to the Alleghany Subdivision line other than the 1947 realignment at Fort Spring and Lowell was the 1972-74 elimination of some double track. Up to that point the line had been completely double-tracked after the 1932 addition of the new Big Bend Tunnel, but with decreased traffic, Chessie System made the decision to eliminate almost 1/3rd of its mainline double track. On the Alleghany Subdivision in West Virginia this included a stretch from Pence Springs through Talcott. This served to eliminate the old Great Bend Tunnel bore, which stood derelict until recently. It is now to be the centerpiece of a small park dedicated to John Henry.

Traffic

Historically, the main traffic over the Alleghany Subdivision has been coal, not coal originated, but coming from the southern West Virginia Fields west of Hinton. Locally generated traffic consisted mainly of agricultural and forest products, especially the forest products coming from the Greenbrier Branch. There were never any large industrial or mining activities. The region was and remains very rural in character, with only a few towns of inconsiderable size. In the modern era, after WWII the freight traffic consisted of usually four manifest freights per day, daily local freights handling business to the on-line communities, and the number of coal trains and empties required by the business. In the postwar era up to through the 1960s this averaged about 10 loaded trains east and 8-10 empties west per day. By the 1970s this had fallen off, but then increased and decreased with the ebb and flow of the overseas coal market, because coal was no longer shipped mainly to the northeast, but rather mainly to export. Local freight trains operated each way each day until about 1960 when only one was run, east on day and west the next.

Passenger traffic, of course, consisted of those mainline through trains that C&O operated at any point in time. Additionally there was always at least one local passenger train each day daily. The Greenbrier branch had up to four passenger trains per day. These consisted of two motor cars, each one up and back daily, which was soon cut to one per day until its end in 1957.

After the end of the post-war passenger glut, C&O mainline service settled down to three sets of name trains. *The George Washington* (Trains 1 and 2), passed over the Alleghany Subdivision late at night. The second set was *The Fast Flying Virginian* (Nos. 3 and 6). No. 3 got to White Sulphur early in the morning and often dropped a sleeper from New York on the "pocket track" at that location, and then passed on through the state in the morning hours. In the mid-century era No. 6 got to Hinton around 8 pm in the evening and left White Sulphur at around 9 pm. Both these trains were heavily patronized by people going to the Greenbrier because No. 3 allowed for an afternoon departure from New York with an early morning arrival at White Sulphur, and No. 6 offered an evening departure from White Sulphur for an early morning arrival in New York. Finally, Nos. 4 and 5, *The Sportsman*, were also daylight trains. No. 4 left Hinton in the early morning, passing White Sulphur about 7:30 am, and also carried sleepers intended for White Sulphur Springs-bound passengers. No. 5 arrived White Sulphur at 5:17 pm and Hinton at 6:30 pm. It was also popular with passengers from White Sulphur Springs headed back westward.

Local trains were Nos. 13 and 14, later 13 and 104. They originated at various terminals over time, but traversed the Alleghany Subdivision during daylight.

The local trains were eliminated in 1958, and Nos. 5 and 6 were discontinued in October 1962. Nos. 3 and 4 lasted until May 12, 1968, and Nos. 1 and 2 ended their lives on Amtrak day, May 1, 1971. After that time Amtrak continued to operate one set of trains over the C&O mainline, first using the names of *The George Washington* (westbound), and *James Whitcomb Riley* (eastbound). Over the subsequent 30 years of Amtrak service these trains have had various schedules, and for most of that time have been named *The Cardinal*. Twice they were discontinued entirely for a period of time, and in recent decades have operated only on a three-times-per-week schedule. (See Chapter 7)

One unusual aspect of passenger service on this line was the operation of extra trains that ran to White Sulphur Springs. In the post-war era up to the late 1960s in any given week a number of special sleeping car movements were made to carry passengers to the Greenbrier. If there were just a few cars involved in the movement, they arrived and departed on the regular trains, but for larger movements special trains were operated. In the summer and during springs seasons at the hotel, C&O operated a *Resort Special* train, to take patrons east, leaving White Sulphur in the evenings eastbound to New York. The last of these operated in the 1969.

Statistics (1948)

Distance Terminal-to-Terminal: 77.8 miles
Distance in West Virginia: 47.3 miles
Branches Connecting: 3 (1 in West Virginia: Greenbrier)
Connections with other Railroads: None
Coaling Stations: Ronceverte (75-tons, elevator)
Yards: Ronceverte
Turntables: Ronceverte (100-foot)
Stock Pens: White Sulphur, Ronceverte, Fort Spring, Alderson, Pence Springs, Lowell
Track scales: Ronceverte
Tunnels:
Alleghany, Eastbound (old) 4,743 feet
Alleghany, Westbound (new) 4,751 feet
White Sulphur (double track) 300 feet
Second Creek (double track) 2,067 feet
Ft. Spring (double track) 2,806 feet
Mann's, Eastbound (old) 982 feet
Mann's, Westbound (new) 916 feet
Big Bend, Eastbound (new) 6,168 feet
Big Bend, Westbound (old) 6,500 feet (*)
Little Bend (double track) 692 feet (**)
(*) - Retired, track removed 1974
(**) - Retired, bypassed, sealed (1970)

Construction work on the new bore at Big Bend Tunnel was about complete when this photo was taken in 1931. The old tunnel to the right is the one where John Henry was supposed to have raced the steam drill in the early 1870s. It remained in service, finally giving C&O a double track mainline all the way from Clifton Forge to Cincinnati, until 1972 when the old tunnel was deactivated, and the line became single track again. (TLC Collection)

J-3 class Greenbrier type 4-8-4 No. 606 takes daylight local passenger train No. 13 west at Hilldale, located between Big Bend and Little Bend Tunnels in June 1947. MW Cabin is seen in the background. Note the speed limit sign showing 45 mph for passenger trains and 20 for freight. (Gene Huddleston Photo)

Track chart for MP 340-355 showing Talcott and Big Bend Tunnels through to Avis.

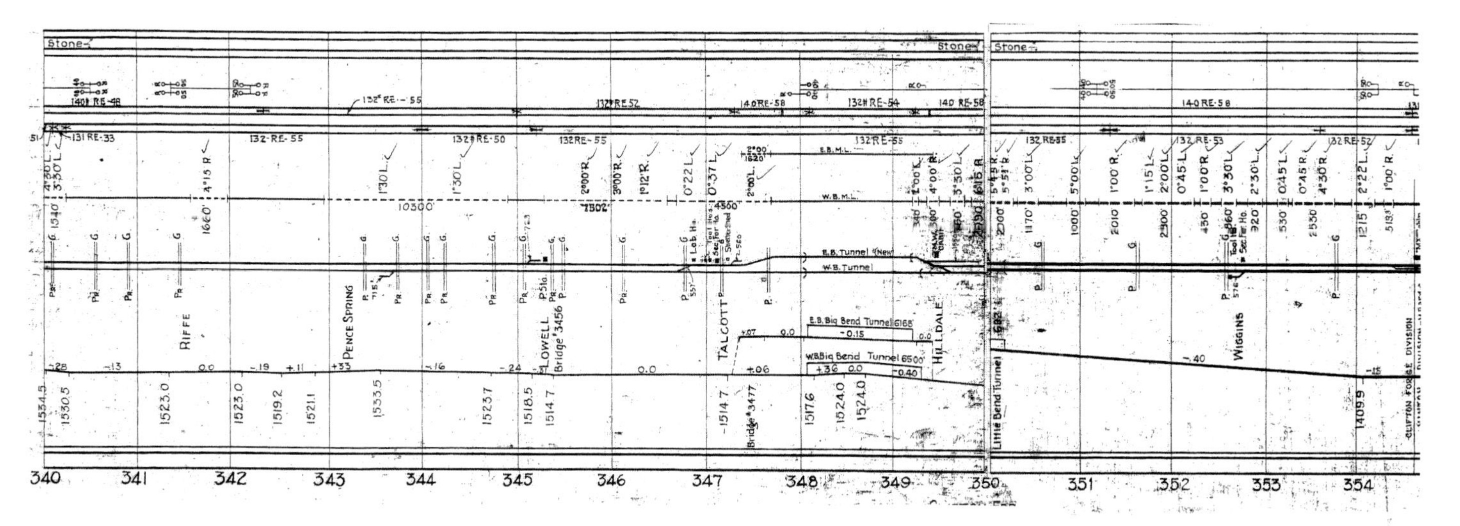

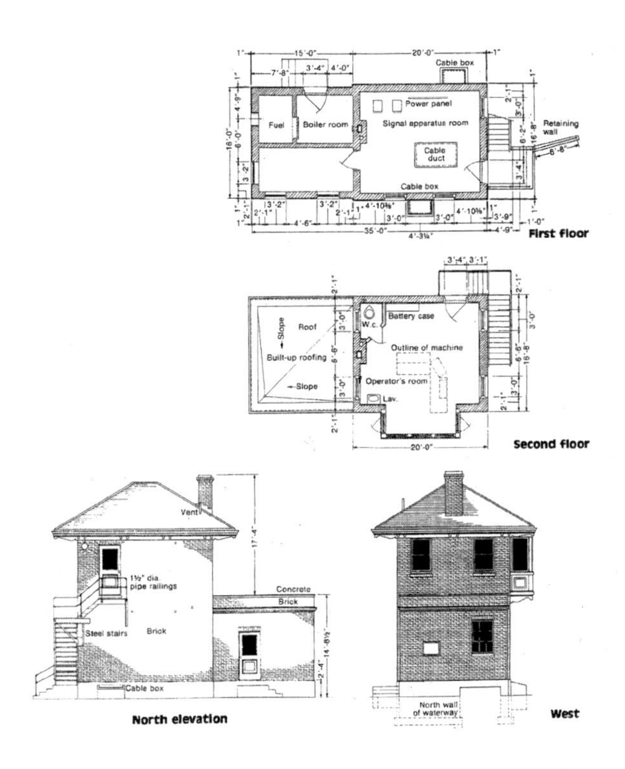

These drawings show the layout of a standard C&O signal tower/cabin of the 1930s. A number of these structures were built to replace older wooden cabins in the era from the 1920s into the late 1930s. MW Cabin at Hilldale was built to this standard. (Courtesy Carstens Publishing)

drawn by Julian Cavalier

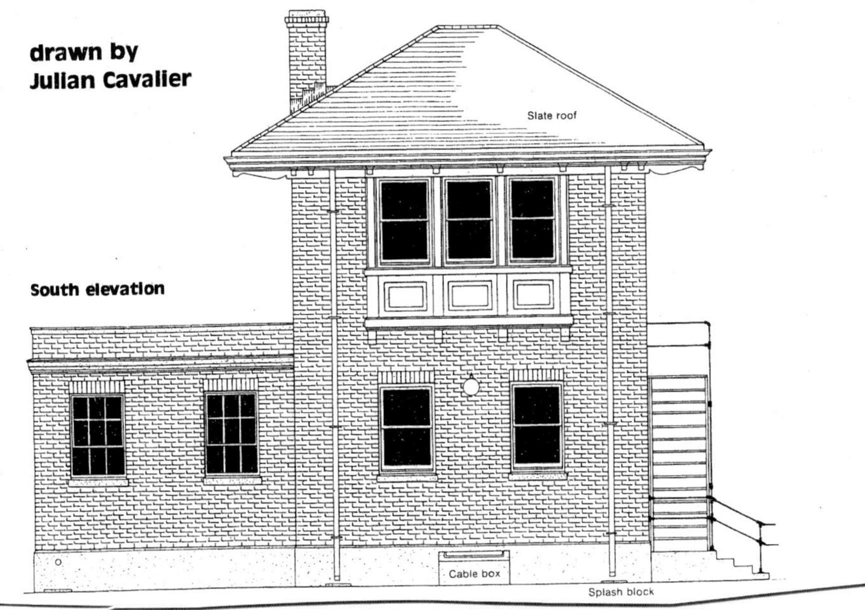

MW Cabin was located west of the Big Bend portals and is seen here after it was replaced by CTC installation in the early 1960s. The tunnel at left is the western portal of the old bore, which had a huge ventilation fan installation installed in 1919 and later removed. The one at right is the newer (1931) bore. (T. W. Dixon, Jr. photo)

Less than a mile west of Big Bend, the C&O mainline plunged into the short, curved Little Bend Tunnel, which was a double track bore that was eliminated in 1970 when the large cut was made as shown in this photo taken after the new line was completed, July 25, 1970. (T. W. Dixon, Jr. photo)

H-8 No. 1608 pushes hard as it accelerates a coal train eastbound out of Hinton's Avis yard in Sept. 1949. The H-8 pushers ran all the way from Hinton to Alleghany, 49 miles. By the time they returned light to Hinton the crew's day was over, so essentially every eastbound train had to have two H-8s and two crews out of Hinton. In the 1890s-1920s period the pushers operated out of Ronceverte, so they could handle several train movements with one locomotive and crew. (Charles H. Kerrigan photo)

Three branch lines connected with the Alleghany Subdivision: the Hot Springs Branch from Covington to Hot Springs, and the Potts Creek Branch from Covington to Bess, both in Virginia; and the Greenbrier Branch in West Virginia. The Greenbrier branch is the only one within the scope of this book.

This line was proposed in the 1890s as a way to tap not coal, which was the reason for almost all C&O branches, but lumber in the vast virgin forests of Greenbrier and Pocahontas counties.

The line ran originally about 101 miles to the small town of Winterburn, but by our mid-century era it was operating 98.1 miles with the end of track at Bartow. At Durbin, 95.6 miles up the line a connection was made with the Western Maryland Railway. Otherwise no other connections to a Class 1 railroad were made.

As early as 1865 the people of this region were trying to get a railroad, and they incorporated the Monongahela & Lewisburg, but it come to nothing. In the 1870s a line was projected across Alleghany Mountain from Virginia to Marlinton, (the seat of Pocahontas County after 1891). It was supposed to be part of a grand scheme for a line from Washington to Cincinnati, and yet later to Chicago. Following this scheme a dozen other proposed or "paper" railroads were projected, many looking for iron ore deposits, but none laid a single rail, and the forest resources of the mountain highlands remained locked away from commercialization.

By the early 1890s, prospects for the line improved as powerful men, including former U. S. Senator Johnson N. Camden, and Col. John T. McGraw, became interested in the area and began to make investments. In 1891 Camden projected his West Virginia

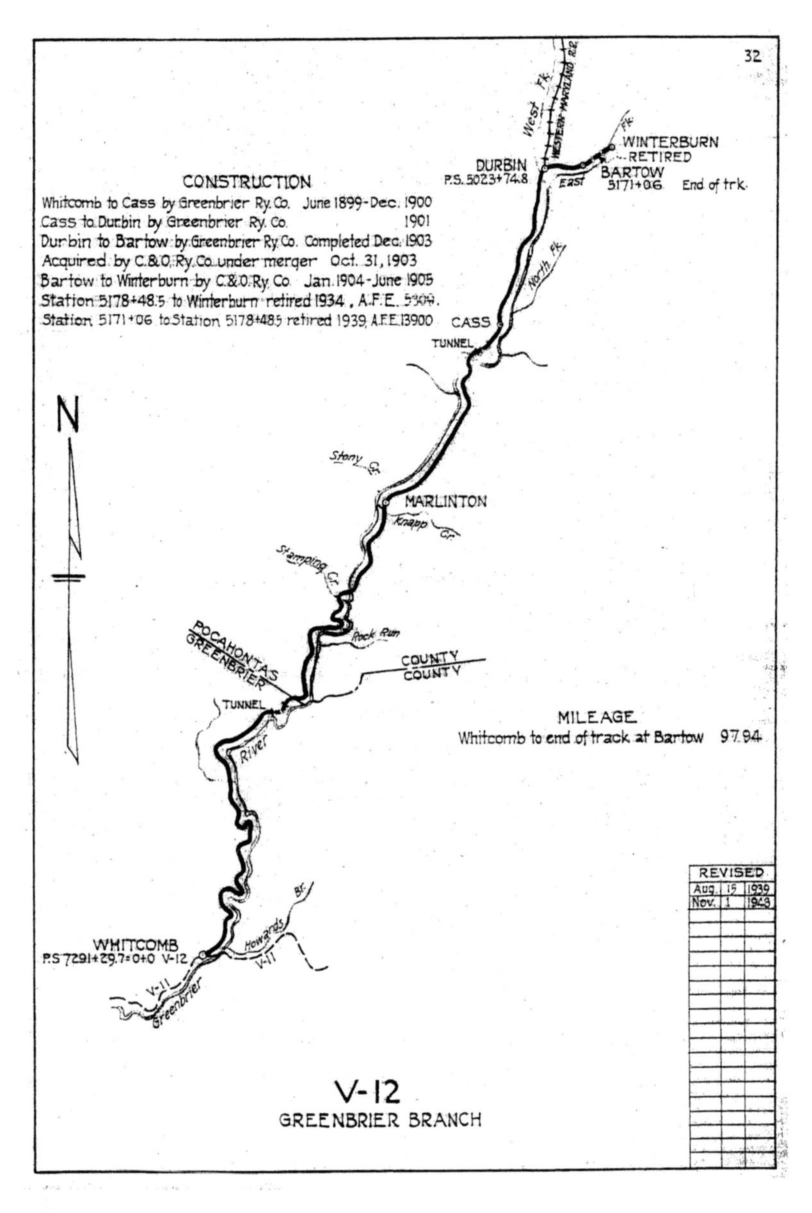

Valuation Index Map showing Greenbrier Branch. Valuation maps were drawn as part of a general engineering survey of each American railroad mandated by Congress in 1913. The study became the basis of all future engineering on the C&O. This is just the index map. Large 2x4-foot drawings were made, each covering 2-4 miles of line with high detail as to tracks, structures, facilities, etc.

and Pittsburg (sic) through Pocahontas and Greenbrier counties to join a proposed extension across the mountain from C&O's Hot Springs Branch, completed in that year from Covington to Hot Springs. It was to come across the gap at Frost and connect at Marlinton. McGraw formed the Pocahontas Development Company and bought land around Marlinton, promoting commercial development. He got the county seat changed from Huntersville to Marlinton in 1891. At least six different railroads were quickly projected from the new town, but the financial panic and depression of 1893 put things on hold. The C&O was not willing to extend any of its lines in this area.

Nothing further happened until 1897 when the West Virginia Pulp & Paper Company built a large paper mill at Covington, Virginia, and persuaded C&O to build the line from Whitcomb up the Greenbrier to reach the company's vast tracts of timber. Originally, the paper mill was sited at North Caldwell, a couple of miles up the projected Greenbrier branch, however it was finally placed at Covington. C&O's board approved the new line in November 1897 and it was built over the next few years using the Greenbrier river route in order to avoid the heavy grades that all other proposed routes would have entailed.

The first train arrived in Marlinton on October 26, 1900, the line was opened to Durbin May 26, 1902, and the final extension was completed March 1904. The construction was done by the Greenbrier Railway, a subsidiary wholly owned by C&O, which was merged into C&O October 31, 1903. The line was initially called "Greenbrier Division," and offices were established at Ronceverte.

The first 20 years of operation saw the installation of a mammoth saw mill at Cass owned by W. Va. P & P. and construction of numerous other lumbering operations along the line, many of which operated their own logging railroads.

In 1923 C&O created a new "fast freight line" to forward expedited freight between Midwestern points and the Northeastern states using the Greenbrier line and interchanging with Western Maryland at Durbin, which operated the bridge to the Pennsylvania Railroad at Hagerstown, Maryland. Called the "Durbin Route" in C&O advertising, it was apparently successful in getting freight to and from the Northeast without going through Washington and Baltimore, but it fell prey to the Depression of the 1930s.

In 1930 the two sets of passenger trains on the line were changed to motor trains operated by a set of C&O's new Brill gas-electric motor cars, each with a coach trailer. In 1933 the Bartow-Winterburn line was abandoned, and traffic continued to fall. The big mill at Cass continued high rates of production though most of the smaller loggers closed.

By 1941 the daily local freights were cut back to one every other day, but wartime traffic improved the situation for a few years. After the war there was little left along most of the line except a trickle of farm products and pulpwood.

In 1957 the last gas-electric trains were discontinued. In 1960 the Cass mill closed, and the alternate-days local freight used Hinton rather than Ronceverte as its terminal. Effective December 31, 1978, the line was abandoned. The last freight actually traveled the line on December 27th-28th. The right-of-way was given to the state which converted it into a biking/hiking trail which is in use today. For a while the line from Cass to Durbin was used by the state-owned Cass Scenic railroad for excursions, but the great flood of 1985 washed it out. The last remnant of the line is a short stretch from just south of the station at Cass to the old lumber railroad connection, now used by the scenic railroad's trains, and about 4-5 miles out of Durbin which is operated by the Durbin & Greenbrier tourist railroad.

Statistics (1948)

Distance 97.9 miles
Branches connecting: None
Connections with other Railroads: Durbin (Western Maryland)
Coaling Stations: Marlinton, 200 tons from trestle
Wyes: Durbin, with Western Maryland, Unlimited tail track.
Yards: None
Stock Pens: Renick, Seebert, Beard, Marlinton, Clover Lick, Barstow
Track scales: None
Tunnels: Droop Mountain, 402 feet, Sharps, 511 feet

Dist. from Ft. Monroe	Tel. Calls	Station No.	Code No.	STATIONS
319.8		320	1012	†Whitcomb.....W Va
321.6		R2	1060	North CaldwellW Va
323.3		R4	1061	†Camp Alleghany...W Va
325.3		R6	1062	†Hopper........W Va
328.5		R8	1065	†Loopemount...W Va
330.8		R11	1068	Keister........W Va
333.9		R15	1070	Anthony.......W Va
336.0		R17	1072	†Woodman.....W Va
341.4		R22	1076	Spring Creek..W Va
344.6	RN	R25	1078	④**Renick**.......W Va
347.9		R27	1080	†Golden........W Va
349.4		R30	1082	†Horrock.......W Va
350.4		R31	1084	Rorer.........W Va
351.8		R33	1086	†Droop Mountain.........W Va
355.7		R37	1090	†Spice Run.....W Va
357.0		R38	1092	†Locust........W Va
358.3		R39	1094	Beard.........W Va
359.1		R40	1096	‡Den Mar......W Va
361.5		R42	1100	†Burnsides.....W Va
362.4		R43	1102	†Kennison.....W Va
365.6	SB	R46	1104	Seebert.......W Va
367.9		R49	1106	†Watoga.......W Va
369.1		R50	1108	†Violet.........W Va
372.0		R53	1110	†Buckeye......W Va
374.7		R56	1111	†Stillwell.......W Va
375.9	MO	R57	1114	④**Marlinton**.....W Va
380.8		R62	1119	Thorny Creek.W Va
382.1		R63	1121	††Clawson......W Va
384.4		R65	1123	†Harter........W Va
386.4		R67	1125	Big Run.......W Va
390.9		R72	1129	Clover Lick...W Va
394.2		R75	1131	Stony Bottom.W Va
396.7		R77	1133	†Sitlington.....W Va
398.7		R79	1135	†Raywood......W Va
400.5	CS	R81	1139	④Cass.........W Va
404.5		R84	1142	Wanless.......W Va
407.9		R89	1146	Hosterman....W Va
411.8		R93	1148	†Boyer.........W Va
412.5		R94	1150	†Whiting.......W Va
415.4	DR	R96	1152	①④Durbin.....W Va
416.4		R97	1154	Frank.........W Va
417.9		R98	1156	Bartow........W Va

④–Coupon Stations.
†–No Siding.
††–Passing Siding only.
‡–Private Siding only.
①–Junction with connecting line.

Station list for the Greenbrier Subdivision taken from the August 1948 issue of C&O Officers, Agents, Stations, Etc. (TLC Collection)

Since the Greenbrier Subdivision was built when C&O was using its 1890 standard depot design, most of the station structures built along the new line conformed to this standard. Typical is North Caldwell, seen here in the early 1960s, with a baggage truck still standing by even though the last passenger train ran in October 1957. The station is preserved today, converted to a residence and removed from the old right-of-way. (TLC Publishing Collection)

Profile showing gradually ascending line as Greenbrier Subdivision followed the river to its headwaters. (C&O Hist. Soc. Coll.)

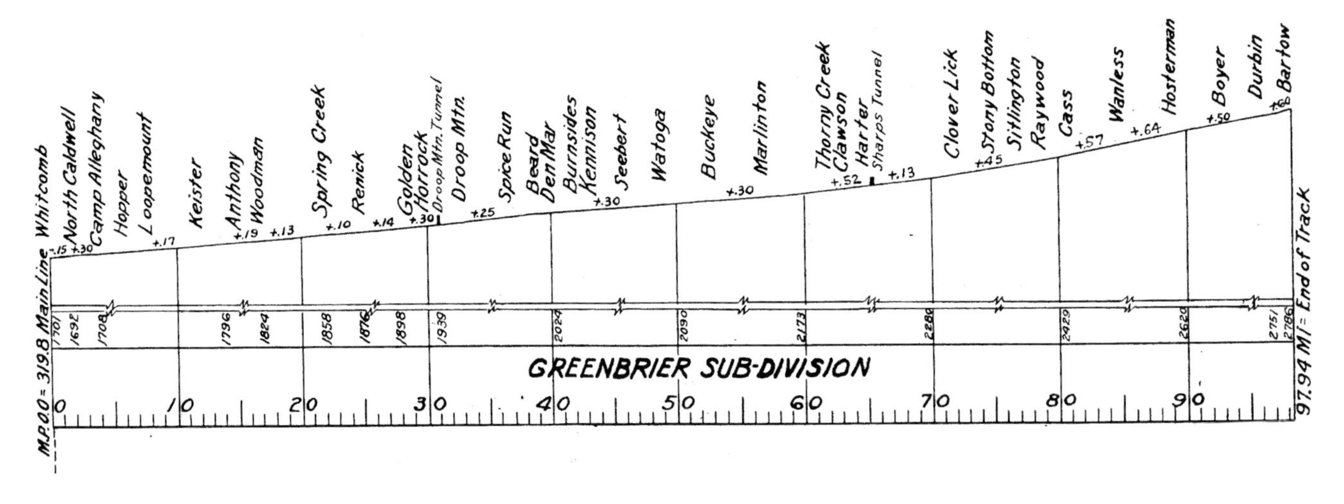

Motive power on the Greenbrier line after WWII consisted of Mikados of various classes, and an occasional 2-6-6-2. The widely used general purpose K-4 class 2-8-4 was also used even though its power greatly exceeded what was needed. Here No. 2760 has the local freight at Renick, in 1953. Within a year the ubiquitous GP9s would be in charge of all remaining service on the line. (Wendell A. Scott photo, TLC Collection)

From the 1920s through 1940s C&O used 2-6-6-2s on Greenbrier trains. This 1945 view taken from the passenger train shows H-4 No. 1414 with a mixed freight somewhere north of Renick. (Charles A. Brown photo, TLC Collection)

C&O used Brill gas-electric motor cars on many of its branch line runs after 1930. On the Greenbrier trains a second "trailer" car was almost always needed to accommodate the traffic. In this scene at Marlinton No. 9055 and trailer are doing a brisk business on June 26, 1945 (Charles A. Brown photo, TLC Collection)

GREENBRIER SUBDIVISION

Calls	Hours Open	WESTWARD FIFTH CLASS. 147 Daily Ex. Sun.	SECOND CLASS. 143 Daily Ex. Sun.		TIME TABLE No. 135. In Effect Sunday, Sept. 26, 1948. STATIONS.	Distance from Whitcomb	EASTWARD SECOND CLASS. 142 Daily Ex. Sun.	FIFTH CLASS. 150 Daily Ex. Sun.	FIFTH CLASS. 146 Daily Ex. Sun.	Side Track Capacity in Cars (41 ft.)
		L AM	L PM				A PM	A AM	A PM	
----	------------	7 30 [150]	----------		BARTOW	98.1	----------	7 30 [147]	--------	o 16
					2.5					
DR	6.00a.m. to 3.00p.m. Ex. Sun.	7 50	1 40 [142]	Wy	Durbin	95.6	1 15 [143]	7 15	2 45	o 54
					7.5					
----	------------	8 12	f 1 53 [146]		Hosterman	88.1	f12 42	--------	1 53 [143]	o 12
					7.4					
CS	8.00a. to 5.00p. Daily Ex. Sun.	9 05	s 2 10	W	Cass	80.7	s12 23	--------	1 00	p 85 o103
					9.6					
----	------------	9 30	s 2 30	W	Clover Lick	71.1	f12 00	--------	12 35	p 35 o 14
					8.8					
----	------------	9 55	f 2 48		Clawson	62.3	f11 38	--------	12 15	p 27
					6.2					
MO	8.30a. to 5.30p. Daily Ex. Sun.	10 30	s 3 03	W	Marlinton	56.1	s11 23	--------	11 30	p 55 o157
					10.3					
SB	8.00a.m. to 5.00p.m. Daily Ex. Sun.	10 58 [142/146]	s 3 27		Seebert	45.8	s10 58 [147/146]	--------	10 58 [147/142]	p 32 o 49
					7.3					
----	------------	12 07	f 3 42		Beard	38.5	f10 40	--------	10 00	p 63
					13.7					
RW	8.30a.m. to 5.30p.m. Daily Ex. Sun.	12 40	s 4 10	W	Renick	24.8	s10 08	--------	9 15	p 50 o 20
					3.2					
----	------------	12 50	f 4 16		Spring Creek	21.6	s 9 58	--------	8 55	o 12
					7.5					
----	------------	1 10	f 4 32		Anthony	14.1	f 9 42	--------	8 35	p 59 o 4
					12.3					
----	------------	1 45	f 4 56		North Caldwell	1.8	s 9 14	--------	8 05	p 35
					1.8					
----	------------	1 50	f 5 00		WHITCOMB	.0	9 10	--------	8 00	----------
		A PM	A PM				L AM	L AM	L AM	
		147 Daily Ex. Sun.	143 Daily Ex. Sun				142 Daily Ex. Sun.	150 Daily Ex. Sun.	146 Daily Ex. Sun.	

This page from the September 26, 1948 C&O Clifton Forge Division employee timetable shows the schedule for passenger and freight trains on the Greenbrier branch. Nos. 142 and 143 were the gas-electric motor trains. Nos. 146 and 147 were the local freights. No. 159 was just a short turn between Bartow and Durbin, apparently to pick up freight at the large tannery there. Note that the passenger trains had regular stops only at Durbin, Cass, Clover Lick, Marlinton, Seebert, and Renick, with all others as flag stops. There were actually many other flag stops not listed here as well. (TLC Collection)

Marlinton was another of the several standard stations on the Greenbrier Subdivision. It had the additional small office building seen to the left in this photo. This building was originally across the tracks from the station. The depot was saved and renovated for local visitor bureau use, but unfortunately burned to the ground in 2008. However it is expected that a replica will be built to replace it so important had it become to the community. (TLC Collection)

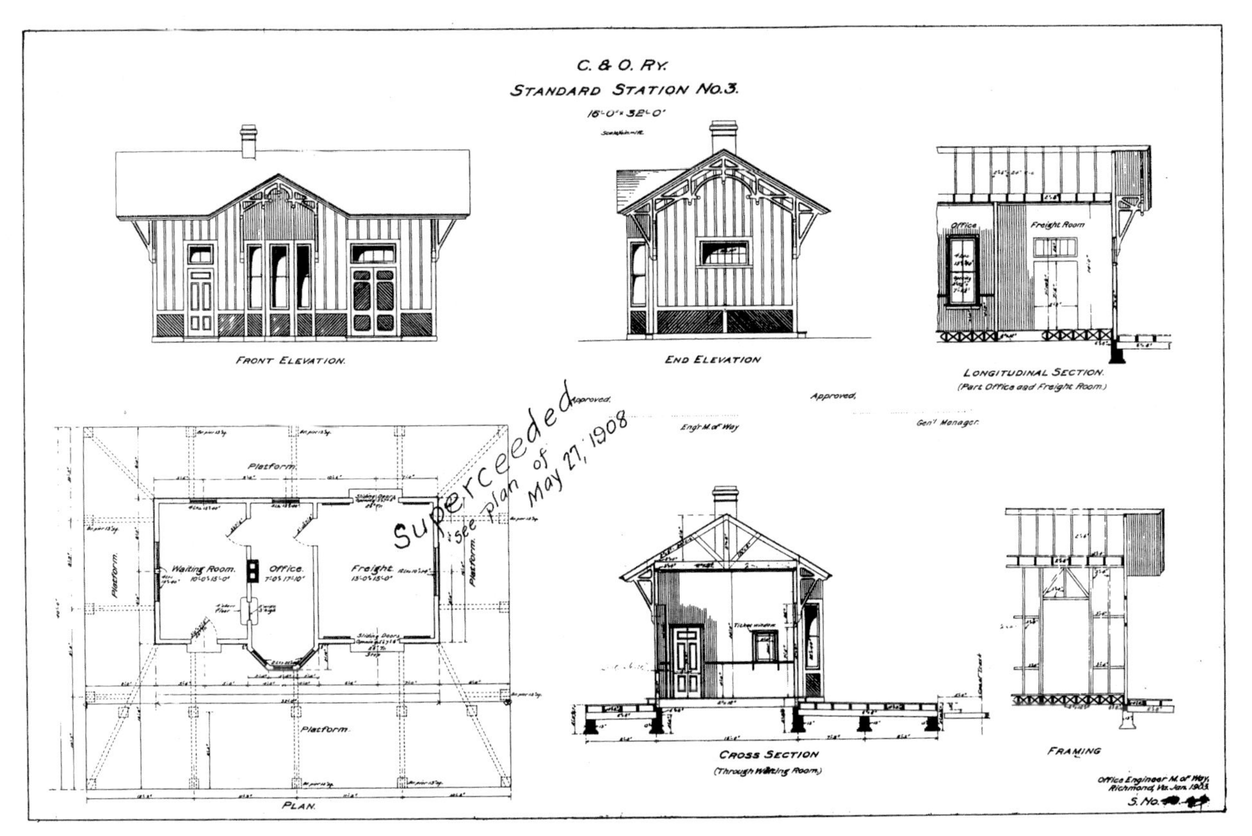

This C&O standard drawing from 1892 shows the type of building that populated the Greenbrier Subdivision in profusion. The standard was used all across the system in the 1890-1908 period, when so many new stations were erected. This drawing shows the smallest of the standards. This was simply expanded as needed in an almost modular form, adding waiting rooms/doors/windows, and freight doors as needed to accommodate local business. This standard became emblematic of the C&O to modern railfans and modelers. (C&O Historical Society Collection)

This drawing shows the verge board decorations that set the C&O standard station apart and so endeared it to people. (C&O Historical Society Collection)

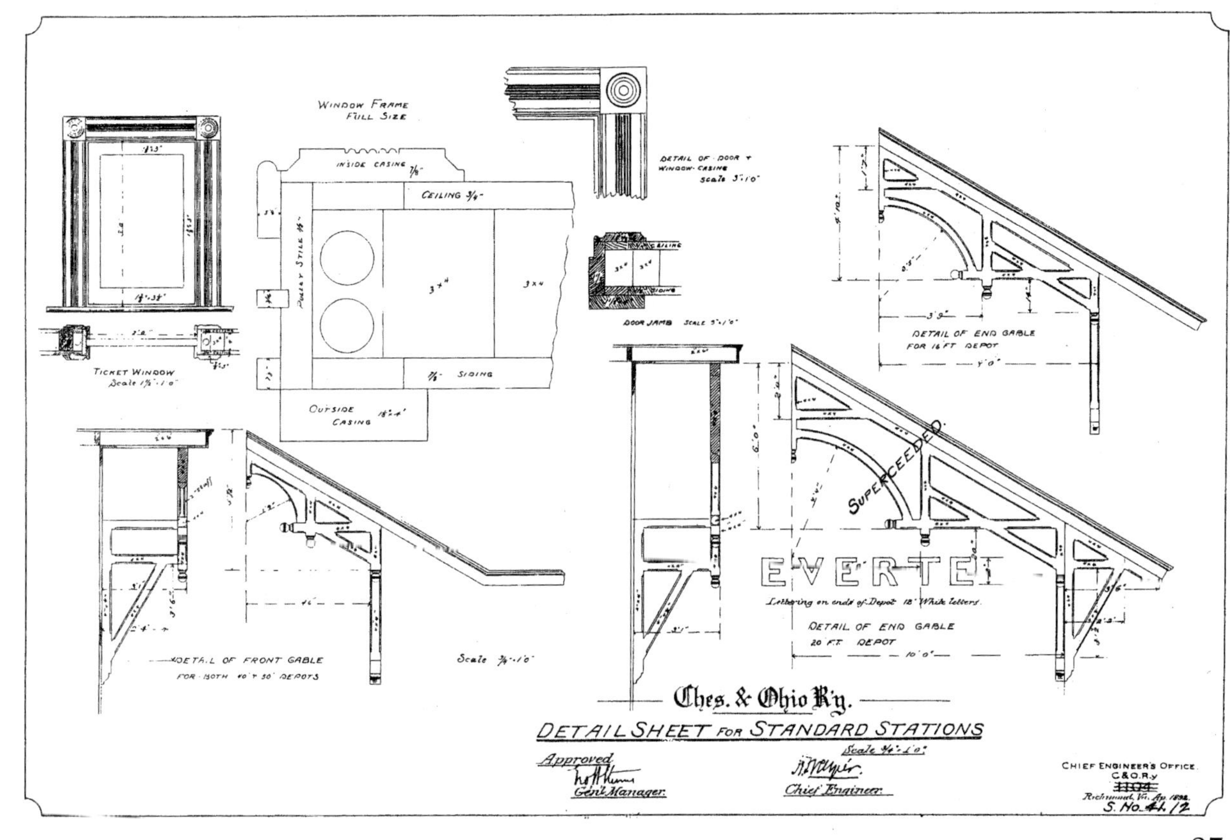

Cass was always the biggest revenue station on the Greenbrier branch because of the large lumber mill here, but its business was done through this standard combination depot. This station burned in 1915 and was replaced by a simpler one, which was taken over and used by the Cass Scenic Railroad State Park, but it burned in the 1970s and was again replaced by a modern version of this style. (C&O Historical Society Collection, Image COHS-520)

The huge band sawmill at Cass owned first by West Virginia Pulp & Paper Company and later by Mower Lumber Company, was one of the largest in the eastern U. S., and supplied C&O with a very large freight business on this line. Wood used in the Wright Brothers airplane came from Cass. (TLC Collection)

Durbin was the point at which C&O and Western Maryland met. Here a WM passenger train from Elkins, W. Va., is stopped at the C&O Durbin depot in 1945. (John Krause photo, TLC Collection)

The Alleghany Subdivision ended at the entrance to Avis yard, which was at the eastern edge of the Hinton yard complex. At that point the New River Subdivision began and ran 73.2 miles to Handley, West Virginia, where it joined with the Kanawha Subdivision.

Unlike the Alleghany, the New River Subdivision was intersected by numerous branch lines, built for the extraction of coal from the New River Coal Field.

Hinton itself was created by and for the C&O in 1871-73 as the mainline was being built westward through the state. It was a logical point to install a division point because it was at the end of the heavy Alleghany grade, and the easier New River topography, and land was available near the month of the Greenbrier as it emptied into New River.

Initially C&O installed a roundhouse, engine servicing facilities, and a couple of yard tracks. As the line's business, especially coal, grew in the 1880s and 1890s, the terminal and yard were greatly expanded, but because of the topography of the area, it didn't have much room between the steep hillside and the river, so in 1919 a new yard was built at Avis, just to the east. The old or "lower" yard at Hinton constricted to just two mainline tracks as it passed the passenger station, then expanded again into the multiple track Avis yard. These tracks were long enough that eastbound coal trains could be assembled here and dispatched over the Alleghany Subdivision to Clifton Forge. Hinton, as all the facilities of the C&O in West Virginia, was built almost exclusively for coal traffic. Most passenger trains just passed through. Crews on interdivisional manifest freights ran through from Russell, Ky. to Hinton without change at Handley, the western division point separating Hinton and Kanawha Subdivisions.

Hinton had no industry or business other than the C&O and the retail and service businesses that grew to support its employees. The town eventually reached a population of 8,800 in 1925, but declined after that, and today has hardly a 1/3rd of that population.

The roundhouse and engine facilities were steadily expanded and upgraded over the years. A 800-ton concrete coaling station was built in 1929 to replace the old trestle-type facility that had been used since the 1890s. This huge monolithic concrete tower is one of the few C&O structures left today, now overgrown by vegetation and hardly recognizable. A sizeable freight station was built on a steep siding at the end of one of the city streets, and served the town's many businesses, including meat packing and wholesale grocery companies which in turn served the retail businesses to the west in the coal fields. This generated a good quantity of incoming and outgoing freight both as car-load lots and less-than-carload freight.

The passenger station still standing today (owned by the city and being refurbished and preserved) was built in 1892, but modified considerably over the years, including the restoration from a fire. It ultimately held the Hinton Division offices in its upper floors, as well as the dispatchers for both the New

A profile of the New River Subdivision mainline shows a steadily ascending eastbound grade as the line follows the New River, which is descending as it runs to the west, connecting with the Gauley River at Gauley.

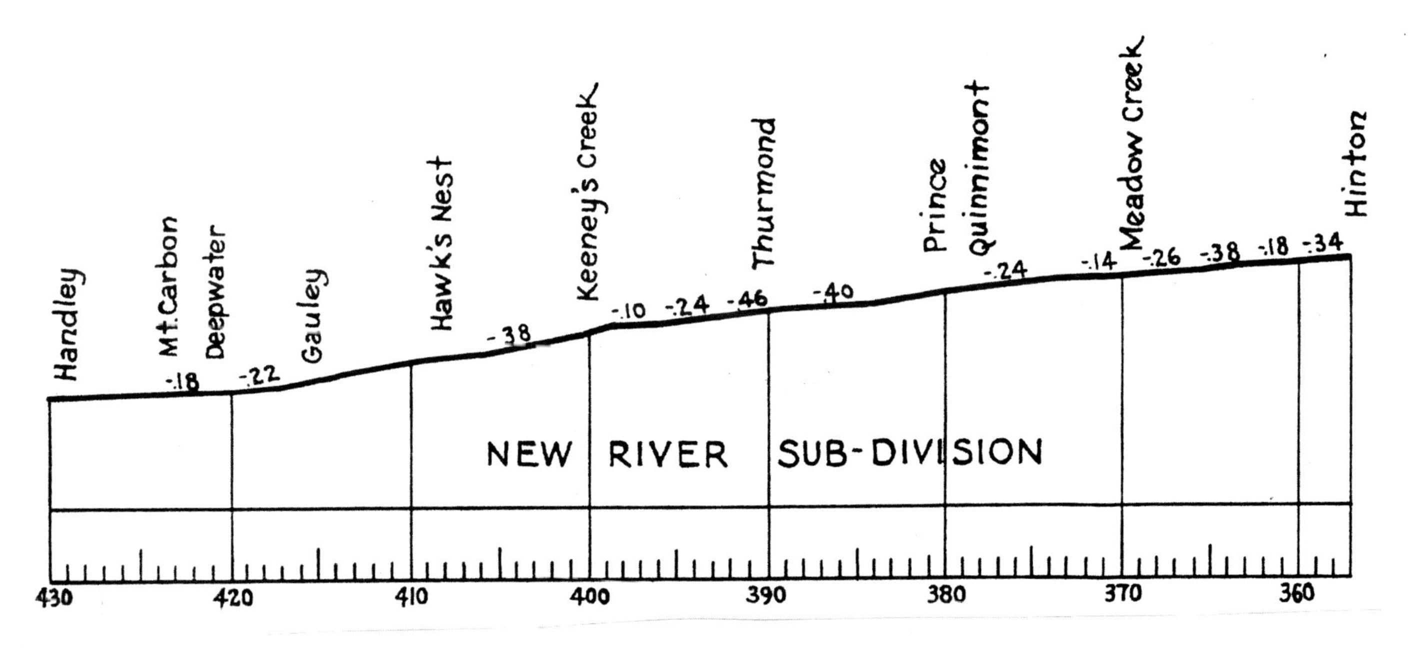

Dist. from Ft. Mon-roe	Tel. Calls	Sta-tion No.	Code No.	STATIONS
354.6	*MX	355		M. X. Cabin--W Va
356.5		356½	1054	Avis----------W Va
357.0	*HX	357	1165	④**Hinton**-------W Va
	*H			" Dispatcher's Off.-
358.0	*CW	358		C. W. Cabin---W Va
360.0		360	1168	Barksdale-----W Va
361.3		361	1170	Brooks--------W Va
362.0	RK	362		††R. K. Cabin--W Va
366.3		366	1175	Sandstone-----W Va
369.6	*MD	369	1177	②④Meadow Creek-------W Va
374.3		374	1183	Glade---------W Va
378.7	*QN	379	1185	②④**Quinnimont** W Va
380.0	*NI	380	1200	②④†**Prince**-----W Va
383.2		383	1372	McKendree----W Va
385.3		385	1373	‡Thayer--------W Va
386.1		386	1374	‡Dunfee--------W Va
387.9		387	1376	Claremont-----W Va
388.6		388	1377	Beechwood Jct. W Va
389.1		389	1378	‡Stone Cliff----W Va
389.4	*CS	390		††C. S. Cabin--W Va
390.8	*DU	391	1380	②④**Thurmond**--W Va
391.9		392	1500	†Dimmock-----W Va
392.4		392½	1501	†Rush Run-----W Va
393.8		393	1503	‡Beury---------W Va
394.4		395	1505	‡Fire Creek----W Va
395.2		395½	1506	†Pennbrook----W Va
396.4		396	1508	E. Sewell------W Va
397.6	*ED	397	1510	④**Sewell**-------W Va
399.3		399	1526	Caperton------W Va
400.4		400	1527	②Keeneys Creek W Va
401.4		401	1524	East Nuttall--W Va
401.6		402	1542	Nuttall--------W Va
404.3		FA	1545	‡④Fayette-----W Va
405.6		406	1549	‡Ames---------W Va
408.6		409	1552	②Hawks Nest--W Va
408.9	*MA	409½	1558	②Macdougal---W Va
410.8		411	1560	Cotton Hill----W Va
415.0	*GU	414		G. U. Cabin---W Va
415.2		415	1565	①②④Gauley---W Va
416.1		416	1610	†Old Gauley----W Va
417.9		418	1614	Kanawha Falls W Va
421.3	*VN	422	1616	①Deepwater---W Va
422.1		423	1621	①†West Deep-water-------W Va
423.7		424	1618	②Mt. Carbon--W Va
425.3		425½	1641	†Eagle---------W Va
427.5	CN	428	1645	④**Montgomery**--W Va
428.2		428½	1647	②Morris Creek Jct----------W Va

④–Coupon Stations.
*–Day and Night Telegraph Offices.
①–Junction with connecting line.
②–Junction of Sub-division shown elsewhere.
†–No Siding.
‡–Private Siding only.
††–Passing Siding only.

New River Subdivision station listing from August 1948 issue of C&O Officers, Agents, Stations, Etc. book.

River and Alleghany Subdivisions after the installation of CTC signal operations. The large red brick station had a passenger ticket office, waiting room, and lunch room facilities for the passengers. Express business was also handled on the first floor's west end. Business here was brisk, especially in the high era of the coal mining from the 1920s to the 1950s. In addition to the mainline name trains (see Chapter 8), Hinton was the terminal for several local passenger trains. The New River local trains were usually made up here westbound and terminated eastbound, as was the same for Alleghany Subdivision locals. Over the years this pattern changed, in that some local trains operated through to and from different, more distant terminals including Clifton Forge and Charlottesville in the east and Huntington in the west. In the post-WW II era on which this book concentrates most closely, the remaining locals usually worked through Hinton after about 1950.

Since Hinton was a division point where steam locomotives were always changed, it needed a large roundhouse/machine shop force to handle running repairs, and to service locomotives between runs. The larger locomotives were needed for eastbound trains over the Alleghany grade, and lighter ones were used to the west. There was always a variety of locomotive types present at Hinton, ranging from the very largest, the H-7 simple articulated and the monumental H-8 2-6-6-6 Allegheny types, to the smaller classes, such as F-15 Pacifics and 2-8-2 Mikados. Switchers of the 0-8-0 variety were also used for heavy yard work, and 0-10-0s during certain periods.

West of Hinton the mainline is laid along the New River in a fairly open valley until it reaches Sandstone, about eight miles, where it enters the gorge of the New River. This is the defining feature of the line and in many ways of the C&O in West Virginia. For the next 49 miles, until the line reaches the mouth of New River at Gauley, the line is laid along the very edge of the rapid river, in what was a wild and remote region in 1870. The construction

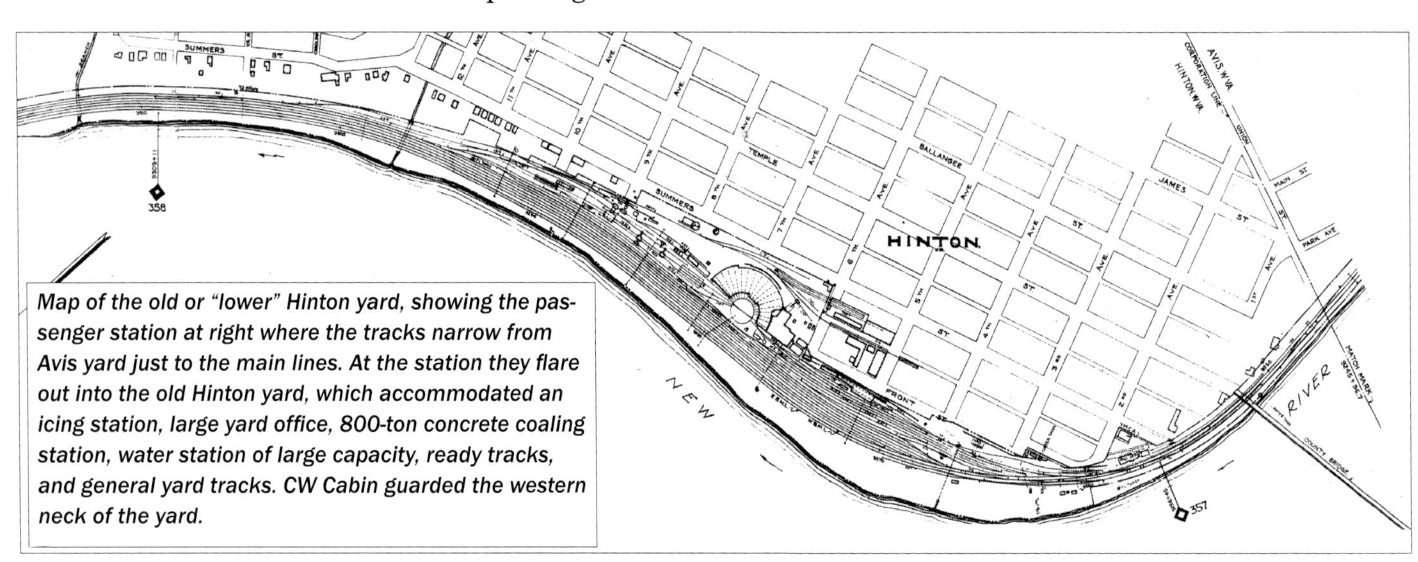

Map of the old or "lower" Hinton yard, showing the passenger station at right where the tracks narrow from Avis yard just to the main lines. At the station they flare out into the old Hinton yard, which accommodated an icing station, large yard office, 800-ton concrete coaling station, water station of large capacity, ready tracks, and general yard tracks. CW Cabin guarded the western neck of the yard.

Rolling through Avis, L-2a class 4-6-4 Hudson No. 310 has local Train No. 13 tow in July 1948. Normally the territory of the larger J-3/J-3A class 4-8-4 Greenbriers, Hudsons were seldom used east of Hinton, so this is a rare photo. (Gene Huddleston photo, C&O Hist. Soc. Coll., Image COHS-1209)

work was difficult and the region remained dangerous for a long time because of frequent washouts and landslides. Easily accessible coal seams existed right along the mainline in this area, and were opened early. These mines started the C&O's coal business, which expanded without stop into modern times.

By 1890 the Hawks Nest Branch was constructed, using an older narrow-gauge right-of-way to access a mine up the ravine toward Ansted. It was among the first of C&O's coal-only branches.

Over the period 1900-1920 C&O built scores of coal branch lines in southern West Virginia, so that by the post-war era, the New River Subdivision had few mines still in production on the mainline, but had large production from the branches. As each of these branches was built it had to have facilities to service the locomotives and stage the cars being used to transport the coal. The maps and data accompanying this chapter will more fully explain this system.

In the earliest era, 1873 to 1889, the operating regions of the C&O were divided so that trains ran Hinton to Cannelton (later renamed Montgomery). When the C&O was rebuilt, refurbished, and expanded beginning in 1889 after its ownership transferred from C. P. Huntington to the Vanderbilt and Morgan interests, the yard and terminal facility at Handley was built at milepost 429, only a few miles west of Montgomery. It was in 1890 that the districts were established (later called subdivisions). This is when the Kanawha and New River Subdivisions got their designations. Handley yard was, at the time of our study at mid-20th Century, assigned to the Kanawha Subdivision, with the New River Subdivision ending just to the east at Morris Creek Junction.

The story of the construction of the New River Subdivision mainline was one of adventure and difficulty because of the rugged terrain that had to be crossed. Southern West Virginia was, in effect,

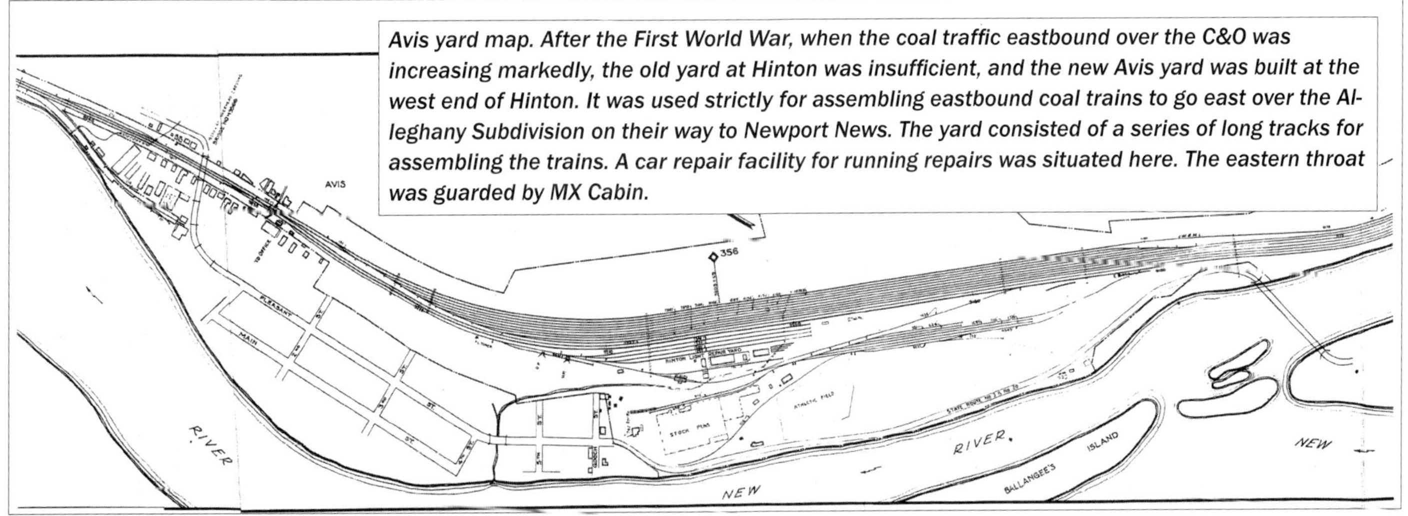

Avis yard map. After the First World War, when the coal traffic eastbound over the C&O was increasing markedly, the old yard at Hinton was insufficient, and the new Avis yard was built at the west end of Hinton. It was used strictly for assembling eastbound coal trains to go east over the Allegheny Subdivision on their way to Newport News. The yard consisted of a series of long tracks for assembling the trains. A car repair facility for running repairs was situated here. The eastern throat was guarded by MX Cabin.

a wilderness with only one major semi-improved road in the area in the form of the old James River & Kanawha Turnpike. In some places C&O's locating engineers had to be lowered down the steep gorge cliff sides in order to lay out a route for the railroad through the rugged region. The gorge walls closed in on the river and allowed little area at the bottom for the C&O, so space for it had to be blasted and dug out of the steep sides to form a narrow shelf along which the rails could be laid. However, once the line was in operation and mines began to be opened, people flowed into the area and in the last quarter of the 19th century the area was a beehive of activity. By the time of our mid-20th Century treatment, most of the mines and associated towns along the mainline were extinct or almost so because the coal that was easily accessible near the mainline had played out and the branch lines had become the center of coal mining activity and associated population.

Hinton figured large in C&O passenger train operations. Dining cars were often dropped and picked up here, based on schedules. C&O covered more trains with fewer cars by attaching them only when necessary to serve meals. Here No. 4, the eastbound Sportsman is at right and No. 3, the westbound FFV is arriving at Hinton passenger station in May 1957. The S-2 Alco switcher has a diner which will be attached to No. 3. The streamlined coaling station at right was erected specifically to serve the huge M-1 class steam-turbine-electric locomotives that C&O bought in 1948. They were a failure and this facility stood unused until it was demolished in the early 1960s. (Gene Huddleston Photo, C&O Hist. Soc. Coll., Image No. COHS-2423)

The large brick passenger station at Hinton had a restaurant in the east (near) end, and divisional offices upstairs. After the early 1960s installation of Centralized Traffic Control the New River and Alleghany dispatchers operated their CTC boards from here as well. The Railroad YMCA building is up the hill to the right. Avis yard is behind the photographer and the old Hinton yard just beyond the station. (T. W. Dixon, Jr. photo)

West of the passenger station, was a large shed-style engine house built in 1911 to accommodate the new Mallet locomotives that were too long for the old roundhouse. Called the "Mallet House," it hosted most of the big mainline locomotives for their between-run servicing. Here H-8 2-6-6-6 No. 1621 is ready for action on an eastbound train as it simmers next to the Mallet House in the fall of 1947. (Gene Huddleston photo, C&O Hist. Soc. Coll., Image No. 1403)

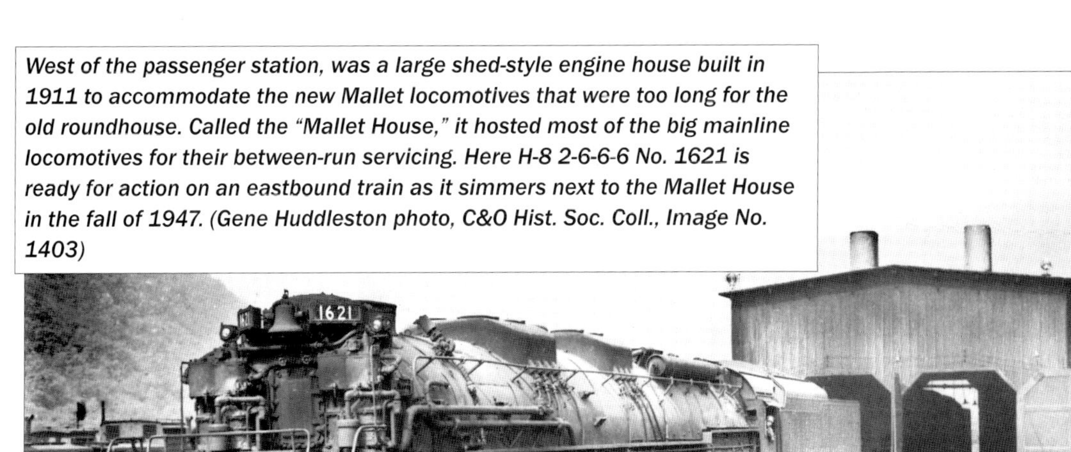

Looking down on the engine terminal at Hinton, the light F-15 class Pacific type No. 432 and 2-8-0 No. 1053 are ready for work. The F-15 was probably for a local passenger run and the 2-8-0 for a local freight or work train. (C&O Hist. Soc. Coll., Image no. COHS-1200)

The 800-ton concrete coaling station at Hinton, with the sand house a left and the huge 100,000-gallon water tank in the distance were the main features of Hinton yard in this 1946 scene. (C&O Ry. Photo, C&O Hist. Soc. Coll., Image CSPR-215)

CW cabin, one of C&O's standard brick towers, stood guard at the west throat of the Hinton yard. Here the operator is about to hand up orders in the early 1970s. (T. W. Dixon, Jr. photo)

Looking down on the mainline and the New River at Brooks, where the River begins to narrow, an H-8 takes an empty coal train west in July 1945. (C&O Ry. Photo, C&O Hist. Soc. Coll., Image no, 57.126)

Roaring west at Brooks, three miles out of Hinton, H-8 No. 1609 takes a empty train towards the coal fields in December 1946. (B. F. Cutler photo, C&O Hist. Soc. Coll., Image No. 1519)

The easternmost coal branch on the New River Subdivision was where the Nicholas Fayette & Greenbrier Railroad (see Chapter 5) joined the mainline. Bringing coal down from the Greenbrier coal fields, 2-6-6-2s were used for taking empties up the steep looped tracks and bringing coal down. Here a couple of H-4 2-6-6-2s are at Meadow Creek's small six-track interchange yard in 1952. Before the elimination of switchbacks on the NF&G, 2-8-2s were used in this service. (B. J. Kern Photo, C&O Hist. Soc. Coll., Image COHS-2766)

The station at Meadow Creek was similar to many other simple, rectangular, undecorated depots that C&O built as it expanded its mainline through West Virginia in the early 1870s. When this photo was taken in 1935 it was still a very active station. (William Monypeny photo, TLC Collection)

About 12 miles west of Hinton the C&O passes Sandstone Falls on New River in some very scenic territory. In the summer of 1956 a set of ABBA F7s powers an eastbound coal train at this location. (C&O Ry. Photo, C&O Hist. Soc. Coll., Image No, 10393.141)

MD Cabin controlled the C&O/NF&G interchange at Meadow Creek, and was built to look similar to contemporary C&O brick towers, except it was built as a wooden frame structure. Note the standard C&O privy and the 10-ton coal house on either side. (T. W. Dixon, Jr. photo)

Quinnimount was home to this very distinctive structure, unique on the C&O, which served both as a signal cabin and as the local yard office. The building endured into the 1970s, ensuring its fame. (T.W. Dixon, Jr. photo)

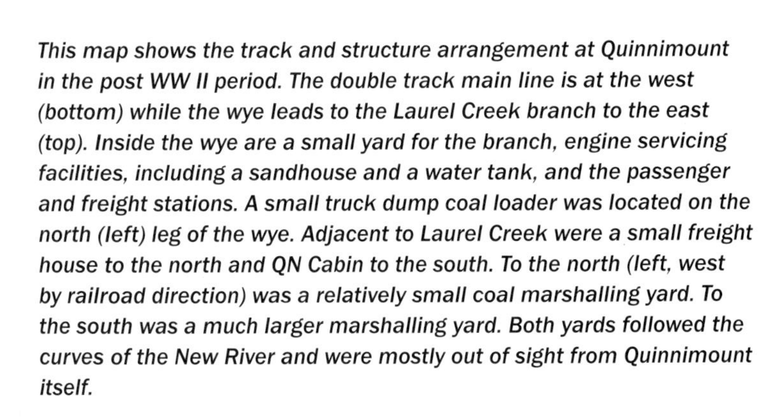

This map shows the track and structure arrangement at Quinnimount in the post WW II period. The double track main line is at the west (bottom) while the wye leads to the Laurel Creek branch to the east (top). Inside the wye are a small yard for the branch, engine servicing facilities, including a sandhouse and a water tank, and the passenger and freight stations. A small truck dump coal loader was located on the north (left) leg of the wye. Adjacent to Laurel Creek were a small freight house to the north and QN Cabin to the south. To the north (left, west by railroad direction) was a relatively small coal marshalling yard. To the south was a much larger marshalling yard. Both yards followed the curves of the New River and were mostly out of sight from Quinnimount itself.

Quinnimont yard, the junction point of the Laurel Creek Branch, was also a point at which coal was assembled from that branch and from the Piney Creek Branch, which entered the mainline about a mile west of here. Quinnimont consisted of only a few yard tracks, arranged in a wye, with a passenger and freight station, pump house, water station, engine ready track, and yard office (in the distance in this 1956 photo) in the center. Note that the station is of the C&O standard design, but has been modified with the addition of a back wing. (Chesapeake & Ohio photo, C&OHS Collection, Image No. CSPR-10393.147)

In this 1957 view of Quinnimount you can clearly see QN Cabin in the distance, the freight house and the water tower. Also of interest are the section labors' homes along the right side of the tracks. The tracks at the left are a parking track for trains off the Piney Creek branch, the westbound and then eastbound main lines, and the west yard. (Gene Huddleston photo, C&OHS Collection, Image No. COHS-2951)

Only a mile west of Quinnimont yard is Prince, which is the junction point for the important coal-hauling Piney Creek Branch, serving a maze of other branches in the Beckley coal fields area. It was at this point that C&O built its most modern mainline passenger station in 1946. There was a plan to replace a number of old stations with new ultra-modern buildings, but it was cancelled because of declining passenger traffic and financial issues. Since the Prince depot had been started before the program ended, it was finished and today is a unique oddity. Its design was according to the precepts of the Mid-Century Modern architecture with the best facilities that could be built. The concrete and brick structure, with its accompanying platform and shed is still in service by Amtrak. In this photo, K-4 2-8-4 Is arriving with mail and express train No. 103 with a long train of head-end cars in June 1946. The station is so new that the large station name signs have not yet been installed atop the canopy ends. The track merging from the right is the Piney Creek Branch. (C&O Ry. Photo, C&O Hist. Soc. Coll., Image No. CSPR-580)

Stretcher's Neck Tunnel is located within sight west of the Prince depot, and is the only tunnel remaining on the New River Subdivision after the short Pope's Nose and Shoo-Fly tunnels were daylighted in the 1930s. Here a brace of F7s, led by 7079 brings a coal train east out of the standard concrete portal in 1956. (C&O Ry. Photo, C&O Hist. Soc. Coll., Image No. CSPR-10393.143)

H-6 2-6-6-2 No. 1489 is arriving at Prince with a coal train from Raleigh assembly yard on Piney Creek Branch in September 1947. Its train is on the bridge across New River. It came down the grade from Raleigh with two 2-6-6-2s. One cut off and ran light over the bridge, and is waiting for this train to pull ahead, where it will couple on again and proceed to Quinnimont to drop its loads for pickup by a mainline train. (C&O Ry. Photo, C&O Hist. Soc. Coll., Image No. CSPR-1171)

The Stone Cliff shelter station was one of C&O's standard flag-stop stations that dotted the system. This one was a little different in that it incorporated a canopy over a portion of the platform. Stone Cliff was at the eastern end of the Thurmond yard. This 1935 photo was taken from a C&O local passenger train exchanging passengers. (William Monypeny Photo, C&O Hist. Soc. Coll., Image No, 3040)

One of the locations that has received a great deal of publicity in the modeling and railfan historical press is Thurmond, C&O's mainline coal assembly terminal about 11 miles west of Prince, in the deepest part of the New River Gorge. This scene from June 1946 shows the large depot at left with G-7 2-8-0 No. 975 and H-4 2-6-6-2 No. 1465 about to enter the terminal area. The bridge leads across New River with the Loup Creek Branch, which connected with numerous other branches in the Beckley area coal fields. (C&O Ry. Photo, C&O Hist. Soc. Coll., Image CSPR-301)

Early in the diesel era, an ABA set of F7s leads an eastbound coal train out of Thurmond, while a string of camp cars and wreck crane sit on the siding in August 1953 during the steam-diesel transition years. (Gene Huddleston photo, C&O Hist. Soc. Coll., Image No. COHS-1485)

Alco S-4 switcher No. 5112 is in charge of a mainline local freight train in summer of 1954. It has just replaced a K-1 2-8-2 Mikado on this run. Engineers on local freights were usually the most senior, and the man in the cab here seems to prove it. (Gene Huddleston photo, C&O Hist. Soc. Coll., Image No. COHS-3438)

This night photo brings out all the detail in the well-weathered Thurmond depot in 1972. The big building was left over from the coal boom years. The upper floor held an operator, clerks' offices, and even a coal company office. (Ron Piksor photo, TLC Collection)

Brakeman and conductor ride the tender of G-7 2-8-0 No. 975 backing into Thurmond with a mine run from the Kenney's Creek Branch which joined the mainline at MP 440.4, about nine miles west of Thurmond. This run used two of the old Consolidations, right up to the end of steam as this summer 1953 scene attests. The 2-8-0s were used because of the short tail track on the switchbacks on the branch. (Gene Huddleston photo, C&O Hist. Soc. Coll., Image No. COHS-1281)

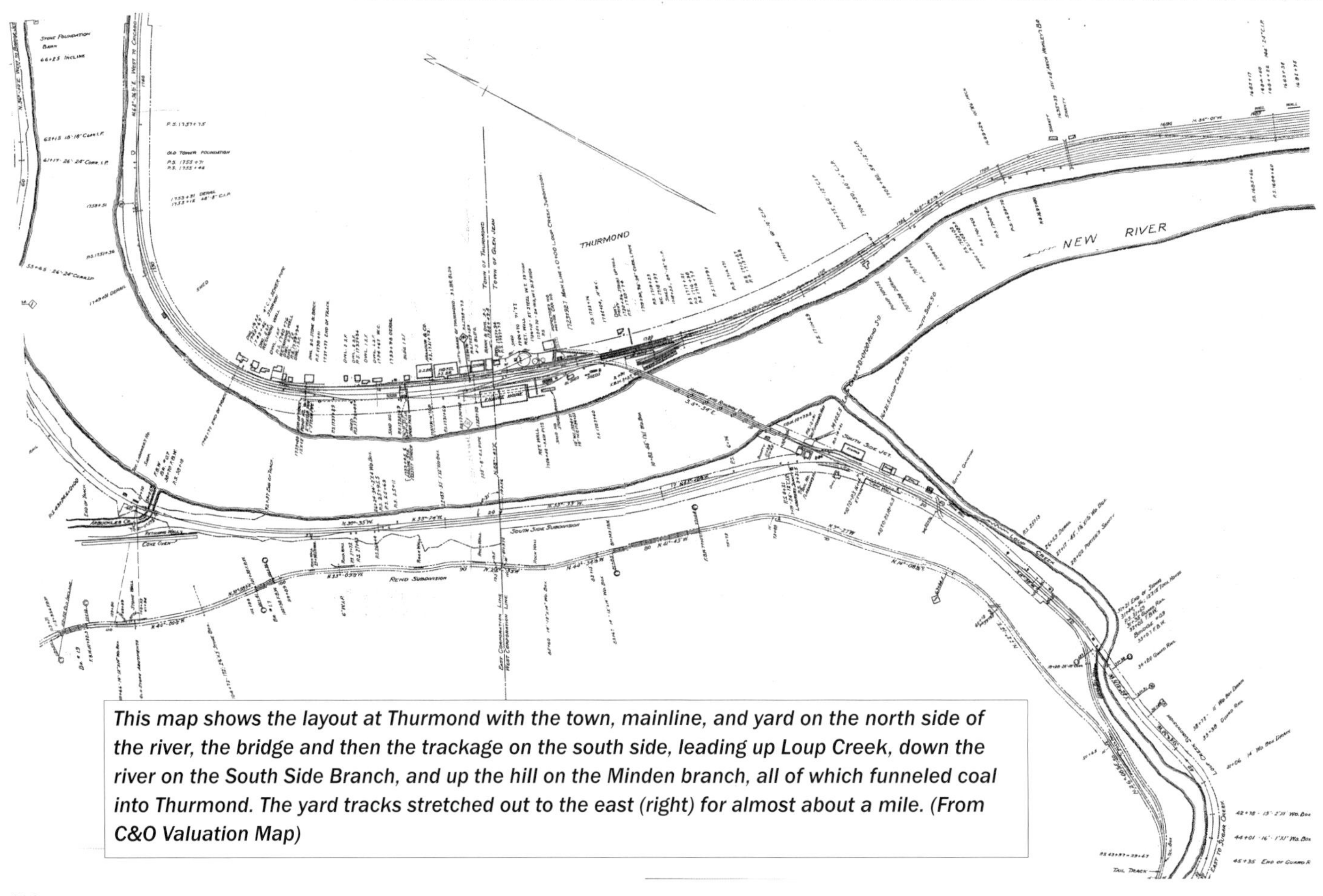

This map shows the layout at Thurmond with the town, mainline, and yard on the north side of the river, the bridge and then the trackage on the south side, leading up Loup Creek, down the river on the South Side Branch, and up the hill on the Minden branch, all of which funneled coal into Thurmond. The yard tracks stretched out to the east (right) for almost about a mile. (From C&O Valuation Map)

In the last decade and a half of steam the H-8 2-6-6-6s were the mainstay for the mainline trains. Here No. 1624 has an eastbound getting under way after taking water at Thurmond in September 1955, in the last year of steam operations. The train will pick up loads at the east end of Thurmond yard to fill out to 142 cars. (Gene Huddleston photo, C&O Hist. Soc. Coll., Image No. 1203)

Drawings prepared by the Historic American Engineering Record branch of the National Park Service show the 500-ton Fairbanks Morse concrete coaling station at Thurmond. (Historic American Engineering Record)

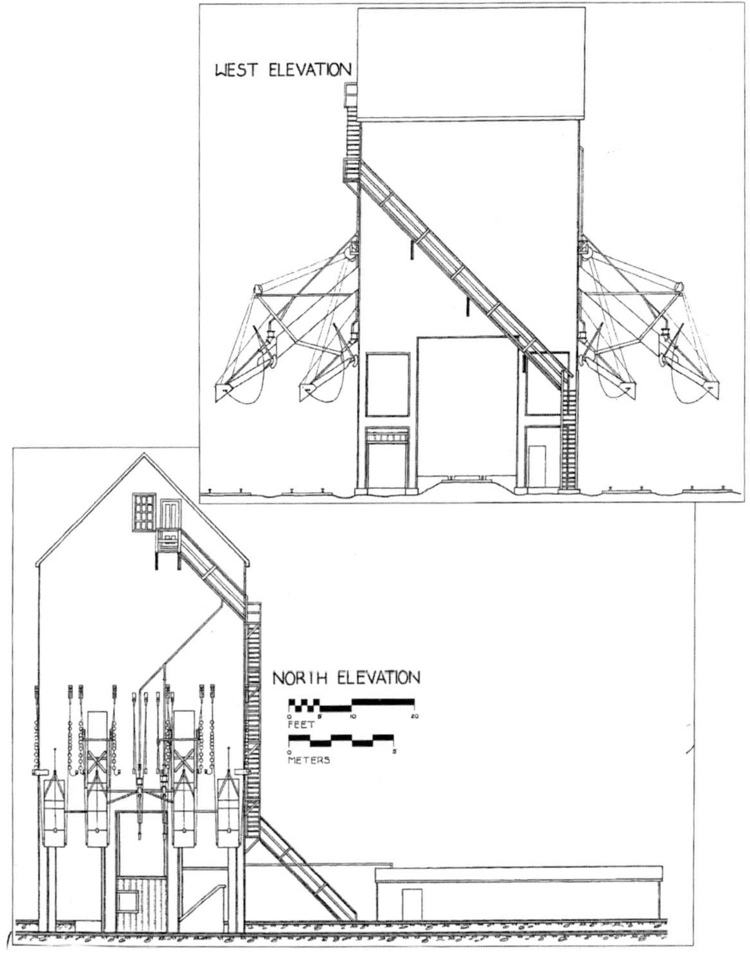

Southern Coals Corporation's mine at Cunard is pictured here in June 1954, with its long monitor carrying coal from the seam high up the side of the gorge down to the tipple on the C&O's South Side Subdivision. The South Side Subdivision ran from across the river at Thurmond 7.7 miles to Bridge Junction, opposite Sewell. (C&O Ry. Photo, C&O Hist. Soc. Coll., Image No. CSPR-10057.W9A)

Stations

Because the New River Subdivision was built through a fairly remote and largely undeveloped region, what stations/towns existed along the line were essentially products of the coming of the railway and the building of coal mines. Most of these small towns, coal camps, and mines have now disappeared and the New River Gorge area has largely returned to nature. In fact today the gorge is covered by a National Park called, appropriately enough, the *New River Gorge National River*.

The first station of any consequence west of Hinton was Sandstone (MP 366.3) which, in the early days, had a large business in lumber and was a station for the immediate region.

Beyond Sandstone by only three miles is Meadow Creek (MP 369.6). It was of no consequence until it became the outlet for the Sewell Valley Railroad, a line built by the owners of the Meadow River Lumber Company of Rainelle, about 20 miles from the gorge. This mill became the largest hardwood lumber mill in the world, and the Sewell Valley delivered its lumber to the C&O at Meadow Creek. In the 1920s C&O decided that it would like to have this line to tap the just opening Greenbrier coal fields in Greenbrier and Nicholas counties. C&O bought it and other line owned by Meadow River Lumber, the Greenbrier & Eastern. These were consolidated with some new trackage to create the Nicholas, Fayette & Greenbrier Railroad Company. This company was owned jointly by the C&O and the New York Central. The NYC connected with the NF&G at Swiss, where its Gauley branch led down to Gauley Bridge (opposite Gauley on the C&O), and on to Charleston and Columbus. NYC generally moved coal from mines located on the western end of the new line, while C&O coal came mainly from mines at the east end. The NF&G coal region developed well and by the post-war era was producing a large quantity of coal, much of which found outlet over the C&O. C&O operated on the NF&G as though it were simply another coal branch. NF&G owned little equipment, so C&O locomotives which were used (as well as NYC locomotives) were serviced at the Rainelle terminal and yard. In 1947 one of C&O's major post-war right-of-way improvements was made when the switchbacks between Meadow Bridge and Meadow Creek were eliminated and replaced by loop tracks. When this occurred, the class K-1 light 2-8-2 Mikado type locomotives that had been used extensively on this branch were replaced by 2-6-6-2 Mallets, which then remained almost exclusive power here until the end of steam. NYC also used the Rainelle terminal but it served only a few mines at the western end of the road. It usually used 2-8-2 Mikados.

At Glade (MP 374.3), a mining short line connected via a large bridge across New River. This operation, along with many early mines along the New River, had played out by mid-century and the station and community receded.

At Milepost 378.4 Quinnimont was an important point. It was the terminal/assembly yard for several

At Sewell, where the narrow gauge Mann's Creek Railroad connected with C&O, was the last of C&O's depot/tower combination structures to stand, being demolished in the mid-1960s. (Gene Huddleston photo, TLC Collection)

mines on the 6-mile-long Laurel Creek Branch. Also, in the 1870s, when C&O first arrived, a large iron furnace was built here which by 1878 employed 600 men. Of course, all these people had to live nearby, creating a community not only of iron workers but of miners as well. The iron operation was gone by the late 1880s, but coal mining continued, and Quinnimont yard was an important point on C&O until modern times. It was arranged as a large wye with the Laurel Creek line coming in from the north and branching both east and west to join the mainline running along the river at the bottom of the triangle forming the wye.

Quinnimont had a passenger station, freight station, large yard office and operator's tower (called "cabin" on C&O), as well as a water station (with a wooden tank on very tall legs), and locomotive sanding and servicing facilities. It did not have an engine house or machine shop, but facilities for coaling locomotives by clam-shell crane directly from cars, as needed.

The yard served as a collecting point for coal coming down the Piney Creek Branch, which entered the mainline about a mile to the west as well as from the Laurel Creek Branch.

The point at which the Piney Creek Branch reached the mainline was Prince, and C&O placed a large passenger and freight station here. Although there was no town at this location, it served as the transfer point for trains coming to and from the Piney Creek Branch. The Piney Creek Branch ran 15 miles to Raleigh and Beckley (and well beyond), where it branched out into several other lines that tapped a maze of mining operations in the region. This coal was assembled at Raleigh yard, and then sent to Quinnimont as mentioned before.

In the post-war era C&O built an ultra-modern passenger depot at Prince as part of its improvement program. This type of station was planned for many locations along the line, but as it happened only the one here was actually built, in 1946. The station seems completely out of place in its isolated position in the gorge. (See page 47) However, it was there just to serve as the transfer point for people taking the connecting branch line passenger trains to and from Beckley, one of the state's largest coal centers. After the branch passenger train was discontinued in 1949, the station still served as the passenger station for Beckley as people came by auto or taxi down the mountain road to board mainline trains. It still has a good business for Amtrak's *Cardinal* today.

NI Cabin, the operator's tower at Prince, was the last standard wooden frame C&O tower to stand, being demolished in the early 1980s.

Sewell was also the location of the last fully active coke ovens on the C&O. The operation is seen here in June 1954. The Mann's Creek Railroad delivered the coal to the tipple in the background. Some of the coal charged the ovens, and their coke production was then loaded into C&O hoppers for shipment to steel mills. By this time much larger coking operations, usually located near the steel mills were producing most of the supply of coke. The Mann's Creek stone 2-stall engine house is seen in the background. (C&O Ry. Photo, C&O Hist. Soc. Coll., Image CSPR-3388)

At milepost 383.2 was the village of McKendree, remote and easily reachable only by train, it was once the site of a large hospital dedicated to serving miners of the region. Thayer was another nearby mining community.

The next major station is Thurmond, once an active center of the coal trade of the region and locus of a great deal of history, story, and legend. At milepost 389.1 is the small station of Stone Cliff (See page 48) which marks the eastern extremity of the Thurmond complex. Its major yard consisted of several long tracks for storage and assembly of coal loads and empties. The station itself is at MP 390.8. A large two-story frame depot was erected in 1905 to replace one of C&O's standard depot/tower combined stations that burned. Behind it was a one-story frame freight station that was cantilevered over the New

More of the geographical context of the gorge is seen at the traditional overlook at Hawks Nest, where tourists have stopped to watch C&O trains far below since the park was established in the 1930s. At the south (right) end of the bridge the two main lines, separated on both sides of the river at Sewell, join again, on the south side. (C&O Ry. Photo, C&O Hist. Soc. Coll., Image No. CSPR-3053)

A coal train, almost invisible at the bottom of the gorge, near Cotton Hill in the summer of 1954. The old location of Pope's Nose Tunnel is about where the caboose is seen, before it was eliminated in the 1930s. (C&O Ry. Photo, C&O Hist. Soc. Coll., Image No. CSPR-3397)

River because of restricted space at this location. Just west of the station was the engine terminal consisting of sanding facilities, ready tracks, a long two-stall engine house (that could accommodate four locomotives), and west of it a concrete 500-ton coaling station, built in 1922. Just west of here the yard ends.

Near the tracks beside the terminal facilities was the main business area of Thurmond, which consisted of a number of multi-story brick commercial buildings that abutted the C&O mainline so closely there was no room for vehicular traffic in front of them. Thurmond bragged for many years that its main street was the C&O. The residences dotted the steep hillside behind the commercial block. Thurmond never had more than a few hundred citizens, but its wealth was great because it served as a headquarters for several coal operators' offices and a very strong bank. At one time Thurmond generated more freight revenue for the C&O than its largest cities, because so much of the coal that came down to the mainline from the branches in the region was billed from this point. Across the river from the station was the Dunglen Hotel, which had a reputation as an infamous gambling locale and vice center. W. D. Thurmond, on whose land the town was built, insisted on strict morality ordinances for the town, so that element tended to congregate around the rambling frame Dunglen across the river out of Thurmond's reach.

Near the station, the Loup Creek Branch crossed New River on a heavy combination through truss and girder bridge. On the south side of the river the Loup Creek Branch was joined by the Minden Branch, coming from mines located up a very steep grade. The Loup Creek Branch itself went about 11 miles to Price Hill and Macdonald. It connected with several other branches serving the Beckley coal area. All the production from these numerous branches was funneled over the Loup Creek line into Thurmond for assembly. The South Side Subdivision also connected at South Side Junction, near that end of the Thurmond New River bridge. It served mines to the west on the south side of the river and also funneled its production across the Loup Creek Subdivision bridge into Thurmond. (All covered in Chapter 5)

In the past thirty years Thurmond has been a tourist Mecca of sorts first because of white-water rafting on this portion of New River, and secondly because the National Park Service targeted it for preservation and restoration as a typical mining community. A huge amount of money was spent to restore the station, which is today a gem for the National River tourist trade. However the engine house and ancillary facilities burned before they could be restored. Although the Park Service owns the whole town now, little additional work has been done for restoration.

Several mines along the mainline were located west of Thurmond, and at MP 394.4 the station at Fire Creek served the mining community there. It had an excellent example of the C&O's standard combined station/tower building that was found at several West Virginia locations on the Alleghany and New River Subdivisions. Between there and Sewell (at MP 397.6) several other mines were situated along the mainline tracks. Sewell was the location for two more of the combined station/tower structures, one at the East end of its yard (East Sewell), and one at the west end. The narrow gauge Mann's Creek short line railroad connected here, dumping its coal into standard gauge C&O cars at this point. A large bank of coke ovens also operated here up into the 1950s, probably the last such operation on the C&O. The town of Sewell had about 600 people at its height, but as with the other mining communities of the region it is now vanished. The remnant of the coke ovens can still be found in the undergrowth.

The Sewell station itself survived to the early 1960s as the last example of the standard station/tower combined building. At Sewell the mainline separates, with one track crossing the river while the other continues to hug the north bank. Thus, C&O is located on both sides of New River until Hawks Nest is reached at MP 408.6.

Numerous mines and communities dotted the line west of here including a large tipple at Kaymoor which operated into later days. The National Park Service has preserved the ruins of this operation and its history and operation have been documented by the Historical American Engineering Study.

Beyond Thurmond by about ten miles, the Keeney's Creek Branch left the main line to serve mines in that area (MP 400.4). It was one the steepest lines on the C&O with a 4.6% grade at one point. In the early days of the 20th Century C&O purchased Shay geared locomotives which were used on the Keeney's Creek line because of this grade. They were also used on the Minden Branch across from Thurmond, and Thurmond served as their base of operations. C&O was one of the few Class I railroads ever to operate Shays in any quantity, but they were gone by the mid 1920s, replaced by 2-8-0s and 2-6-6-2s.

Several more small mining communities were in operation west of this point until the major settlement of Hawks Nest was reached (MP408.6). At this point the Hawks Nest Branch served a couple of mines a few miles to the north and the town of Ansted at the top of the gorge. Hawks Nest had a considerable community, but nothing is left. Another of the depot/tower station buildings was used here. At this point the mainline on the north bank of the river crosses over to the south side and joins the line coming in on that side of the river from Sewell.

Hawks Nest is also the site of a large dam that was built here in the 1930s to divert a large amount of New River water through a long tunnel, exiting at a hydro-electric plant further down river. This was the site of one of America's worst industrial disasters when hundreds of the workers who bored the tunnel died of silicosis because of the type of rock encountered in the work. The dam backs up New River at this point for several miles. Hawks Nest is the site of an old state park that has an overlook

L-2 Hudson (4-6-4) No. 303 passes the neat brick Cotton Hill depot in 1952 with No. 6, the eastbound Fast Flying Virginian. Cotton Hill depot served the county seat of Fayetteville, a few miles distant by highway. There were no other structures at Cotton Hill itself–just the station. (C&O Ry. Photo, C&O Hist. Soc. Coll., Image No. CSPR-3057)

At Gauley a C&O bridge connected with the New York Central's line at Gauley Junction. C&O also operated its Gauley Branch up that river from this point. The photo, from a ca. 1920-era postcard shows the bridge and the Gauley station on the south side of the river. (TLC Collection)

that looks down on the C&O as it crosses the river.

MacDougal was the station name on the south side of the bridge here, and it also had a station even though it was within sight of the Hawks nest station just across the river.

Only about a mile west (MP 410.8) stands to this day the station at Cotton Hill. There is no town there and there never was. Rather, this station served the town of Fayetteville, a few miles by road to the south. The brick depot building at this point which is now used by CSX as office and storage for signal maintenance forces, was built in 1942, and loaded its last passengers in 1968.

Five miles westward, the New River and Gauley River join to form the Great Kanawha. C&O had a station at this point, which is roughly opposite the town of Gauley Bridge on the north bank of the river. A bridge from Gauley to Gauley Bridge allowed C&O to connect with the New York Central's Gauley Branch at this point, and to serve mines on its own Gauley Branch, which paralleled the NYC on the opposite side of Gauley River.

Deepwater is reached at MP 421.3. This is where C&O connected with the Virginian Railway's mainline. Over the years much interchange between the two competing coal-haulers has occurred. At one time Virginian passenger trains operated by trackage rights on C&O to Charleston and Huntington. This was changed in the 1930s to the New York Central instead.

Mt. Carbon station at MP 423.7 was the junction of the Powellton Branch, a short coal line going about five miles to the south.

Montgomery is at MP 427.5. It was once known as Cannelton after the "cannel" coal type that was mined in the region. It grew to a considerable town and eventually hosted West Virginia Institute of Technology (later a branch of West Virginia University). It had a large passenger station of brick design in the era we are treating in this book, and the students helped make it a principal passenger train stop.

At MP 428.2 the New River Subdivision ends and the Kanawha Subdivision begins. This is also Morris Creek Junction, at which the short Morris Creek Branch intersects the mainline. About a half mile beyond Morris Creek Junction is Handley yard, the eastern terminal of the Kanawha Subdivision.

Motive Power

It is hard to generalize the pattern of steam locomotive use on the New River Subdivision and its various branches, but some observations can be made. For the mainline passenger trains, the early small locomotives gave way soon after the turn of the 20th Century to the Atlantic (4-4-2) and Pacific (4-6-2) types, and as the Pacifics became more powerful and the trains heavier the Pacifics were the standard west of Hinton. When the first 4-6-4 Hudson types arrived in 1941, they were used west of Hinton to Huntington and sometimes through to Cincinnati or Detroit (after *The Sportsman* service was inaugurated in 1930) on the mainline trains. The heaviest, most modern Pacifics were still seen in this service and on the local passenger runs after WWII. The light F-15 class Pacifics were often used in local and branch line service. This ended when the C&O dieselized its passenger operation within a very short time between late 1951 and early 1952, with E8 passenger diesels handling mainline trains from that point until the end. Most branch line passenger trains were gone after 1949 and those remaining generally used gas-electric cars.

In the early era, freight trains saw the standard 4-6-0 and 2-8-0 types, followed by 2-8-2s in the early part of the 20th Century. During the era 1911-1923 C&O bought 2-6-6-2 Mallets and put them to work on its heaviest work. Just as they dominated the Alleghany Subdivision coal and freight trains in this era so did they on the New River as well. Although the H-7 2-8-8-2 simple articulateds, which arrived 1923-26, were mainly intended for the Alleghany grade, they were also used on the New River even though the clearance on some of the tunnels was very tight. The 1930s tunnel improvement program eliminated all the tunnels on the line except for Stretcher's Neck Tunnel just west of the Prince station, which was double tracked and of sufficient size to handle the biggest of C&O's power from that date forward. It is 1,588 feet in length and is built on a curve.

When the 2-6-6-6 Alleghany types arrived in quantity during the war they were also put to work on coal and freight west of Hinton, but they seldom operated west of Handley on the Kanawha Subdivision.

Taken from a C&O westbound local passenger train, the Kanawha Falls depot is seen in this 1935 photo. This point was important in the early days as a major stopping point in the region. The large hotel here once served as a meal stop for C&O trains before 1890, when dining cars were introduced. (William Monypeny Photo, TLC Collection)

In 1930 C&O acquired the fabulous Lima Super Power T-1 class 2-10-4 Texas type, but it was used exclusively on the heavy coal trains out of Russell, Kentucky, up the Northern Subdivision to Columbus and on to Toledo. These engines could not go east because of weight limitations on the Big Sandy Bridge at Catlettsburg, Kentucky. When this bridge was strengthened in 1948, the T-1s then were occasionally used on interdivisional fast freight runs between Russell and Hinton. Their use on the New River was rare, though.

Local freights rated a 2-8-2 Mikado in our era. Consolidation type 2-8-0s were used on some branch line passenger trains and mine runs, while most mine runs on the branches were handled by 2-6-6-2 Mallets right up to the arrival of diesels.

Switching operations at Hinton consisted of 0-10-0 and 0-8-0 switchers, while Raleigh, Quinnimont, and Thurmond usually had 0-8-0s. Consolidation 2-8-0s were also used as switchers, and larger 2-6-6-2s could be used as needed on heavy cuts of coal cars.

Dieselization was swift, occurring all over the C&O between 1949 and 1956. GP7s and GP9s were the models that essentially dieselized the main and branch lines of the New River. Alco S-2 and S-4 model switchers replaced 0-8-0s at Handley and Hinton, as well as supplanting 2-8-2s on local freights. F7s were occasionally seen on fast freights on interdivisional runs, but they were rare, the GP7s and GP9s dominating. These two EMD models were so versatile and well-liked that they could handle almost any job. Most steam had been removed from service by early 1955, but an upsurge in traffic resulted in more trains than there were diesels to handle. While waiting for new GP9s to arrive, C&O pulled some of its stored steam back into service, and for a short time, ending in late 1956, the New River Subdivision saw the last stand of mainline steam on the C&O.

When the SD18 EMD models arrived in 1963, and after trials on heavy trains on the Alleghany and New River Subdivisions, most were transferred to work on Cincinnati Division and as switchers at Russell (and a few remained at Handley for road work). The GE U25B units of the same era lasted a short while before transferring to C&O's Michigan lines leaving the GP7s and GP9s in control on the New River lines until the arrival in the late 1960s of bigger, more modern power in the form of EMD SD35s and SD40s.

Other diesels to operate on the New River in the era of this book were Baldwin AS-616's which were used in pairs out of Raleigh on the coal trains down to Quinnimont and empties back, but they were soon supplanted as more GP9s arrived.

Traffic

The traffic on the New River Subdivision was, in a word, coal. The Alleghany Subdivision had solid coal trains headed east, but New River had not only solid trains of coal headed both east and west (though primarily east), it also had the many mine runs and assembly and staging of the coal as it was gathered from the many mine branches, and the distribution of the empty cars back to the mines over these branches. This necessitated a system of marshalling yards where the loads could be assembled and the empties distributed. Yards of this type on the New River Subdivision were: Quinnimont, Raleigh, Thurmond, Gauley, Rainelle, and Meadow Creek.

In addition to the coal traffic, the C&O's manifest freight trains passed over the New River Subdivision on their much longer runs between major end-point terminals and beyond. In the era we are treating in this book, usually four such trains operated on a regularly scheduled basis. Local business required local freights along the mainline, usually handled by 2-8-2s, and branch line local freight business was usually handled on coal trains and mine shifters.

Of course, mainline passenger trains passed over the New River Subdivision on their longer operations across the system, and major stations supplying the most passengers for these trains were: Hinton, Prince, Thurmond, and Montgomery. A number of local passenger trains were in operation in the earlier days to supply frequent service to the many small and otherwise isolated coal mining communities along the mainline, but as these communities declined with the playing out of coal seams close to the main line, the number of locals decreased as well, until just two were in operation in the 1950s, both of which were gone in 1958. (See Chapter 8)

Local branch line passenger service was supplied to accommodate folks along almost all the branch lines, but most of this was gone after 1949.

Statistics (1948)

Distance 73.2 miles
Branches Connecting: (see Chapter 3)
Coaling Stations: Hinton, 800 tons; Quinnimont (from cars by crane); Thurmond , 500 tons
Turntables: Hinton, 115 feet; Stone Cliff (Thurmond), 100 feet; Meadow Creek, 35 feet; K&M Junction, 80-feet (on NYC)
Wyes: Meadow Creek, Quinnimont
Yards: Hinton, Quinnimont, Thurmond
Stock Pens: Hinton, Sandstone
Track scales: Hinton, Avis yard, 200-ton; Hinton, West yard, 150-ton; Meadow Creek, 100-ton; Gauley, 150-ton
Tunnels: Stretcher's Neck, 1,588 (double track)

L-2a Hudson, common power for the name trains west of Hinton, is seen here August 23, 1951, with No. 6, The FFV, passing the double-spouted water tank at Mt. Carbon. The line at left is the short Powellton Branch. (Gene Huddleston photo)

Montgomery was at the very western edge of the New River Subdivision. A sizeable town, it was first called Cannelton after the type of coal mined in the region in the era just before and after the coming of the C&O, but was later renamed Montgomery and ultimately became the location for West Virginia Institute of Technology. The students provided additional passenger traffic for C&O at this point. The large brick passenger station is seen in this 1970 photo is now gone. (T. W. Dixon, Jr. photo)

C&O's coal country begins west of Hinton. At first the coal came from mines located along the main line, but by the 1890s branch lines tapping coal fields distant from the mainline began to be built. This continued into the 1920s. Nine branches actually joined the New River Subdivision main line, but there were many more that branched from these main stems. This chapter will explain and present maps and photos showing many of these.

The whole arrangement is fairly complicated, and many operations are not clearly known at this remove in time. Some of the lines are still very much in operation on today's CSX, but many more have been abandoned or are inactive, and some have been sold to short line operators. The picture painted in this chapter attempts to depict the situation as it was about 1950.

The following branches are involved in this treatment. These are as shown on the C&O employee timetables of the era. Branch lines entering the New River Subdivision main line:

- Nicholas, Fayette & Greenbrier Railroad (Although an semi-independent operation jointly owned by C&O and NYC, it was treated as just another coal branch as far as C&O operations went.)
- Laurel Creek SD - junction at Quinnimont
- Piney Creek SD - junction at Prince
- Loup Creek SD - junction at Thurmond
- South Side Subdivision - junction at Thurmond and Sewell
- Hawks Nest SD - junction at Hawks Nest
- Gauley SD - junction at Gauley
- Powellton SD - junction at Mt. Carbon

Each of these will be listed in this chapter and subsidiary branches feeing their lines will be shown.

Nicholas Fayette & Greenbrier Railroad

The NF&G was incorporated in 1930 and was jointly owned by the C&O and the New York Central. The C&O connection was at Meadow Creek (MP 369.6, about 15 miles west of Hinton), and the NYC junction was at Swiss, at the western end of the NF&G. The C&O also had access to the western end from a connection between its Gauley Branch and the NYC near Swiss. The NF&G began as a lumber company short line in 1906, when the Meadow River Lumber Company was incorporated to operate a mill at the new town of Rainelle (named for the Raine family which owned the mill). The company eventually owned 125,000 acres of timberland in Greenbrier County.

To haul its forest products to the C&O the Raines built the Sewell Valley Railroad in 1908-09, connecting with the C&O at Meadow Creek, a distance of about 20 miles. As with many logging roads, it was steep climb up from the C&O beside New River to reach the mill at a much higher elevation, and the new railroad incorporated four switchback tracks to negotiate the steep grades.

The big mill here eventually became the world's largest hardwood lumber mill, at its height producing over 200,000 board-feet of lumber per day, all of which was shipped via its Sewell Valley Railroad to the C&O, amounting to a very large revenue stream for C&O.

Meanwhile, the Loup & Lookout Railroad was built connecting C&O's Keeney's Creek Branch with timberlands in the same region, and by about 1911 it built a line connecting with the Sewell Valley. The L&L was owned by the Raines as well.

The first coal mine in the region opened in 1913, and in 1921 yet another railroad was built in the region, called the Greenbrier & Eastern, extending further into coal and timber lands, completing the system of lines that were under the control of the Raine family and their Meadow River Lumber Company.

In the 1920s new coal mines opened along the lines and it soon became evident that coal would eclipse lumber as the prime traffic from this area. In this era the New York Central and C&O were engaged in a dispute before the Interstate Commerce Commission about which had rights to haul westbound coal from the Greenbrier-Gauley coal fields. New York Central's line entered West Virginia at Point Pleasant and ran along the Kanawha River to Charleston, thence to Gauley Bridge and up Gauley River. It also served the rich coal area northeast of Charleston, and was, along with C&O, N&W, and VGN, an important carrier of coal in southern West Virginia. NYC's line in West Virginia was operated by its subsidiary, the Kanawha & Michigan Railroad.

The C&O built its Gauley branch in 1893 from Gauley Junction, just across the river from its mainline station at Gauley, to Belva, and in 1916 extended this line to the mouth of Rich Creek. This was in direct competition with NYC in the area. The ICC saw the vigorous contest between C&O and NYC for this coal business as counterproductive and duplicative, so it told the two roads to get together and divide up the territory or the ICC itself would do so. As a result, in an agreement dated December 15, 1925, the two roads formed a new company called the Nicholas, Fayette & Greenbrier Railroad which was incorporated in June 1926. NYC and C&O jointly leased the company, which was a combination of the Loup & Lookout, Greenbrier & Eastern, and Sewell Valley. The joint operation actually began in 1932. Mont Raine, who had been with the old lines, served as the Assistant Superintendent of the NF&G into the early 1950s.

Throughout the 1930s-1950s era coal ruled supreme on the NF&G, new lines were built, and the C&O took its loads to Meadow Creek over the old Sewell Valley, while NYC took its traffic via Swiss and the connection with its Gauley line. Meanwhile, Meadow River Lumber's "big mill" continued a large production, which went to market mainly via the C&O. Meadow River's Shay-powered log trains traveled over the NF&G to particular points and then took branches that the lumber company built to get to the woods, so in effect the log trains had trackage rights over the NF&G.

The main engine terminal and yard was at Rainelle, and almost all equipment on the line was supplied by C&O and NYC. Through World War II C&O K-1 2-8-2s were standard because of the short tail tracks on the switchbacks. NYC also used 2-8-2s almost exclusively. In 1947 C&O completely rebuilt the line from Meadow Bridge down to Meadow Creek, eliminating the switchback operation and replacing it with broad loops to gain the altitude. This was part of C&O's realignment and right-of-way improvements in the late 1940s that wrought large changes in the layout of the mainline, added branches, and made this large improvement to existing "branches." After this work, C&O used 2-6-6-2s almost exclusively to power trains to and from Rainelle and to serve the mines.

Complicated arrangements allocated the revenue received from traffic handled by NF&G, but as far as operations went, C&O served the larger portion of the line and carried the most coal from it. Though NYC locomotives came to Rainelle for servicing, they kept their work toward the western end of the line.

When dieselization occurred, GP7s and GP9s became the standard power for C&O, and most NYC operations seem to have been road switchers of the GP9 variety also. This continued until the early 1970s when GP40s and more modern power began to populate the Rainelle terminal and the NF&G lines.

Operationally, the NF&G trains were treated as regular C&O branch line runs. The company with its joint lease arrangement continued until the NS-CSX-Conrail division/merger, when the NF&G was divided between CSX and NS, with CSX receiving the portion of the NF&G east of Swiss, and NS receiving the part west of there.

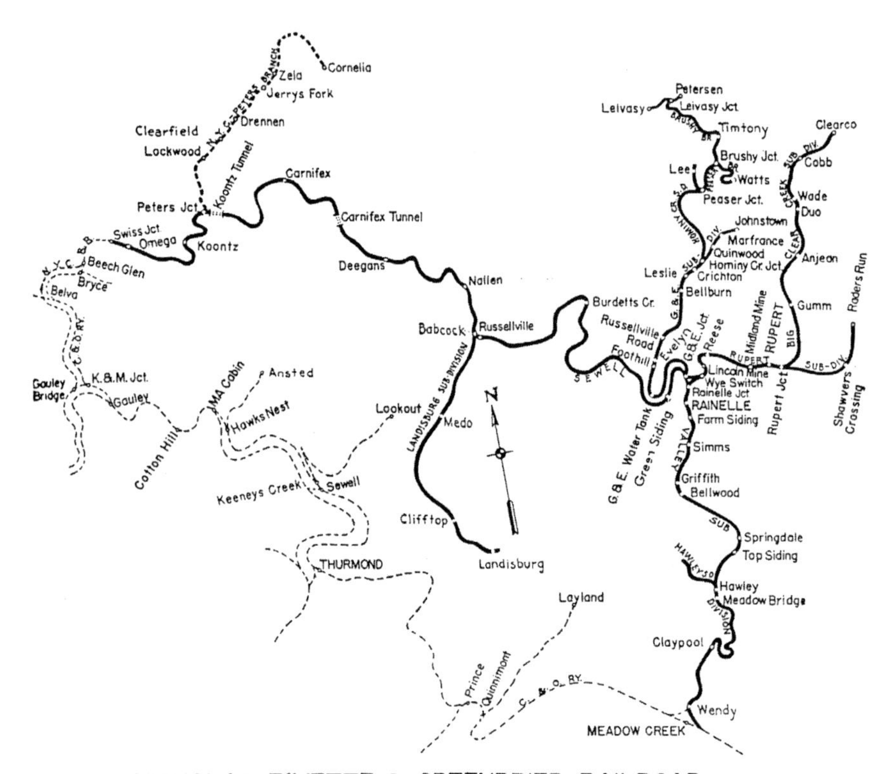

Map of the NF&G at its height, showing its relationship with C&O and NYC connections. (C&O Historical Magazine, August 1990)

The mid-century era of this book NF&G was one of C&O's important coal traffic sources and figured importantly in the New River Subdivision operations. Coal coming from the NF&G mines mainly went east to Hinton, but some also went west. Essentially all the coal coming from the NF&G to the NYC was westbound.

Composition of the NF&G:

- Sewell Valley Subdivision- Meadow Creek to Swiss: 67.5 miles
- Hawley Branch - Hawley to end-of-line: 2.1 miles

Miles from Hawley	HAWLEY TO END OF TRACK — WESTWARD — STATIONS (LEAVE)	
.0	Hawley	....
2.1	End of Track	....
	ARRIVE	

Miles from End of Track	END OF TRACK TO HAWLEY — EASTWARD — STATIONS (LEAVE)	
.0	End of Track	....
2.1	Hawley	....
	ARRIVE	

Miles from G. & E. Junction	G. & E. JUNCTION TO JOHNSTOWN — WESTWARD - SECOND CLASS — STATIONS (LEAVE)	207 Daily Except Sunday P. M.
.0	G. & E. Junction	3.40
3.0	Evelyn	f 3.46
4.7	Russellville Road	f 3.51
7.5	Bellburn	s 3.59
8.3	Leslie	s 4.02
8.9	Crichton	s 4.04
9.0	Hominy Creek Junction	4.05
9.8	Quinwood	s 4.09
10.6	Marfrance	4.12
11.1	Johnstown	......
	ARRIVE	P. M.

Miles from Johnstown	JOHNSTOWN TO G. & E. JUNCTION — EASTWARD - SECOND CLASS — STATIONS (LEAVE)	210 Daily Except Sunday P. M.
.0	Johnstown	......
.5	Marfrance	4.15
1.3	Quinwood	s 4.18
2.1	Hominy Creek Junction	4.20
2.2	Crichton	f 4.21
2.8	Leslie	f 4.23
3.6	Bellburn	f 4.26
6.4	Russellville Road	f 4.33
8.1	Evelyn	f 4.38
11.1	G. & E. Junction	4.44
	ARRIVE	P. M.

Eastward trains are superior to westward trains of the same class, unless otherwise specified.
No. 207 has right over No. 210 G. & E. Junction to Marfrance.
Trains 207 and 210 will stop on signal at Foothill and Bryant.

Miles from Hominy Creek Junction	HOMINY CREEK JUNCTION TO LEE — WESTWARD — STATIONS (LEAVE)	
.0	Hominy Creek Junction	....
4.2	Peaser Junction	....
5.1	Lee	....
	ARRIVE	

Miles from Lee	LEE TO HOMINY CREEK JUNCTION — EASTWARD — STATIONS (LEAVE)	
.0	Lee	....
.9	Peaser Junction	....
5.1	Hominy Creek Junction	....
	ARRIVE	

Miles from Peaser Junction	PEASER JUNCTION TO WATTS — WESTWARD — STATIONS (LEAVE)	
.0	Peaser Junction	....
1.7	Brushy Junction	....
3.9	Watts	....
	ARRIVE	

Miles from Watts	WATTS TO PEASER JUNCTION — EASTWARD — STATIONS (LEAVE)	
.0	Watts	....
2.2	Brushy Junction	....
3.9	Peaser Junction	....
	ARRIVE	

Miles from Brushy Junction	BRUSHY JCT. TO PETERSEN — WESTWARD — STATIONS (LEAVE)	
.0	Brushy Junction	....
4.5	Leivasy Junction	....
5.4	Petersen	....
	ARRIVE	

Miles from Petersen	PETERSEN TO BRUSHY JCT. — EASTWARD — STATIONS (LEAVE)	
.0	Petersen	....
.9	Leivasy Junction	....
5.4	Brushy Junction	....
	ARRIVE	

Miles from Leivasy Junction	LEIVASY JUNCTION TO LEIVASY — WESTWARD — STATIONS (LEAVE)	
.0	Leivasy Junction	....
.9	Leivasy	....
	ARRIVE	

Miles from Leivasy	LEIVASY TO LEIVASY JUNCTION — EASTWARD — STATIONS (LEAVE)	
.0	Leivasy	....
.9	Leivasy Junction	....
	ARRIVE	

Miles from Rainelle Junction	RAINELLE JUNCTION TO JETER — WESTWARD—SECOND CLASS — STATIONS (LEAVE)	
.0	Rainelle Junction	......
.2	Wye Switch	......
1.0	McRoss	......
4.3	Mill Creek Road	......
7.1	Rupert	......
7.2	Rupert Junction	......
9.3	Shawvers Crossing	......
11.1	Jeter	......
	ARRIVE	

Miles from Jeter	JETER TO RAINELLE JUNCTION — EASTWARD—SECOND CLASS — STATIONS (LEAVE)	210 Daily Except Sunday P. M.	
.0	Jeter	......	......
1.8	Shawvers Crossing	......	......
3.9	Rupert Junction	.....	......
4.0	Rupert	......	......
6.8	Mill Creek Road	......	......
10.1	McRoss	......	......
10.9	Wye Switch	4.47	......
11.1	Rainelle Junction	4.48	......
	ARRIVE	P. M.	

Miles from Rupert Junction	RUPERT JUNCTION TO CLEARCO — WESTWARD—SECOND CLASS — STATIONS (LEAVE)	
.0	Rupert Junction	......
3.4	Gumm	......
5.9	Anjean	......
10.0	Duo	......
11.6	Cobb	......
13.1	Clearco	......
	ARRIVE	

Miles from Clearco	CLEARCO TO RUPERT JUNCTION — EASTWARD—SECOND CLASS — STATIONS (LEAVE)	
.0	Clearco	......
1.3	Cobb	......
3.1	Duo	......
7.2	Anjean	......
9.7	Gumm	......
13.1	Rupert Junction	......
	ARRIVE	

Station listing showing NF&G lines, from 1948 employee timetable. (TLC Collection)

- Rupert Branch - Rainelle Jct. to Raders Run: 11.2 miles
- Big Clear Creek Branch - Rupert Jct. to Clearco: 13.1 miles
- Greenbrier & Eastern Branch - G&E Jct. To Johnstown: 11.1 miles
- Hominy Creek Branch - Hominy Creek Jct. to Lee: 5.1 miles
- Brushy Branch - Brushy Jct. to Peterson: 5.4 miles
- Peaser Branch - Peaser Jct. to Watts: 3.9 miles
- Landisburg Branch - Landisburg to Babcock: 12.8 miles
- Peters Branch - Cornelia to Peters Jct.: 13.8 miles

NF&G had little equipment of its own, but this caboose was included. It appears to be ex-C&O in appearance. Photographed at Rainelle September 9, 1948. (Everett Young Collection)

SEWELL VALLEY SUBDIVISION BETWEEN MILEPOSTS 3 AND 7

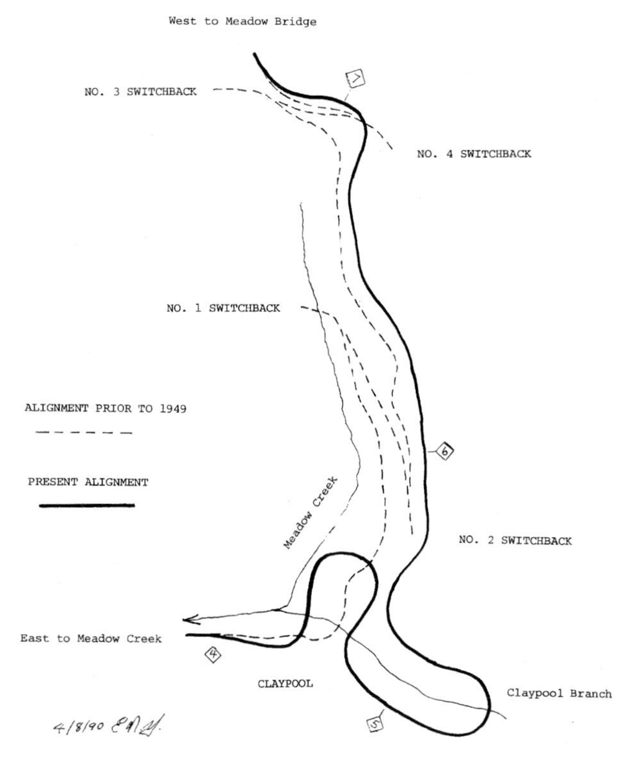

When C&O was involved in major right-of-way realignments and improvements following World War II, it selected the NF&G line leading from Meadow Bridge down to the New River SD at Meadow Creek as part of the work. The old switchbacks which had been inherited from the Sewell Valley were changed into loops as shown on this map. (Map by E. N. Young, courtesy C&O Hist. Soc. Coll.)

This 1952 view of the new loop tracks shows a 2-6-6-2 on the head of a train ascending with mostly cars filled with ballast. Three levels of track can be seen. (B. J. Kern photo, C&O Hist. Soc. Coll., Image No. COHS-2772)

At a later date three GP9s are in charge of a coal train descending the loops downgrade in April 1958 on its way from Rainelle to Meadow Creek. (Gene Huddleston photo, C&O Hist. Soc. Coll., Image No. COHS-3447)

The engine terminal at Rainelle in 1952 was fully equipped as seen in this 1952 scene. At left are several C&O 2-6-6-2s, the standard power for C&O, while two NYC 2-8-2 rest closer to the large corrugated steel engine house. At right is the water station, sanding tower and cinder conveyor. To the right is the trestle style coaling station. (B. J. Kern Photo, C&O Hist. Soc. Coll., Image No. COHS-2644)

This 1931 drawing shows the profiles of the various NF&G lines. It has been revised through 1949 to incorporate the re-aligned route between Meadow Bridge and Meadow Creek. It can be seen that grades on this line still run over 3%. (C&O Ry. Drawing 9932, C&O Hist. Soc. Coll.)

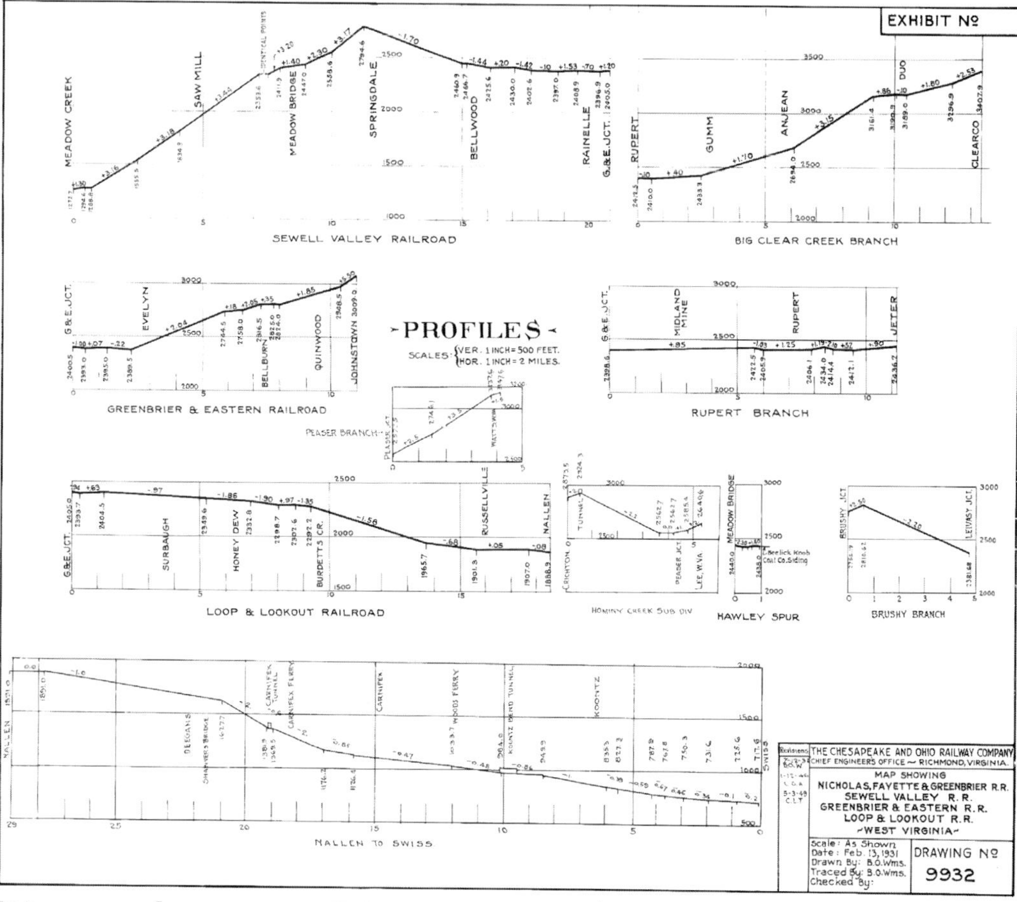

Two NYC 2-8-2s with a C&O caboose is a truly joint operation at Rainelle in 1952. (B. J. Kern photo, C&O Hist. Soc. Coll., Image no. COHS-2788)

Passenger service was maintained on NF&G using a couple of old gas-electric motor cars inherited from the Sewell Valley. No. 121 has just left the flag-stop at Duo, at the top end of one of the original switchbacks, in 1936. Passenger service on NF&G was discontinued in early 1949. (Glenn Grabill photo, TLC Collection)

The Imperial Smokeless Coal Company's Quinwood No. 2 mine at Lee was typical of mines in the Greenbrier field served by the NF&G, seen here in June 1954. (C&O Ry. Photo, C&O Hist. Soc. Coll., Image No. CSPR-10057.K5)

Laurel Creek Subdivision

The Laurel Creek Subdivision ran 5.8 miles between Quinnimont yard on the main line and Layland at the end of track. It was a very old piece of railroad, having been built originally in 1873 by the Quinnimont Coal Company in order to serve its mine at Brownwood and to convey coal down to the big iron furnace at Quinnimont. The line was extended to Hemlock Hollow (about 0.3 miles from Brownwood) in 1890, this time by the Robins Coal Company, and in 1902 C&O completed the line 0.3 miles to Layland, the ultimate end of line, under contract with the owners. The line was purchased and operated as part of the C&O system as of January 1, 1905. The end of the line at Quinnimont served as two legs of the wye that formed the yard there, the mainline being the third.

Quinnimont early became an important point because of this branch bringing coal to the large iron furnace that was installed inside the wye tracks at Quinnimont. At one time the furnace employed 600 men and could ship its pig iron via the C&O to northeastern markets as cheaply as the Pennsylvania iron works could send theirs. The furnace got its ore from Virginia, but by the 1880s this ore was proving to be sparser and less valuable that new deposits from the Midwest, feeding the great steel mills of the North-

Dist. from Ft. Monroe	Tel. Calls	Station No.	Code No.	STATIONS
378.7	*QN	379	1185	④**Quinnimont**....W Va
381.8		T3	1188	‡Export..........W Va
382.5		T4	1190	‡Laurel..........W Va
383.5		T4½	1193	†Big Q...........W Va
383.7		T5	1195	‡Brownwood....W Va
384.0		T5½	1197	‡Hemlock Hollow.......W Va
384.4		T6	1198	Layland........W Va

④–Coupon Stations.
*–Day and Night Telegraph Offices.
†–No Siding.
‡–Private Siding only.

east and Midwest, completely eclipsing the production of the C&O region in Virginia and West Virginia. By the turn of the 20th century Quinnimont was just a C&O operating point, and the mines along Laurel Creek were just part of the overall production coming from the New River coal fields. In 1950 there were four active coal mines on Laurel Creek, at Laurel, Greenwood, Hemlock Hollow, and Layland. The branch has a maximum grade of 3.87%, the mine at Layland being reached by a switchback. Coal from all four mines on the line was from the Fire Creek Seam.

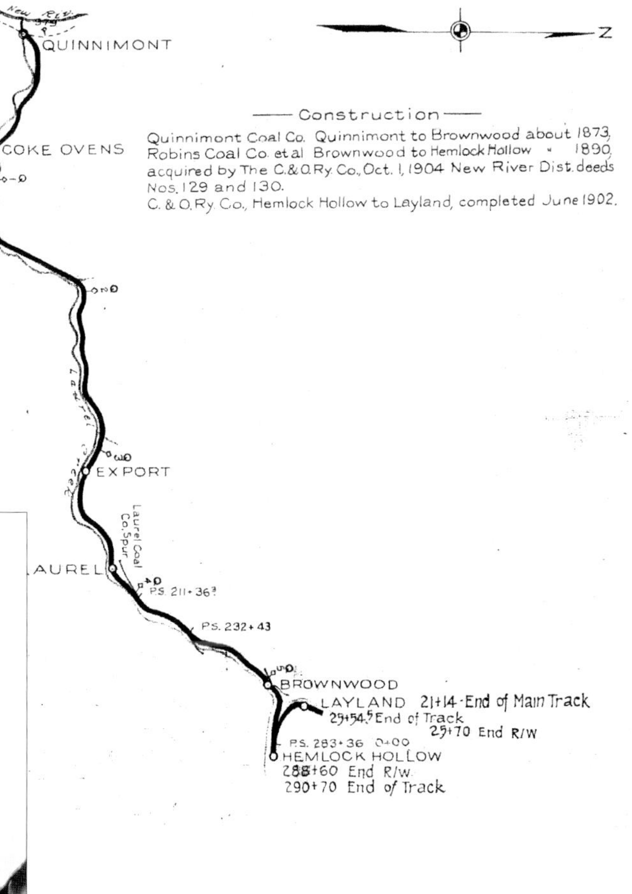

Valuation index maps showing the Laurel Creek Subdivision. (C&O Hist. Soc. Coll.)

The large tipple of the New River & Pocahontas Consolidated Coal Company at the end of the Laurel Creek line, as it appeared in June 1954. (C&O Ry. Photo, C&O Hist. Soc. Coll., Image No. CSPR-10057.G6)

Piney Creek Subdivision

The Piney Creek Subdivision leaves the mainline at MP 380.0, opposite the Prince depot and runs 28.49 miles to Lester. It not only had mines along its route, but connected with many other C&O branches which served to funnel coal to the marshalling yard at Raleigh and thence down to Prince. After joining the main line at Prince, Piney Creek Branch trains traveled a mile farther east to Quinnimont yard, where the loads would be picked up by New River Subdivision trains and taken east or west. In the mid-century period coal trains were operated on the line by 2-6-6-2s of the H-4, 5, and 6 classes. Often two would be used for the trains descending the grade to Prince and to haul empties back. The main terminal was Raleigh, which is close to Beckley.

According to C&O valuation records, construction was completed across a through-truss bridge over New River (which is still in use) to Raleigh in July 1901. An extension to Beckley Junction was completed in September 1903, and from there to end of line in August 1905. The Eccles spur was acquired from the Crab Orchard Coal and Land Company in 1927.

On the south side of New River, just beyond the end of the bridge, the Terry Spur ran 1.7 miles as a branch from the Piney Creek SD.

At Blue Jay Junction, 11.5 miles up the line, the Glade Creek & Raleigh branch joined.

From Raleigh, the Raleigh & Southwestern Subdivision was joined, while the Piney River & Paint Creek Subdivision joined at Mabscott (Beckley Junction). Not only did it serve numerous coal mines, but also the city of Beckley.

From this point the line meandered onward joining the Surveyor Subdivision. In this area C&O lines began to mesh with lines operated by the Virginian Railway, which also tapped into the New River coal fields in competition with C&O.

The yard at Raleigh was an important coal marshalling yard/collecting point which handled all these branches. This yard had full scale facilities and a considerable storage yard trackage. From it, mine shifter runs radiated to all the mentioned areas to distribute empties and pick up loads which were consolidated at Raleigh for shipment to Quinnimont.

Right: Valuation map showing the Piney Creek Subdivision and connecting lines

Lower Right: Simple line map showing Piney Creek Subdivision and the several branches that fed into it (Extract from C&O employee timetable, 1958)

Dist. from Ft. Monroe	Tel. Calls	Station No.	Code No.	STATIONS
380.0	*NI	380	1200	④**Prince**........W Va
380.5		W½	1201	‡Royal..........W Va
381.4		W1	1202	††②Terry Jct...W Va
381.7		W2	1206	†McCreery.....W Va
382.9		W3	1208	Norvell........W Va
383.4		W4	1209	‡Wright.........W Va
384.6				††Stonewall....W Va
385.1		W5	1211	‡Jonancy........W Va
385.5		W5½	1212	‡Lanark.........W Va
385.7		W5¾	1210	‡Penman........W Va
386.0		W6	1213	‡Stanaford.....W Va
386.3		W6½	1214	††Dorsey........W Va
388.0		W8	1216	†White Stick...W Va
389.3		W9	1218	‡Pinepoca.......W Va
389.8		W10	1220	††Rodes.........W Va
392.7		W11	1222	‡Raleigh No. 7..W Va
393.2		W11½	1224	†McQuaid.......W Va
393.3		W12	1226	②Blue Jay Jct..W Va
393.6	*RA	W13	1228	②Raleigh.......W Va
394.2		W14	1230	‡West Raleigh..W Va
396.1	BJ	W15	1232	②Beckley Jct ..W Va
396.4		W16	1234	Mabscott.......W Va
396.6		W16½	1235	‡Mabscott MineW Va
396.9		W17	1236	Bickell.........W Va
397.4		W17½	1237	†Westwood.....W Va
398.4		W18	1239	Cabell..........W Va
399.0		W19	1241	††Burks.........W Va
401.5		W21	1243	①Admiralty....W Va
402.1		W21½	......	⑥Eccles Jct....W Va
402.8		W22	1244	†Metalton......W Va
403.1		W23	1245	†Glen White Jct.WVa
403.7		W24	1248	Baylor.........W Va
404.7		W24½	......	⑥Marsh Fork Jct..........W Va
405.4	VO	W25	1250	Surveyor.......W Va
406.2		W26	1252	†Tolleys........W Va
407.1		W26½	1253	†Hoo Hoo......W Va
407.6		W27	1255	Lester..........W Va

④–Coupon Stations.
*–Day and Night Telegraph Offices.
①–Junction with connecting line.
②–Junction of Sub-division shown elsewhere.
⑥–Established for operating purposes only—not a station for passenger or freight business.
†–No Siding.
††–Passing Siding only.
‡–Private Siding only.

Gene Huddleston, writing in the book *Riding That New River Train* (C&O Historical Society, 1989) gives a description of an actual mine run shifter operation out of Raleigh:

"... let's examine [a mine shifter] out of Raleigh in the year 1946. I have reconstructed this from eight train orders my uncle gave me. On the night of June 19, 1946, Extra 1536 (USRA 2-6-6-2, class H-5) was called at ten o'clock to work mines at Sprague, Skelton, and Cranberry on the Piney River & Paint Creek

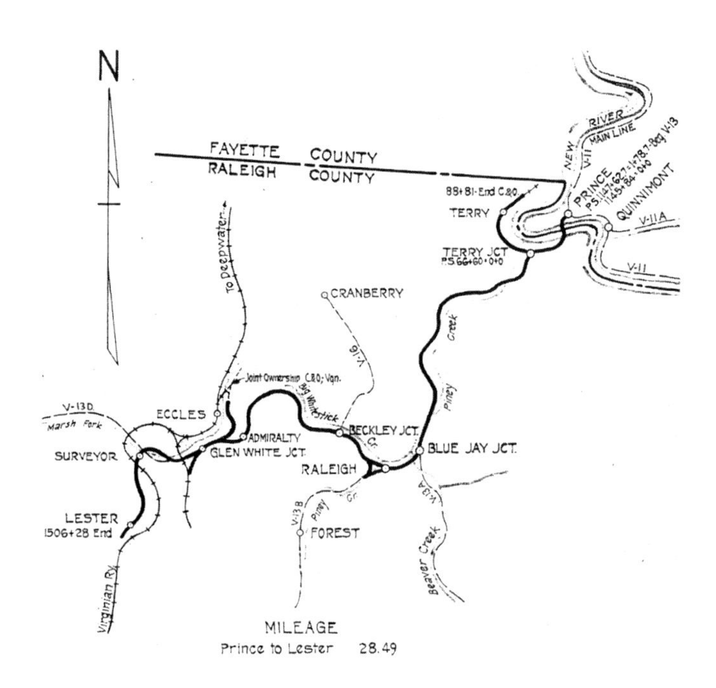

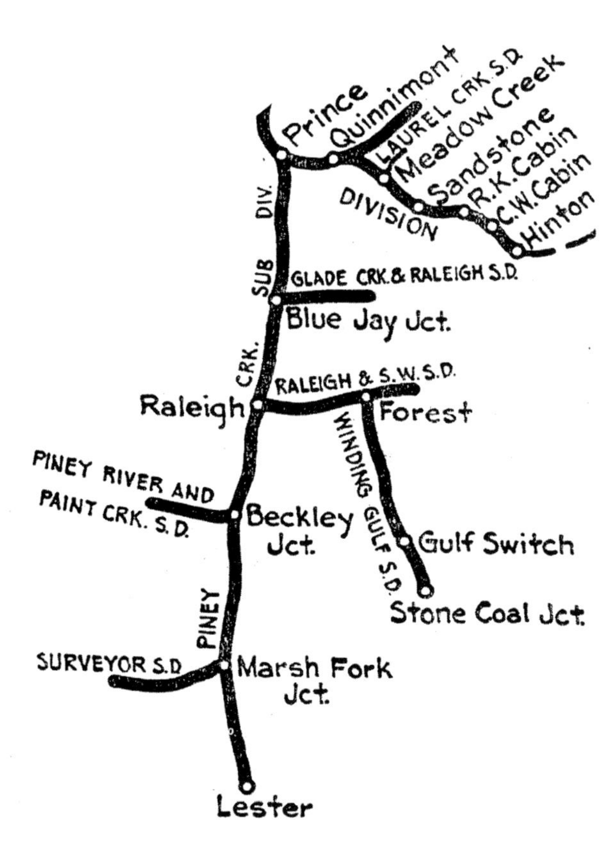

Subdivision, as well as to supply Raleigh No. 6 Mine with empties at Raleigh. The crew as relieved at Raleigh at 7:00 AM after making an hour's overtime."

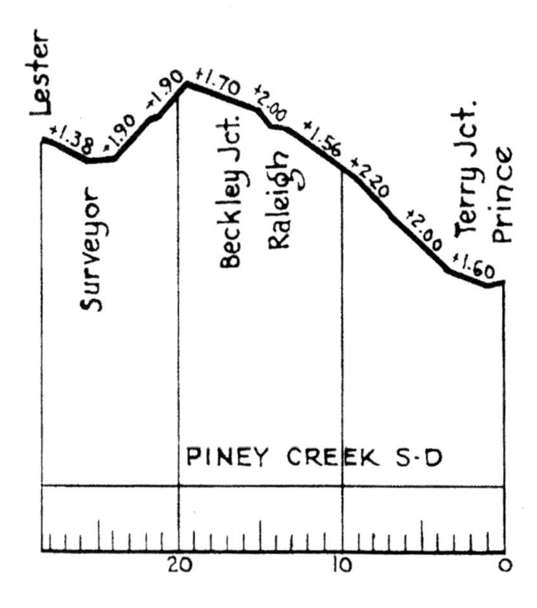

Piney Creek SD profile showing line through Raleigh to Lester.

C&O H-6 2-6-6-2 No,. 1479 with a loaded coal train meets 1475 with empties on the Piney Creek branch in October 1945. This was a busy area as coal from the numerous lines feeding Raleigh yard was shipped down to Quinnimont and empties were taken back. (C&O Ry. Photo, C&O Hist. Soc. Coll., Image CSPR-308)

This loaded coal train coming down the Piney Creek Branch in summer 1953 is typical of trains on this line in the 1930s-1940s decade and into the early 1050s. By the mid-1950s GP7s and GP9s had replaced them. (C&O Ry. Photo, C&O Hist. Soc. Coll., Image CSPR-3728)

The Stanaford mine tipple was located right along the Piney Creek line about six miles up from Prince. Loaded hopper cars sit at left and in a long string in the right background in this June 1954 photo. (C&O Ry. Photo, C&O Hist. Soc. Coll., Image CSPR-10057.A12)

The assembly or marshalling yard at Raleigh was the point for collecting coal from 24 mines located on 6 branches. The compact terminal and yard bent around a curve in Piney Creek. It had a two-stall board-and-batten engine house, a large yard office, a store room made from a former depot structure, a 300-ton cylindrical concrete coaling station, a large capacity water station, and all the normal ready-track facilities needed of servicing steam locomotives. The town nestled around the yard on several sides. Note the yard for the Raleigh Coal & Coke Company mine tipple at the top of the map. (TLC Collection)

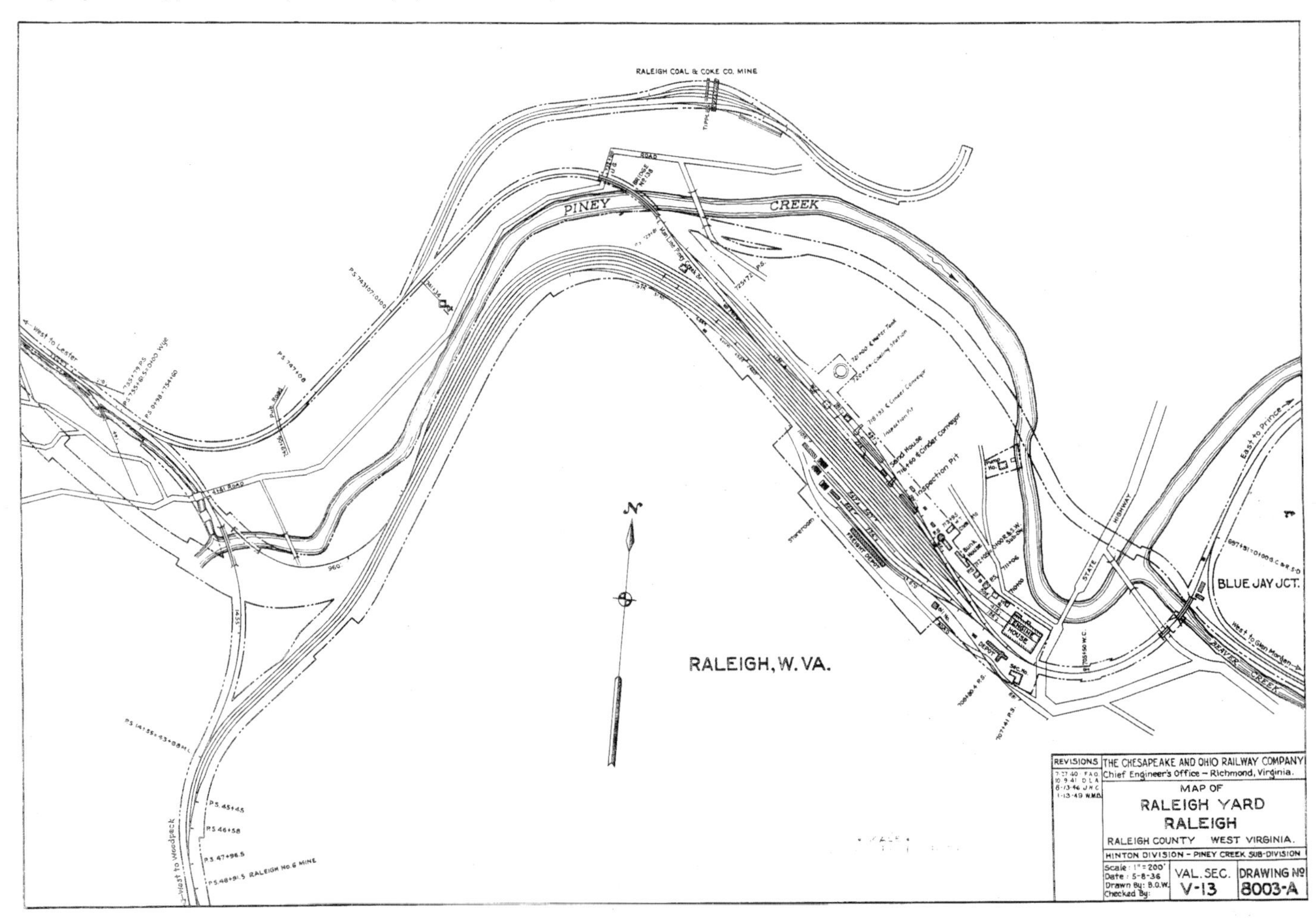

A general view of Raleigh yard as it looked in the late steam era about 1950. The most identifiable feature is the tall concrete coaling station. (J. I. Kelley Photo, D. Wallace Johnson Collection)

Overhead view of the Raleigh engine terminal ready tracks at Raleigh yard shows three C&O 2-6-6-2s ready for action as mine shifters in 1945. (C&O Ry. Photo, C&O Hist. Soc. Coll., Image CSPR-293)

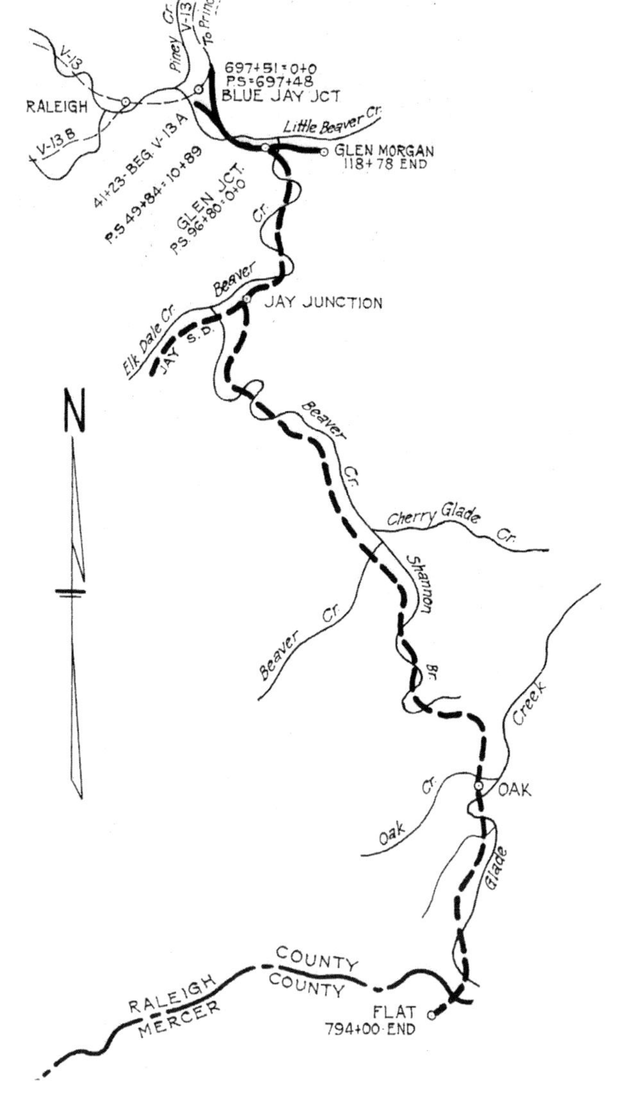

The Glade Creek and Raleigh Subdivision left the Piney Creek line at Blue Jay Junction, 12 miles up the Piney Creek line from Prince and just a mile from Raleigh yard. At the time of this book's era, 1950, it ran only 1.2 miles to Glen Morgan, where the old Blue Jay Lumber Company's mill was located. At an earlier time the line had run south as far as the Mercer county line, and to the New River, which it crossed to connect with the C&O New River Subdivision at Glade, using a high bridge, the piers of which still stand in New River. The line was originally built by Blue Jay Lumber Company starting in 1898, was acquired by the Raleigh & South Western in 1906, and then by C&O after 1910. The major portion of the line was abandoned in 1928, and the short Jay Subdivision was retired in 1940.

Just beyond Raleigh yard the Raleigh & Southwestern Subdivision in 1950 ran as far 5.39 miles, to a location just beyond Forest. The original line had gone on an additional three miles but this was retired in 1943. The line was built as an independent railroad in 1909, and then was acquired by the C&O in 1910, the last portion of the line being finished by C&O in 1912. At our mid-century time period two mines were operating on the line. The Winding Gulf Subdivision, probably the most productive of the lines served out of Raleigh yard, joined with the R&SW at Forest.

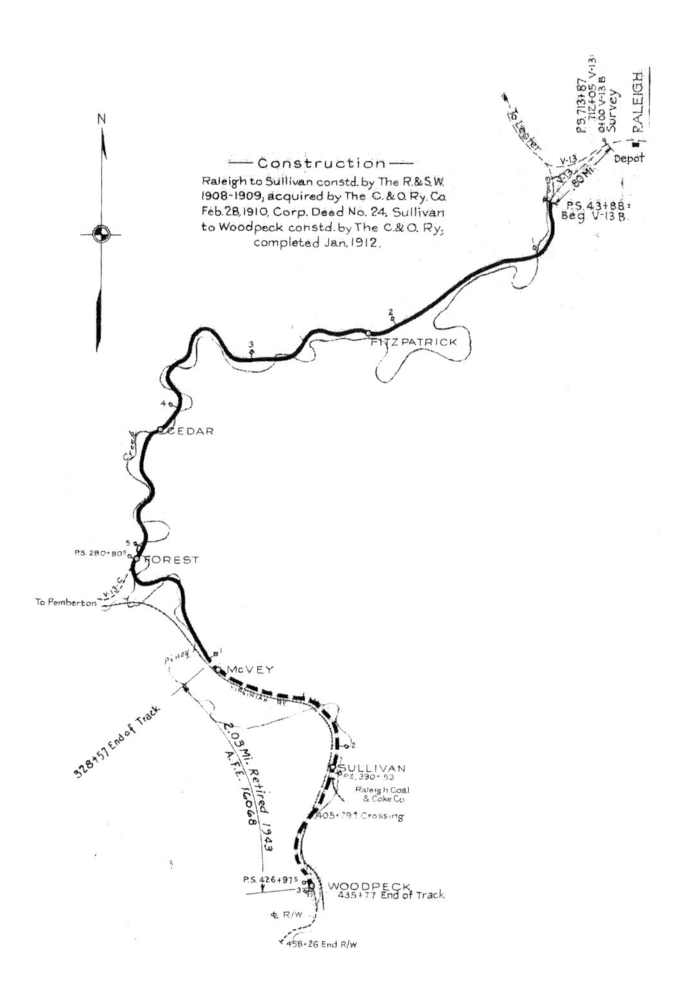

A closer view of the tipple at Crab Orchard in 1954 shows a Virginian car being loaded. In this region C&O and Virginian intersected each other at numerous locations and sometimes served the same mines. Three saddle-tank 0-6-0s brought coal from three miles away and emptied the mine cars into the tipple here for processing. (C&O Ry. Photo, C&O Hist. Soc. Coll., Image CSPR-10057.C5)

H-6 2-6-6-2 No. 1481 works the Winding Gulf Coal Company's Crab Orchard mine on the Raleigh & South Western Subdivision, in October 1945. It appears that the mine has assembled a number of loads of various grades of coal for the shifter to take to Raleigh yard on this particular day. (C&O Ry. Photo, C&O Hist. Soc. Coll., Image CSPR-357)

Winding Gulf Operations

(By Gene Huddleston, reprinted in part from *Chesapeake & Ohio Coal and Color*, with permission)

Winding Gulf traversed an area of rugged beauty, featuring numerous large coal camps, two loops, a switchback intertwined with one of the loops, a high bridge, six tunnels, steep grades, and a crossing at grade with the Virginian, all within a space of about twenty miles. The Winding Gulf field first flourished during World War I and reached the height of its development in the 1920s.

Because coal mining completely governed the development of the Gulf area, one first looks back to 1909 when a developer named Walter Tams, from Staunton, Virginia, first became interested in the field. He organized the Gulf Smokeless Coal Company, and mined just 30,000,000 tons by the time he sold out in 1955. The C&O reached the Gulf about 1911, the Virginian having arrived first, in 1909.

The C&O was slow to get to the Gulf. With Winding Gulf Creek being a tributary to the Guyandotte River it was easier for the Virginian than C&O, because practically all of the Virginian's coal fields were within the upper Guyandotte basin. C&O also suffered a setback when the courts gave the Virginian rights to enter the area in 1906 through Jennys Gap, and thus built through Lester and Slab Fork down to Mullens. From Mullens to the Gulf was a short and easily traversed route along the upper Guyandotte.

Usually, when a competing railroad had reached a mine, there would be little reason for another road to try to serve the same mine. However, the C&O knew, by 1910, when the Virginian was completed, that the road had no western outlet, whereas C&O's own line to Cincinnati provided a long haul to connections there. Virginian's seeking direct access to Piney River and Paint Creek, which C&O ad VGN eventually controlled jointly, along with the White Oak Railroad, motivated the C&O as well.

This development caused C&O to extend its Raleigh & Southwestern line into the Gulf. Getting into and out of the Gulf was not an easy matter. For the Virginian, the climb to the plateau involved two loops, three tunnels, two bridges over the C&O, and a two percent grade. For C&O, the descent was less complicated: two tunnels and a switchback, and a maximum gradient of 1.9%.

Once C&O got into the Gulf it was a fairly easy matter to build along the creek, for the Virginian, in building up to it, had kept to the west bank all the way. But near the confluence of Winding Gulf Creek with the Guyandotte River, there developed a situation similar to that at the switchback and loops – similar in that each road decided concurrently to build up Stone Coal Creek. Surveys along it had revealed exposures of Pocahontas Coal Seams 2, 3, 4, and 6. The difference, though, was that the two roads built no tracks side by side; they jointly built a paper railroad-the Stone Coal Railroad, nine miles long.

The rugged topography kept this from actual construction up the creek for several years, but the line was eventually completed in 1916. At Stone Coal Junction, the junction of the two roads, a small yard for interchange of loads and empties was constructed. For C&O, the layout was fairly simple. Since its tracks were already on the east side of Winding Gulf Creek, it had only to curve sharply to the east to head up Stone Coal Creek. Its interchange tracks were built along this long curve. Virginian's approach was more complex,. First its tracks would have to cross Winding Gulf Creek. From a point midway across the branch line bridge, the Virginian turned northward toward Stone Coal Creek. However, a spur of the hill necessitated a curved tunnel. About a tenth of a mile north of this tunnel was Amigo Junction, the actual junction of the two roads, located about a half mile south of Stone Coal Junction.

At the top of the grade the Winding Gulf Subdivision uses this tunnel with an interesting timber portal supported by additional timber framing above to prevent further erosion of the unstable shale. Here a C&O train features a wooden caboose and GP9 in April 1958. (Gene Huddleston Photo, C&O Hist. Soc. Coll., Image COHS-2961)

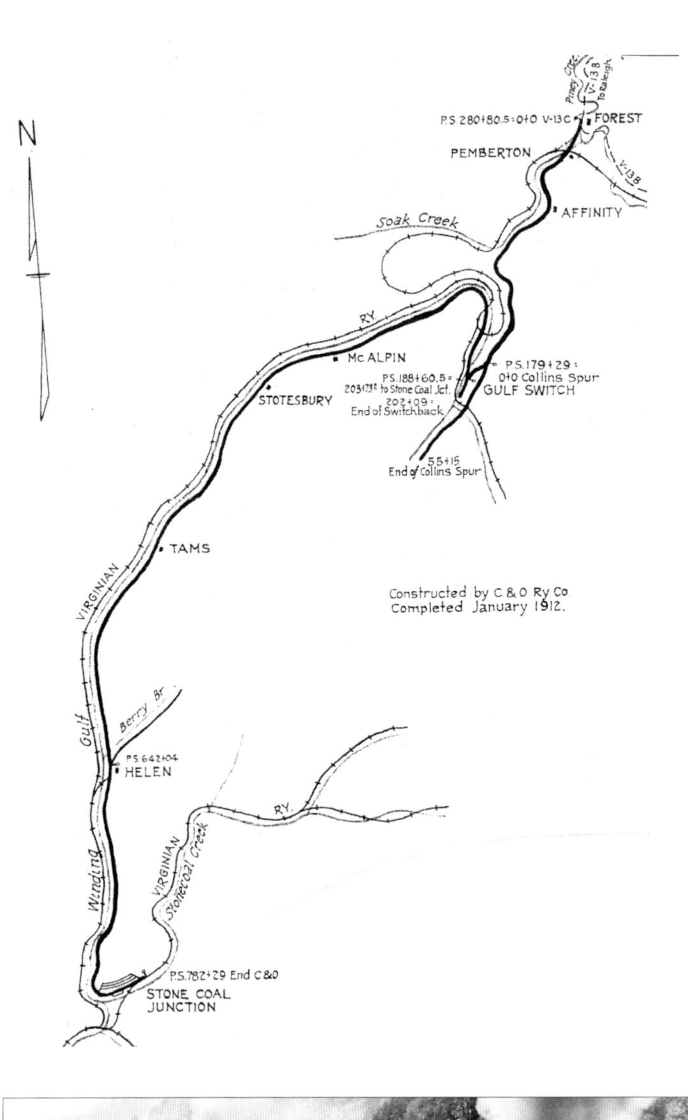

The Winding Gulf Subdivision, joined the Raleigh & South Western Subdivision at Forest and served a number of mines in the "Gulf" region of the Raleigh fields. It ran 14.79 miles from Forest to Stone Coal Junction, where it joined the Virginian Railway. The Virginian also paralleled the C&O and crossed it in the "Gulf" as shown on the map. This area was the center of a great deal of controversy as the new Virginian attempted to enter the region and tap its coal resources at the same time that C&O was trying to do the same. The result was a kind of war between the two construction crews. At length C&O and Virginian served many of the mines in this area jointly, which was the case in the 1950 era of this book. C&O and Virginian jointly operated the Stone Coal Subdivision in this area as well. The topography of the area, coupled with the overlapping of the two railways led to an interesting operation that is perfectly adaptable to today's model railroading. The C&O's Winding Gulf line was completed in 1912. It is one of the few C&O lines that featured a switchback, at Gulf Switch.

The layout of the Winding Gulf lines looked like this near Gulf Switch in April 1958. The line entering the concrete portal tunnel is the Virginian. The line at lower right is C&O, and the line closest to the camera is C&O.(Gene Huddleston Photo, C&O Hist. Soc. Coll., Image No. COHS-2958)

In this scene two 2-6-6-2s, with No. 1418 closest pushing backwards with 24 loads while doubling the steep grade en route from the Gulf coal mines to Raleigh in 1953. (Three Photos: D. Wallace Johnson Photo)

This view shows 1412 backing with 1418 posing on a second doubling of the hill with 19 cars. The old caboose body served as the operators cabin at Gulf Switch.

Headed up the steep grade toward Forest and Raleigh from Gulf Switch the two 2-6-6-2s work hard.

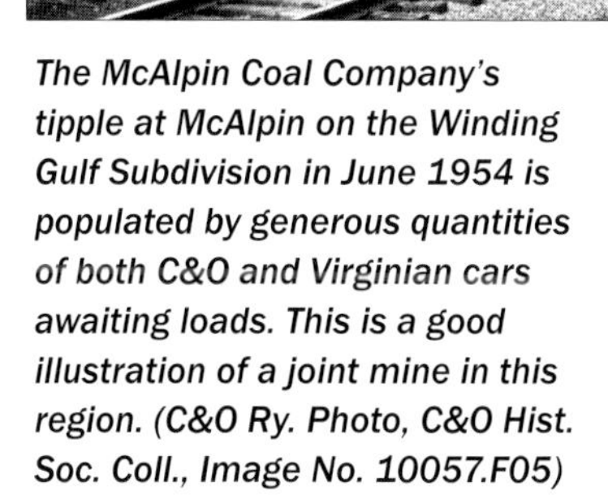

The McAlpin Coal Company's tipple at McAlpin on the Winding Gulf Subdivision in June 1954 is populated by generous quantities of both C&O and Virginian cars awaiting loads. This is a good illustration of a joint mine in this region. (C&O Ry. Photo, C&O Hist. Soc. Coll., Image No. 10057.F05)

Gulf Smokeless Coal Company mine at Tams was of the wooden frame board-and-batten style and is seen here in a June 1954 photo. The accompanying plat shows the layout and how the mine was served by both Virginian and C&O tracks. The photo shows the C&O side of the tipple. (C&O Ry. Photo, C&O Hist. Soc. Coll., Image No. CSPR-10057.E11)

Stone Coal Subdivision

This joint line ran from Stone Coal Junction, at the end of the C&O's Winding Gulf Subdivision to Lynbrook, about nine miles. Mines on this line were served both by C&O and Virginian trains over the same trackage.

Piney River & Paint Creek Subdivision

The Piney River & Paint Creek Subdivision operated 6.38 miles between Beckley Junction, through the city of Beckley and on to Cranberry.

It was constructed by a short line railroad owned by coal baron Samuel Dixon in 1905 to give access to his New River Company mines at Sprague, Skelton, Cranberry, and Prosperity. It joined the C&O at Beckley Junction near Mabscott. He sold the railroad to C&O in 1918. The Virginian was given rights over the line but C&O served the mines almost exclusively.

It was over this line that the branch line passenger train operating on the Piney Creek Branch (until 1949) reached Beckley and served that important coal hub, taking passengers down to the mainline at Prince where they could transfer to the main line trains. In our mid-century era the line also had three large mines.

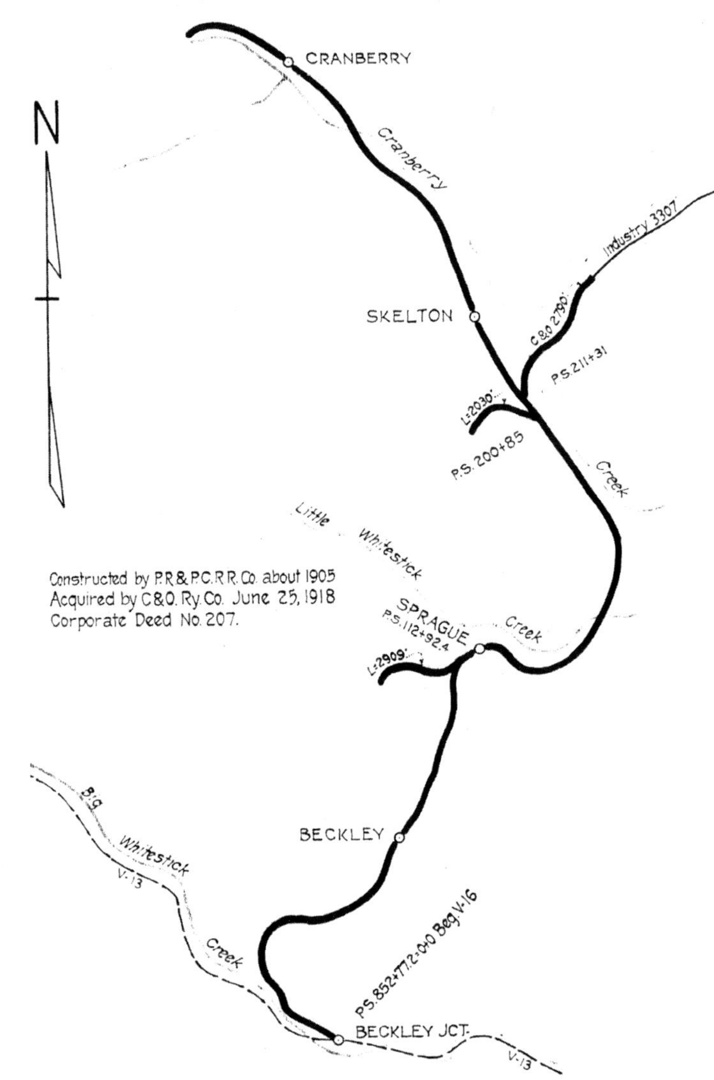

Map showing Piney River & Paint creek Subdivision.

Dist. from Ft. Monroe	Tel. Calls	Station No.	Code No.	STATIONS
396.1	BJ	W15	1232	Beckley Jct.......W Va
397.3		PR1	1277	④Beckley..........W Va
398.3	RG	PR3	1279	Sprague...........W Va
400.6		PR5	1281	Skelton...........W Va
402.1		PR6	1282	‡Cranberry........W Va

The passenger station at Beckley, impressively built of stone, was located on the Piney River & Paint Creek Subdivision. It stood opposite the freight station in downtown Beckley, the railroad being in a cut, necessitating the steps and elevator in this photo. (TLC Collection)

The Beckley Freight station was located above the PR&PC Subdivision tracks, which were in a cut below. This was a joint station with C&O and Virginian serving it. This photo was taken after the VGN/N&W merger and the sign reflects that. (C&O Ry. Photo, TLC Collection)

At the end of the PR&PC Subdivision was the large mine at Cranberry operated by the New River Company, and seen here in 1945 loading coal into C&O hoppers on four tracks. (C&O Ry. Photo, C&O Hist. Soc. Coll., Image CSPR-345)

Mabscott, where the PR&PC subdivision joined the Piney Creek line, had this fairly large standard C&O frame station, which survived into modern times. Beckley and environs had a huge business during the days of the coal boom. C&O Manifest freights set off perishables in refrigerator cars at Quinnimont, which were delivered by shifter for wholesale companies in Mabscott. (T. W. Dixon, Jr. Photo)

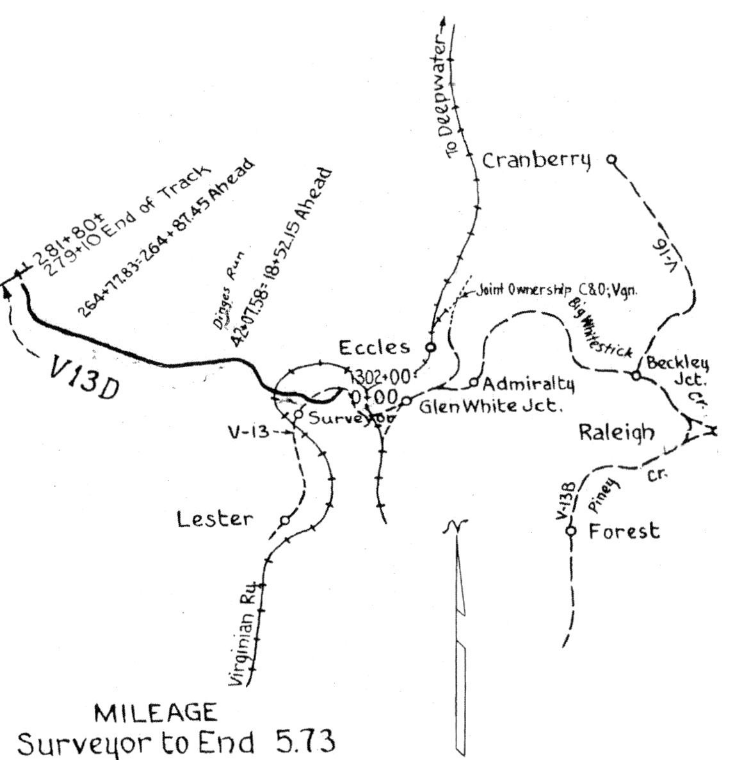

The Surveyor Subdivision ran 5.73 miles from the Piney Creek Branch at Marsh Fork Junction to end of track. It also connected with the Virginian at Surveyor as shown on this map which well depicts the maze of Virginian and C&O lines in the area. The line was built by C&O in 1930 to reach mines, but in the 1950 listing of active mines none are shown on the line.

Lillybrook Coal Company Mine No. 3 at Lillybrook, served by both Virginian and C&O, in June 1954. Only C&O cars are visible in this photo, though.

Lines Accessed from Thurmond

Traveling along the C&O main line from Prince the next major junction and terminal is Thurmond. At this point several branches connected directly and others indirectly, to make it the hub of the New River coal fields from the earliest days up until modern times. From Thurmond mine shifters operated in several directions pulling coal from numerous small branches.

Loup Creek Subdivision

The Loup Creek Subdivision branch line crossed New River from near the Depot at Thurmond and ran up the Dunloup Creek valley to the Beckley area, but didn't connect with any of the branches served by Raleigh and tributary to the Piney Creek line.

During the C&O's renovation and expansion beginning with the change in ownership in 1889, a bridge was built across New River at Thurmond to South Side Junction. The Loup Creek branch was then built up that creek to Glen Jean and Price Hill, a distance of 9.9 miles. At Price Hill Junction it intersected with the Kanawha, Glen Jean and Eastern Railroad, and at Kilsyth Junction with other branches.

The Loup Creek branch and the lines connecting with it proved very lucrative for C&O over the decades, and made Thurmond the great coal hub that it became by the 1920s. This good production lasted into the 1960s.

Rend Subdivision

At South Side Junction the Loup Creek line connects with the Rend (or, as it is sometimes called, Min-

The Loup Creek Branch passenger train is seen here near Glen Jean on July 14, 1948 with its usual consist of an ancient coach and a Harriman-roof combination mail and express car which had a tiny 15-foot Railway Post Office section that accommodated a single clerk. In fact, this run, the Thurmond & Mt. Hope RPO in the Post Office terminology, was the shortest RPO route in America (about 10 miles each way). The power is a G-7 class 2-8-0. (C. A. Brown photo, TLC Collection)

The New River & Pocahontas Consolidated Coal Company (known as Berwind) had this mine at Minden, on C&O's Rend Subdivision south of Thurmond. Note the NRBX Berwind hopper car. This private line of hopper cars was one of the few that operated extensively on C&O trains in the mid-century era. (C&O Ry. Photo, C&O Hist. Soc. Coll., Image No. CSPR-10057.C3)

Map showing route of South Side Subdivision between Bridge Junction, opposite Sewell, and South Side Junction across from Thurmond.

den) Subdivision. This line was originally built by W. P. Rend. It was completed in June 1904 to reach the mine at Minden, and sold to C&O a month later. C&O added an extension in 1916 to reach another mine. In the era of our book there was one mine in operation, owned by the New River & Pocahontas Consolidated Coal Company. This company operated a fleet of their own private hopper cars, lettered "Berwind." These cars were often seen on C&O trains in the pre-1955 era. The 6.23-mile line (including the 1916 extension) climbed steeply high along the south wall of the gorge and could be seen from Thurmond. The branch used a switchback from its South Side Junction beginning point, to gain elevation to climb the side of the gorge and then ascend Arbuckle Creek to Minden.

To cope with the heavy grade, between 1903 and 1908 C&O acquired some huge 4-truck Shay geared locomotives for use on this and other steeply graded lines. Many of these locomotives were headquartered in Thurmond. By the 1920s, though, the Shays were gone, replaced by the usual 2-6-6-2 Mallets on this line.

Price Hill Subdivision

At Price Hill Junction the Loup Creek Subdivision connected with the Prince Hill Subdivision leading to the nearby town of Mt. Hope. The line consisted of 0.69 miles running from Price Hill Junction to a point beyond Mount Hope. This was originally part of the White Oak Railway, and served the depot for Mt. Hope. The White Oak Railway was also met here.

South Side Subdivision

Built 1889-1894 and acquired on completion by C&O, running from South Side Junction along south bank of New River to Bridge Junction opposite Sewell, 7.82 miles. In 1950 one mine was in operation along this line. At Bridge Junction the line actually connected with the eastbound main just before the main crossed the river to Sewell.

White Oak Subdivision

This line was constructed by the Glen Jean, Lower Loup & Deepwater Railway, a wholly owned C&O subsidiary in December 1900, and acquired by C&O Nov. 21, 1901. It ran 3.36 miles from White Oak Junction near Glen Jean about 7.5 miles from Thurmond, and connected with the White Oak Railway. The latter was a joint C&O/Virginian operation. The White Oak Branch had one mine on its line as of our 1950 era, and production from three other mines came in from the White Oak Railway.

Mill Creek Subdivision

This short branch ran 4.5 miles to a large mine at Garden Ground as well as one at Cleve, with its trains entering the Loup Creek Branch at Kilsyth Junction.

Kanawha, Glen Jean & Eastern Subdivision

Acquired by the C&O in 1940, this line was originally built by coal operator William McKell and paralleled C&O's Loup Creek Branch from South Side Junction, opposite Thurmond, to Glen Jean and on to Tamroy on one fork and to a connection with the Virginian Railway at Pax on its second fork. McKell built the line essentially beside the C&O supposedly because he had trouble getting the C&O to supply him with enough cars when he needed them for loads. McKell built the original part of the line in about 1906 and extended it to the Virginian in 1908 when that road was built. After C&O acquired the line in 1940 the parallel track from South Side Jct. to Glen Jean was abandoned (1942), while the remainder of the line continued in use.

Glen Jean Subdivision

The branch was originally the Kanawha, Glen Jean & Eastern Railway, and connected with Loup Creek Subdivision at Sugar Creek Junction, running south to Tamroy on one of its lines and west to the Virginian at Pax on the other. It operated independently until acquired by C&O in 1940 and thereafter operated as C&O's Glen Jean Subdivision. The distance from Sugar Creek Jct. to Tamroy was 4.74 miles and to Pax 6.16 miles. In 1950 two mines were in operation on this subdivision.

The White Oak Railroad

Built as a short line by coal operator Samuel Dixon in 1899, the White Oak Railroad was for the sole purpose of taking coal from Dixon's mines to the C&O since C&O would not build its own branch to his operations. This line extended from C&O's White Oak Subdivision at Carlisle to mines at Summerlee and Lochgelly, near Oak Hill. This railroad also connected with the Virginian when it began incursions into this coal region, connecting at Oak Hill Junction. Dixon eventually sold the line to C&O and Virginian together, who operated it as a joint line. The Virginian did most of the switching for the mines located on this line, however the coal fed to both railways.

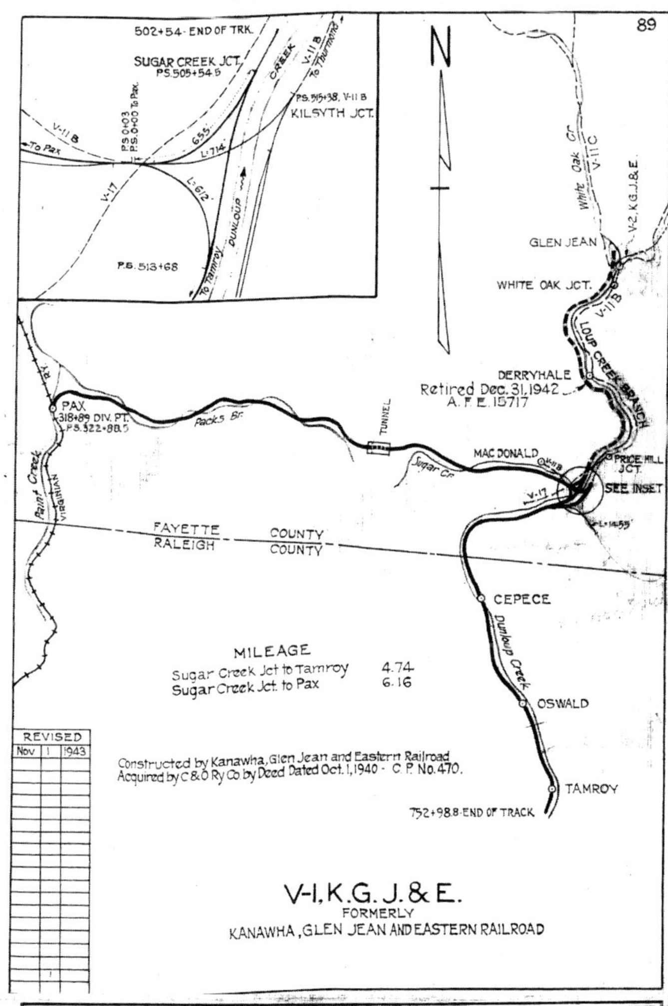

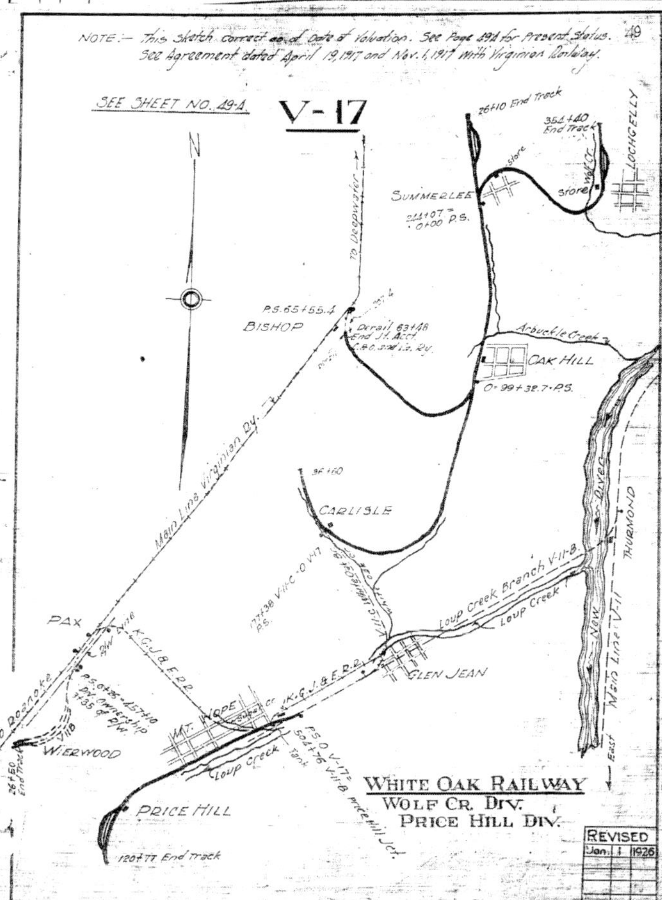

Tipple of the New River Company's Oakwood mine at Oakwood, on the White Oak Subdivision was a fairly large operation with five loading tracks under the tipple. (C&O Ry. Photo, C&O Hist. Soc. Coll., Image No. 10057.B12)

New River Co. Oswald mine at Oswald, W.Va. on the KGJ&E in 1954. (C&O Ry. Photo, C&O Hist. Soc. Coll., Image No. 10057.C05)

Big New River Company's Lochgelly tipple, on the White Oak Railway, is seen here in 1943 with a miner adjusting brakes as he drifts loaded coal cars away from the tipple in preparation for C&O to pick them up. Most mines operated their yards on a gravity system. The empties were positioned by C&O mine shifters on one side of the tipple, on tracks that were slightly up-hill from the tipple, and when needed, mine employees released the brakes and positioned them under the tipple for loading. After loading gravity was again used to move them away to the loaded yard, located down-hill from the tipple. Note the different grades of coal evident here. (C&O Ry. Photo, C&O Hist. Soc. Coll., Image No. CSPR-343)

Keeney's Creek Subdivision

Leaving the mainline at Milepost 400.4 about 9 miles west of Thurmond, the line ran 7.82 miles to Lookout, and used one switchback to help ascend the very steep grades. The line was built by John Nuttall and between 1891 and 1904, but was operated under lease to C&O until it was sold to the later. Even though it utilized a switchback to gain elevation out of the gorge, it still had a 4.17 % grade, one of the steepest on the C&O. When C&O purchased Shay geared locomotives beginning in 1907, they first used on this line. After the end of the Shays in the early 1920s, 2-8-0 Consolidations, operating in multiples of two (one on the front and one on the rear of short trains) were used to carry empties up the grade and bring the loads back. They operated in and out of Thurmond as their collecting yard and terminal.

Hawks Nest Subdivision

Further west (at MP 408.6) the Hawks Nest Branch served a couple of mines to the north near Ansted, running 3.44 miles from Hawks Nest station to end of line beyond Ansted. Originally there was a narrow gauge line installed here in the early days, but C&O built its line to standard gauge, completing it in August 1890. This was one of the first of the many coal branches that C&O built or acquired over the period 1890-1920.

As with other branches from the New River mainline, the climb up Mill Creek from Hawks Nest station to Ansted included a steep 4.2 % grade, one of the heaviest on the C&O. As on the Keeney's Creek line, with its grade of about the same percentage, a runaway track was provided in case a train got away going downhill. The only other place on the C&O with runaway tracks besides Hawks Nest and Kenney's Creek was on the Hot Springs line in western Virginia.

In our 1950-era, the branch had two producing mines. Today much of the old right-of-way of this branch can be traveled via a nature trail that is built on the old right-of-way and is part of the Hawks Nest State Park facilities.

In the mid-century era the line boasted a local passenger train until 1949, and short coal mine shifter runs as needed to supply the two mines. These were operated out of Thurmond as well.

At Hawks Nest the westbound mainline crossed New River and joined the South Main line westward.

Gauley Subdivision

The next branch that is encountered westward along the C&O is the Gauley Subdivision out of Gauley Bridge. C&O's mainline was on the south side of the river west of Hawks Nest as it passed through Cotton Hill and exited the deepest portion of the gorge. At Gauley station, MP 415.2, C&O built a bridge across to the town of Gauley Bridge. The construction of this branch was authorized by the C&O's board in 1892. The section from Gauley to Greendale was opened in 1894 (14.027 miles) and a second line, called the Open Fork Subdivision was built from Open Fork Junction to Bentree in 1904 (3.416 miles).

In 1913-1915 the Gauley & Meadow River Railroad built a branch from Rich Creek Junction on the Gauley Branch to Marshall, which was sold to C&O in 1918. C&O then built this road onward to end of its line in 1930. This became the Gauley & Rich Creek Subdivision.

The lines of the Gauley Subdivision and the Gauley & Rich Creek Subdivision were both closely parallel to the New York Central's lines in this area, C&O occupying one side of Gauley River and NYC the other. A connection from the Gauley & Rich Creek line was made with NYC at Beech Glen, which accomplished a linkage with the NF&G at Swiss. Therefore, the joint NF&G lines were linked with both NYC and C&O at their western end as well as C&O only at the eastern end at Meadow Creek (see page 60)

Another connection was made with NYC at K&M Junction at Gauley Bridge. In the mid-century era of this book C&O maintained a small yard and engine terminal at K&M Junction to serve the branches and interchange with NYC. Consolidation type locomotives were common on these branches in the late steam era and were, of course, replaced by GP7s and GP9s in the early diesel period. In 1950 there were two active mines on the Gauley SD and two on the Gauley & Rich Creek SD. Two more were operating on the Open Fork SD.

Powellton Subdivision

At Mt. Carbon, Milepost 423.7, the Powellton Subdivision left the mainline southward and ran 4.96 miles to Powellton, with another branch of 2.8 miles called the Elkridge Subdivision.

The Powellton line was built in 1885 by the Mt. Carbon Company to reach its mines and was sold to C&O in 1902. C&O built to Elkridge Subdivision to reach mines in that vicinity in 1905. By the 1950 era of this book there was only one mine in operation, on the Elkridge SD.

An interesting feature at Mt. Carbon near the junction of the Powellton branch was a standard C&O 50,000 gallon water tank with penstocks arranged for both the mainline and the branch.

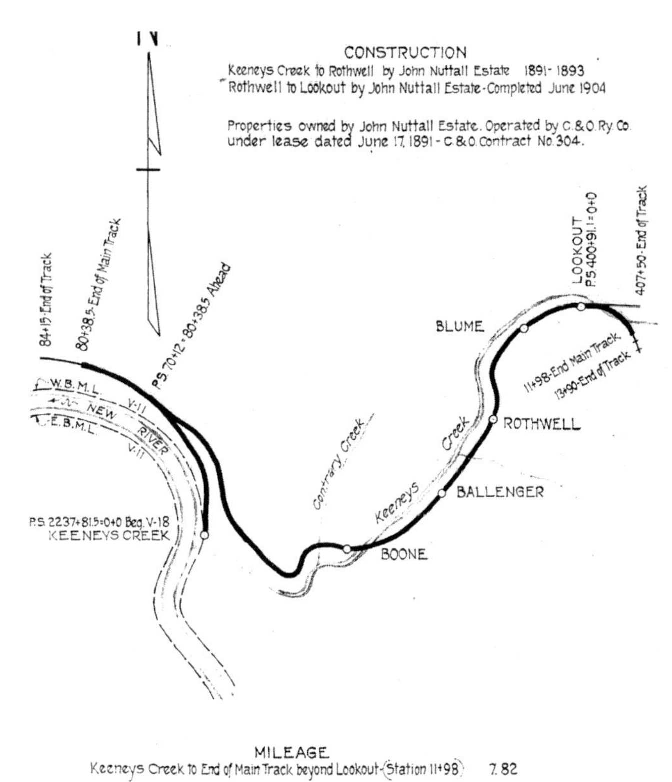

Map showing Keeney's Creek line, running 7.2 miles from the mainline to Lookout. Note the switchback leaving the steepest part of the gorge.

Rare indeed are photos of operations on the Keeney's Creek Branch. In this October 1953 photo the usual G-9 2-8-0 No. 1025 is taking empties up the branch. In 1950 six fairly small production mines were in operation on the branch. (W. H. Odell Photo, TLC Collection)

One aspect of the Keeney's Creek Branch that has been much remarked about is the runaway track which protected the steepest part of the grade. At the time of this book's treatment at mid-century only the Keeney's Creek, Hawks Nest, and Hot Springs branches had such safety tracks. (W. H. Odell, TLC Collection)

Mine shifter with 2-8-0 brings a mine run off the Gauley Branch near Gauley Bridge in July 1953. (J. I. Kelly Photo, C&O Hist. Soc. Coll., Image No. COHS-358)

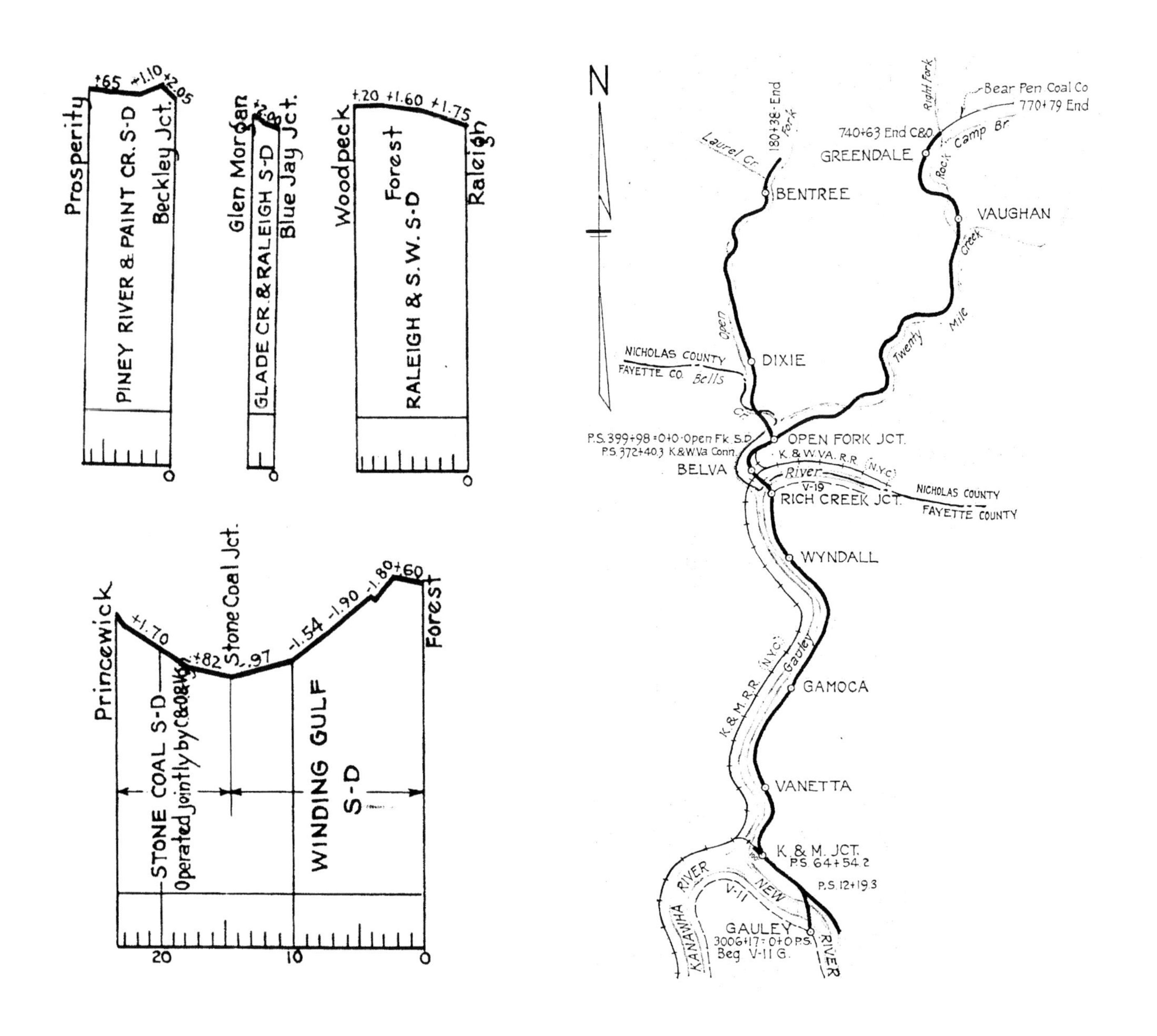

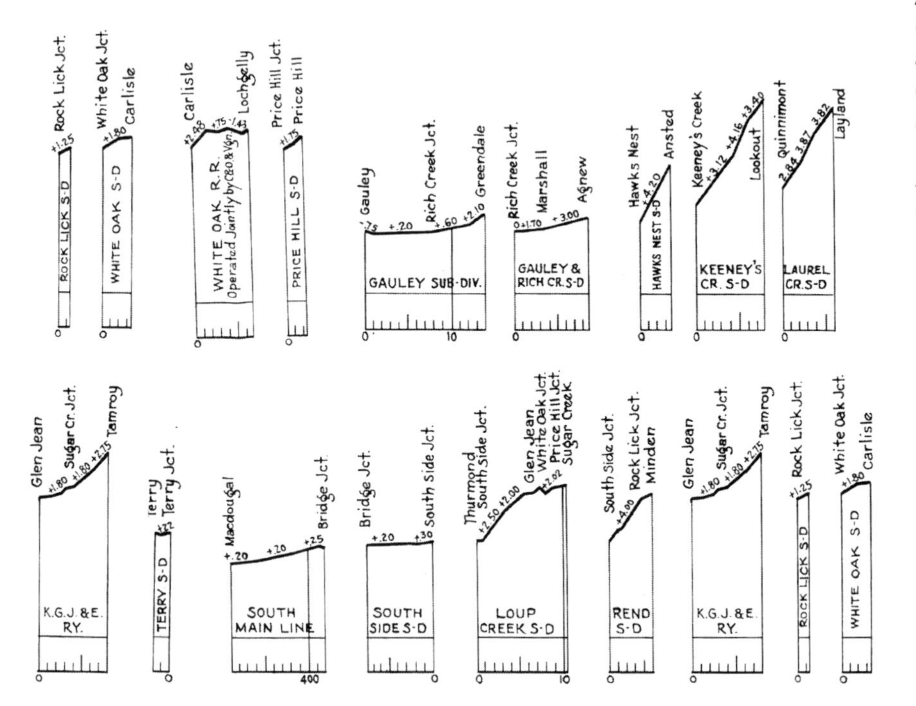

Above: Map showing Gauley Branch. The Gauley and Rich Creek Subdivision branched at Belva and is shown as "V-19" on this map. It connected with NYC and NF&G as well as serving other mines.

Above Left and Left: Profiles of the various New River branches.

6: The Kanawha Sub-Division

The third mainline subdivision on the C&O in West Virginia is the Kanawha, running between Handley, West Virginia, and Russell, Kentucky. The bulk of it was within West Virginia, but it extended 10 miles into Kentucky.

The Kanawha Subdivision's eastern terminal is at Handley, West Virginia, although the subdivision's trackage begins at MP 428.2, Morris Creek Junction, about a mile east of Handley, so that the short Morris Creek Branch could be included. After reaching Russell, at milepost 523.9, the mainline trackage covered in this line was 95.7 miles. Of this about 84.8 miles are in West Virginia.

The mainline exited the New River gorge at Gauley (where the New and Gauley Rivers form the Kanawha), and was laid along the south bank of the Kanawha River from that point to Handley. From this terminal, it ran westward as far as St. Albans, the railroad hugging the river, but at the latter point it continued more directly westward, while the river curved to the northwest. The C&O reached Huntington, and then left West Virginia by crossing the Big Sandy River near its mouth on the Ohio between Kenova, West Virginia, and Catlettsburg, Kentucky, for the last 10 miles in Kentucky. Generally the gradient of the line was easy, as it followed the river, but it had one steep grade located west of St. Albans as it left the Kanawha and entered the geological region known as the Teays Valley, the bed of an ancient extinct river. This grade required the use of pushers on coal trains in both directions in the steam era, and was known as Scary Hill after the name of the station near its summit.

The original C&O line in this area was begun around Charleston in the era before the War Between the States under the control of the Covington & Ohio Railroad, an enterprise sponsored by the Commonwealth of Virginia to connect with the Virginia Central at Covington. After the war, the charter and properties of the Covington & Ohio were merged with those of the Virginia Central to form the C&O (see page 5). Under C&O the line in the west was completed from the new city of Huntington to Charleston in 1871 and to Coalburg and Kanawha Falls by mid-1872. In 1872-early 1873 it was built eastward at the same time that the line from White Sulphur Springs was being built west, and the two construction crews met at Hawks Nest, in the New River Gorge, on January 29, 1873, thus completing the mainline between Richmond on the James and Huntington on the Ohio.

Dist. from Ft. Monroe	Tel. Calls	Station No.	Code No.	STATIONS
428.2		428½	1647	②Morris Creek Junction----- W Va
429.6	*RO	430	1670	Handley------- W Va
431.8	P	431	1672	②Pratt-------- W Va
432.8		432	1720	Hansford------ W Va
433.5		434	1721	Crown Hill---- W Va
435.0		435½	1723	‡Black Cat----- W Va
435.6		436	1725	East Bank----- W Va
437.5		437	1726	‡Coalburg------ W Va
438.1	*CA	438	1730	②④Cabin Creek Junction----- W Va
438.5		439	1900	†Chelyan------- W Va
440.6		441	1902	Winifrede Jct-- W Va
441.6		442	1904	†Chesapeake---- W Va
444.5		444	1905	Marmet------- W Va
448.2		448	1908	South Malden- W Va
449.8		450	1910	Owens-------- W Va
451.8	*KO	452	1912	South Ruffner- W Va
453.6		454	1915	①④**Charleston**-- W Va
			1916	" Depot
			1917	" City
455.2		455	1916	Elk----------- W Va
457.3		457	1918	④South Charleston---------- W Va
458.9	XY	459	1920	Spring Hill---- W Va
465.5	*VF	465	1925	②④**St Albans**-- W Va
466.9		467	2500	Dock---------- W Va
469.6		469	2502	Scary--------- W Va
473.2	*SC	473	2505	Scott--------- W Va
475.1		475	2507	Teays--------- W Va
479.2	*KX	479	2510	Hurricane----- W Va
481.5		481	2513	Culloden------ W Va
485.8	*MI	486	2515	Milton-------- W Va
487.8		488	2517	Yates--------- W Va
490.3		490	2519	Ona----------- W Va
491.9		492	2521	†Blue Sulphur-- W Va
494.7	*BR	495	2525	②Barboursville W Va
498.2		498	2980	†Wilson-------- W Va
499.8		500	2981	‡East Huntington--------- W Va
501.0		501	2982	Guyandotte--- W Va
501.2	*DK	501½		††D. K. Cabin-- W Va
502.4		502	2984	Huntington Shops------- W Va
			2987	Coal Acct.----------
504.0	*HU	504	2986	①④**Huntington**- W Va
			2985	" Tkt Office-----
	*UN			" Disprs' Office---
504.6	*HO	505		H. O. Cabin--- W Va
506.1		506	2988	W. Huntington W Va
507 6		508	2990	Westmoreland- W Va
508.2		509	2991	‡Kellog-------- W Va
510.2		510	2995	Ceredo-------- W Va
511.2	*KV	511		††K. V. Cabin-- W Va
511.3		512	2999	①④**Kenova**----- W Va
			3000	" Tkt Office-----
513.3	*BS	513	4000	②Big Sandy Jct---Ky
514.0		514	4500	④**Catlettsburg**-----Ky
516.0		517	4505	Normal----------Ky
516.6	*SX	517½	4506	Clyffeside-------Ky
519.2	*AU	520	4509	②④**Ashland**------Ky
			4510	" Tkt Office-----
519.5	*AX	521	4510	Ashland Jct------Ky
520.4	*NC	521½		N. C. Cabin-----Ky
521.1		522	4701	Bellefonte-------Ky
523.9	*RU	524	4705	④**Russell**---------Ky

†No Siding.
‡–Private Siding only.
*–Day and Night Telegraph Offices.
①–Junction with connecting lines.
②–Junction of Sub-division shown elsewhere.
④–Coupon Stations.

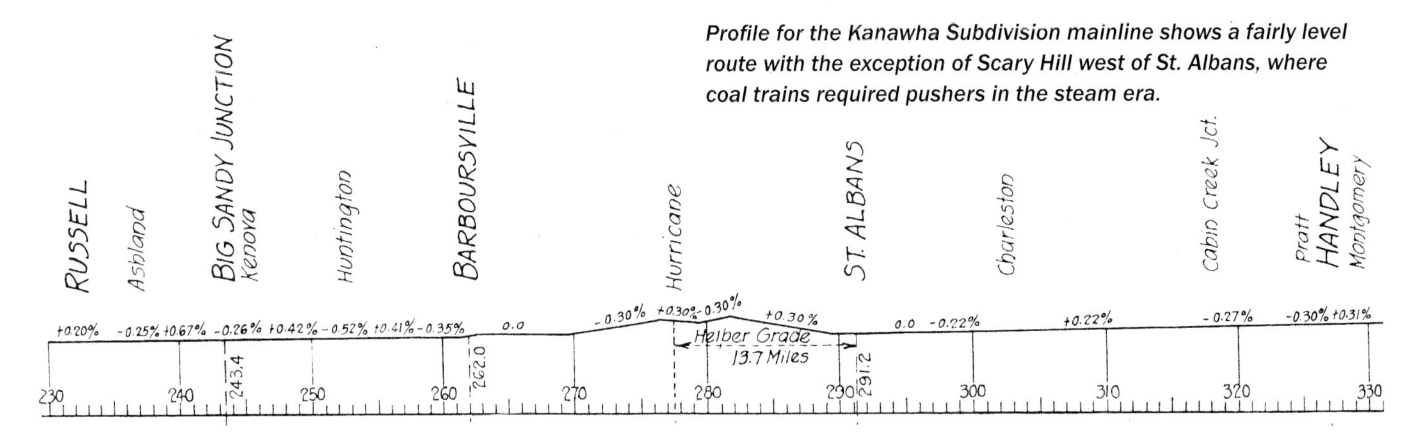

Profile for the Kanawha Subdivision mainline shows a fairly level route with the exception of Scary Hill west of St. Albans, where coal trains required pushers in the steam era.

The operational situation before 1891 is unclear, but trains seem to have had an operational district between Hinton and Cannelton (later Montgomery), where crews and locomotives were changed. In 1889-92 the C&O was completely rebuilt and refurbished by the new owners (see page 5) and Handley was established as the appropriate terminal point joining the New River and Kanawha Subdivisions (or "districts" as they were then called). Handley yard was laid out just a few miles from Montgomery, where the old operational district had ended. This situation continued into modern times.

Handley itself was originally settled in 1875 by owners of a coal company called Wyoming Manufacturing Company, soon after the arrival of the C&O, naming it after one of the officials of the company. It remained a small coal town until 1891 when C&O decided on its new operational arrangement and built the yard, moving its terminal operations from Montgomery. A roundhouse, machine shop, coaling and water stations, and sizeable yard were established. A large Railroad YMCA was built in 1896 to serve as a layover point for crews away from home.

Handley was the division point yard separating the new River and Kanawha Subdivisions. This 1949 photo looking west shows the caboose track, house track filled with camp cars, station/yard office area on the left. the yard tracks at center, and the edge of the roundhouse at right. It was taken from the top of the coaling station. (TLC Collection)

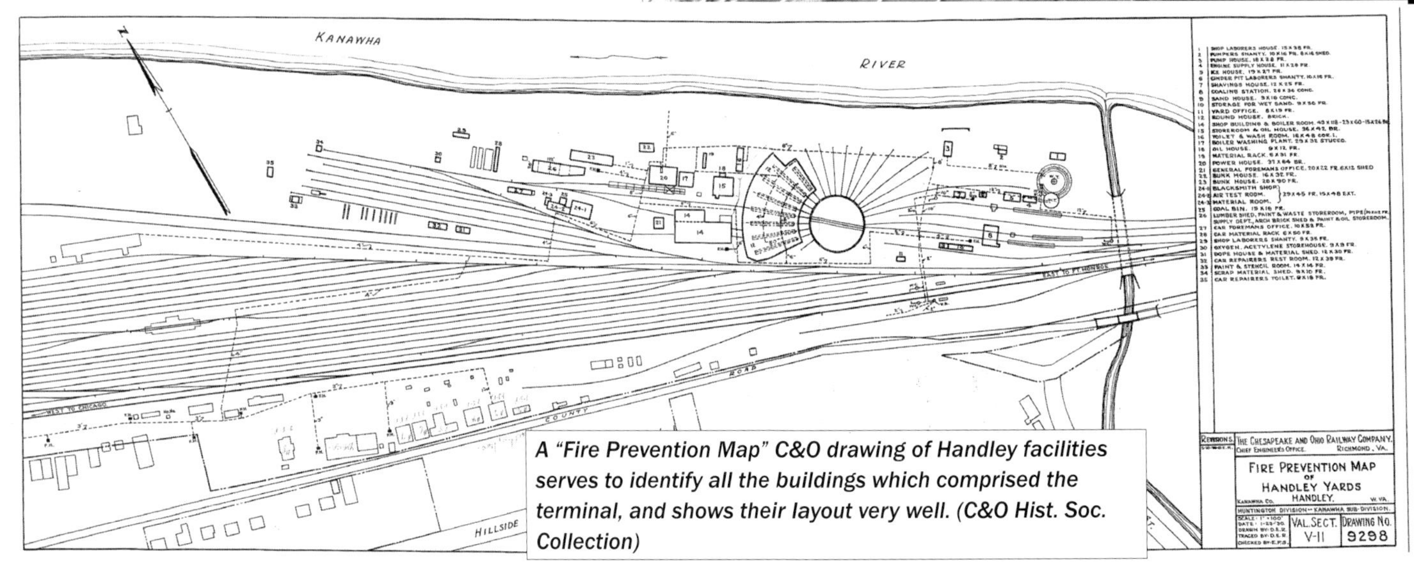

A "Fire Prevention Map" C&O drawing of Handley facilities serves to identify all the buildings which comprised the terminal, and shows their layout very well. (C&O Hist. Soc. Collection)

In 1889 the officials of the new Railroad YMCA movement came to President M. E. Ingalls soon after he took control of C&O and proposed that the railroad locate YMCA operations along the line. He is reported to have said that he would fund a building and facilities for the YMCA at Hinton, and if that wild and raucous town could be tamed by having the Y's good wholesome influence on his crews he would build structures all across the system and lease them to the Railroad YMCA at no cost. In those days the C&O in West Virginia was known as lawless and rough, with the saying being current "No heaven west of Clifton Forge, no God west of Hinton." Over the first few years of the 1890s, the YMCA did its job well, and Ingalls kept his promise, installing large YMCA buildings at all C&O terminals. Handley was one of the larger buildings, though Clifton Forge was the largest. These operations served the C&O's crews admirably, giving them a good clean bedroom, dining hall, reading and relaxation rooms, and a generally wholesome atmosphere which greatly improved morale. This reduced accidents on the C&O in this early crude era of railroading. It was only in the 1970s that the YMCAs were replaced by contractor-operated bunkhouses.

Handley continued as a division point and yard for assembly, collection, and distribution of coal cars to several branch lines until the 1970s. Today its large yard and all the facilities are gone. However, in the mid-century era on which this book centers it was a very important terminal.

West from Handley the mainline passed several coal mining operations that were largely played out and gone by the middle-20th Century, and at MP 437.5 the station at Coalburg was located. This name soon disappeared from C&O station lists in favor of Cabin Creek Junction, just six-tenths of a mile further west. This became important when the Cabin Creek Branch was purchased in 1902. This branch tapped rich coal veins to the south of the main line. A large station and small yard were located here, and with its tower it was an important operational point in the era with which we are dealing.

At MP 440.6, about 2½ miles west of Cabin Creek Junction, a connection was made with the Winifrede Railroad. This was an independent short line that had been in operation since 1853 to carry coal from a mine located several miles to the south, to the Kanawha River where the coal was dumped into barges to carry it to Charleston and as far as Cincinnati, all long be-

The engine terminal at Handley in 1955 was still well populated with steam, though it would be all gone within a year. K-4 2-8-4 No. 2713 is partially visible at right, while two H-8s are visible. The large water tanks and uniquely designed coaling station were landmarks of the yard. (C&O Ry. Photo, C&O Hist. Soc. Coll., Image CSPR-10311)

H-4 2-6-6-2 No. 1473 prepares to go out with a mine run probably to Paint Creek, with the Handley roundhouse in the background, in 1955. (C&O Ry. Photo, C&O Hist. Soc. Coll., Image CSPR-10311.A1)

The steam-diesel transition was well under way as shown by this 1955 Handley photo, with both active steam and F7 diesels near the coaling station. (C&O Ry. Photo, C&O Hist. Soc. Coll., Image CSPR-10311.A7)

The brick machine shop at the rear of the Handley roundhouse, pictured here in 1949, was part of the facility that was built here in the 1890s when Handley was established as the division point. (C&O Ry. Photo, C&O Hist. Soc. Coll., Image CSPR-1459)

The telegraph tower, depot, and yard office complex at Handley is shown here about 1949, but was unchanged from when it was first built about 1892. The yard office is closest the camera, while the station comprises the depot area plus the signal tower (cabin) arranged atop it in a C&O style used in the 1890s. These structures were replaced about 1950 by a modern brick structure. (C&O Ry. Photo, C&OHS Collection, Image COHS-12308)

fore the C&O was ever built. After the coming of the C&O, a good deal of Winifrede coal was interchanged with it, but the line continued to dump a large part of its traffic into river barges, as it does to this day (2010).

Stations west of here, most spaced a few miles apart, included Chesapeake (MP441.6), Marmet (MP 444.5), South Malden (MP 448.2), Owens (MP 449.8), and South Ruffner (MP 451.8), all part of a region that had gotten its start in salt production well before the War Between the States and arrival of the C&O. The area continued industrialization with the coming of coal mining as a major element in the region's economy, and eventually would become part of a large chemical manufacturing region. In the era of this book the region was well populated, one town today running into the other almost without a break.

At MP 453.6 the C&O established its station for Charleston. Although the bulk of the city is on the north side of the river at this point, the C&O's line was on the south side, and at first the station could be reached from the main city only by means of ferry boats and barges. C&O built a line down to the river's edge and transferred freight and passengers there. In the 1890s a vehicular and pedestrian bridge was in place terminating at the C&O station on the south side, thus facilitating the ever-growing traffic. Charleston became West Virginia's second capital city in 1870-75 when the seat of government was moved from Wheeling. After being returned to Wheeling from 1875 to 1885, it came back to Charleston to stay.

In the era of this book, Charleston was a very important station on the C&O. First, it supplied a large passenger traffic not only because it was the state's largest city in the era, but because of the state government activities. Over the years it grew as a manufacturing center with special emphasis on chemicals, and after WWII was one of the major chemical producing areas in the eastern U. S. This supplied a large business to C&O, which had a yard called "Elk Yard" located west of the station by about a mile and a half. This yard is still functional with switcher locomotives stationed there to accommodate the industrial needs still present at this writing. However, Charleston was not an operational terminal, with passenger and freight trains passing through. Its impressive yellow brick Beaux Arts style station was built in 1906 and is today preserved and adaptively reused. Other manufacturing at Charleston included glass and automotive.

To reach the city proper, a railroad bridge was built in 1909 that allowed C&O to serve a large freight station located in the main business district of the city near a similar facility operated by the New York Central. NYC's line coming into the state from Point Pleasant served Charleston north of the river. C&O also had numerous switching operations that were performed from this small yard adjacent to the freight station. Another station, called South

The Charleston passenger station was located across the Kanawha River from the main part of the city, with access via the bridge shown at left in this photo. The long concrete roadway leading down from the bridge actually served as part of the platform shed. The impressive stone and brick station was fitting for the capital city. Today it is preserved and used as offices. (TLC Collection)

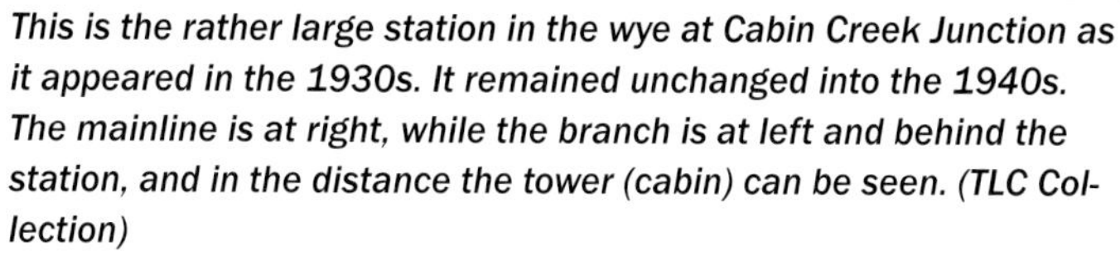

This is the rather large station in the wye at Cabin Creek Junction as it appeared in the 1930s. It remained unchanged into the 1940s. The mainline is at right, while the branch is at left and behind the station, and in the distance the tower (cabin) can be seen. (TLC Collection)

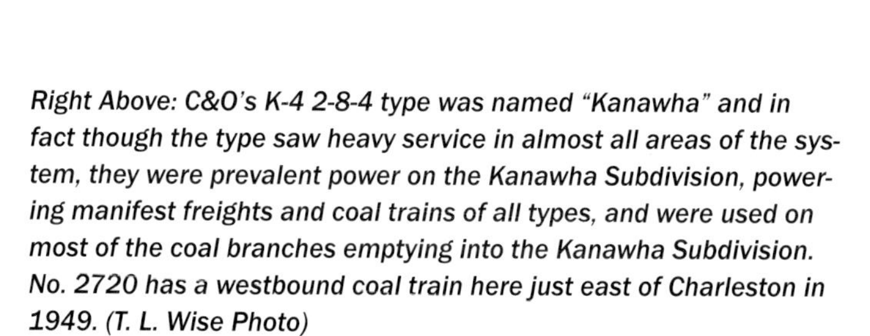

Right Above: C&O's K-4 2-8-4 type was named "Kanawha" and in fact though the type saw heavy service in almost all areas of the system, they were prevalent power on the Kanawha Subdivision, powering manifest freights and coal trains of all types, and were used on most of the coal branches emptying into the Kanawha Subdivision. No. 2720 has a westbound coal train here just east of Charleston in 1949. (T. L. Wise Photo)

Right: Although Charleston had no large operational yard facility, it did, nonetheless have to have facilities to serve the many switchers that handled the large industrial and commercial business of the city. This view of the automatic coaling station at Elk yard shows how the compact facility simply conveyed coal from a pit after it dropped from nearby hoppers, negating the need for a big tower. (TLC Collection)

Charleston, was located about two miles beyond Elk.

Twelve miles west of Charleston is St. Albans (MP 465.5), first known as "Coal's Mouth," because it was situated at the mouth of Coal River, where that tributary joined the Kanawha from the south. The name of the river gives an indication of its importance to C&O. A number of railroad companies were projected to build from the C&O up the Coal River to develop its resources, but only a little progress had been made by 1906 when C&O bought the Coal River & Western and began its own expansion up the river and development of what would become one of the best deposits on the C&O. At this writing the Coal River district is still one of the most important coal producing lines on CSX. In the mid-century era of this book St. Albans had a yard of several tracks, and a coaling station and small engine house. It served in the late steam era as a servicing point for locomotives operating as mine shifters on the Coal River line short of the marshalling yards there (see Chapter 7), as well as the pusher locomotives used on trains west of this point over the Scary Hill pusher district. After the end of steam this operation and all facilities at St. Albans were eliminated except for an operator and yard office at the Coal River branch junction. A sizeable passenger station accommodated a good traffic, and a freight station was connected to it with a long covered platform shed.

From St. Albans the line leaves the river, climbs the Scary Hill grade, and enters the Teays Valley region mentioned earlier. This is really the only operationally difficult area on the Kanawha Subdivision.

In this region the towns of Hurricane (MP 479.2), Culloden (MP 481.5), and Milton (MP 485.8) are principal stations, though they were fairly small. The glass industry was prominent and supplied some business to C&O. Farming and

Because C&O was located on the south side of the river, it built this bridge to reach the main part of the city. It used the line across the bridge to serve a large freight station, many industrial spurs, and to connect with the New York Central (K&M). This late-era photo shows Chessie System units with a train in 1985 not long before the bridge and connection were abandoned. (Jay Potter Photo)

F-17 class heavy Pacific (4-6-2) No. 471 is getting some water as it pauses with a westbound passenger train at the Charleston station in 1949. Pacifics were standard power for passenger trains west of Hinton until they were supplemented by the giant 4-6-4 Hudsons after 1941. (T. L. Wise Photo)

cattle raising were more important here than in the east where mineral extraction was paramount.

At MP 494.7 Barboursville is a town of considerable size in its own right but for C&O it served two purposes in our era. First, it was the junction point for the Logan (or Guyandotte as it was first known) branch, tapping the fabulous Logan coal fields to the south. This branch is at this writing still an important coal producer for CSX. Second, Barboursville was, at mid-century, important because it was the site of

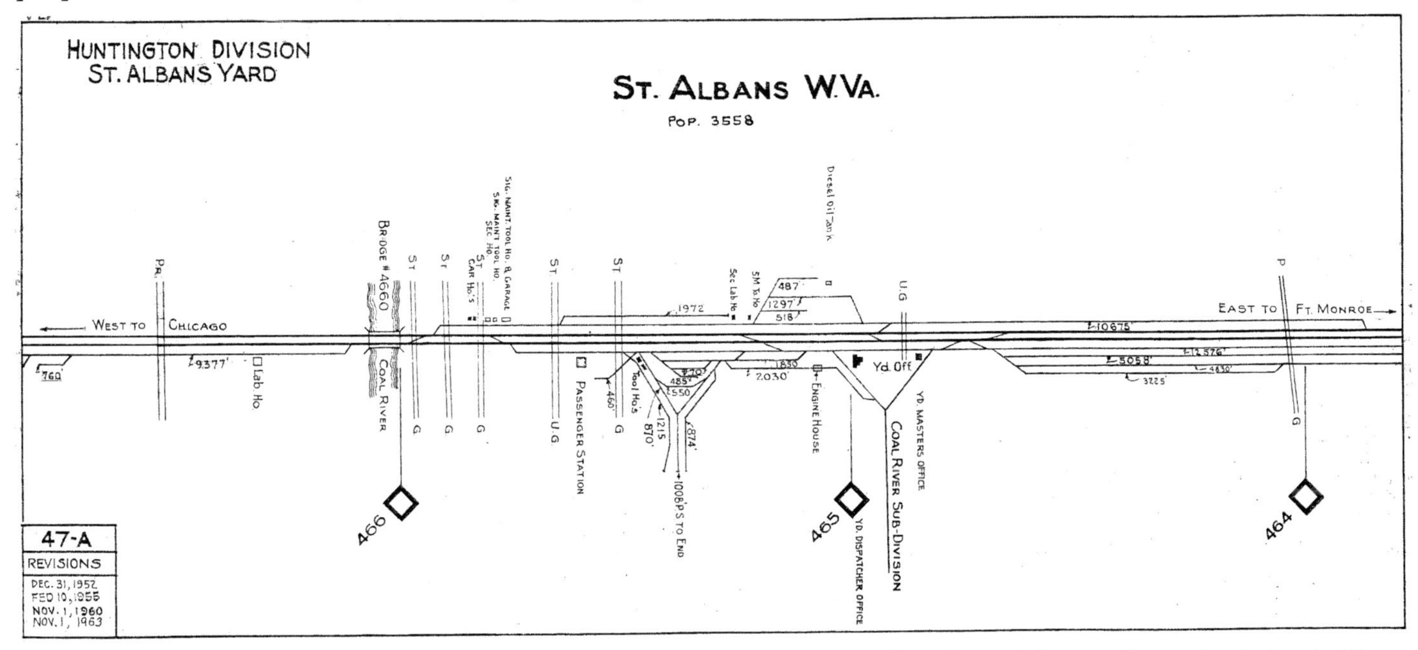

St. Albans yard was long and was intersected by the Coal River Subdivision line arriving from the south by way of a wye located east of the station. This map shows a portion of the layout. The second, truncated wye was the old alignment of the branch. (C&O Drawing, C&O Hist. Soc. Coll.)

St. Albans

By Gene Huddleston

The center of interest at St. Albans was the concrete coaling tower, located about three-quarters of a mile east of the depot and just west of the wye forming the junction of the mainline and the Coal River branch lines. A second wye was located just east of the depot, forming the junction of the old Coal River line which went through the city and curved around a big hill by hugging the river bank. The new line (built in 1923) avoided the curve, a slight grade, and city congestion by tunneling through the hill. Right beside the big coal dock was a one-stall engine house.

Back down the line was the freight house, depot and lunch room, forming an impressive "Railroad Avenue" type compound. Everything is gone now except the depot. [The passenger depot has been converted to a railroad museum.]

Back in the 1940s there would have been stationed here a 4-4-2 for the passenger run to Madison, a Brill gas-electric car for the run up Big Coal, a Consolidation, a K-1 Mikado, and several 2-6-6-2 Mallets, most of which would have been USRA H-5s for Scary Hill pusher service. The other engines were for use on mine runs short of the terminals at Danville and Elk Run. These branches included the Brush Creek, Seth, and Horse Creek Subdivisions. After the H-5 Mallets were scrapped in 1952, K-2s or K-3s [2-8-2s] were generally used on Scary Hill pushers. These pushers coupled on westbound trains near the coal dock and pushed to the summit just east of Teays station. Pushers for eastbound trains (only coal trains required pushers) ran light from St. Albans to Barboursville where they turned on the wye and ran behind the eastbound until it stalled, usually around Milton.

The C&O cut off one of the passenger trains in its wholesale slaughter of passenger service in 1949, but the Brill gas-electric car remained until about 1954, when it was replaced by a Consolidation locomotive. Soon all service was abandoned.

In 1947 Centralized Traffic Control was installed on the main Coal River line, and in that year a new yard office and telegraph office [with the CTC board] was built in the wye. Besides the usual array of Pacifics, Hudsons, Mallets, and Kanawhas passing through St. Albans in the late 1940s one could have seen a G-7 class 2-8-0 with inside piston valves, used on the local freight that ran between Elk yard and Barboursville.

In September 1956 a manifest freight train, Advance 92, derailed and struck the coal dock, weakening it so much it had to be demolished.

General view of the St. Albans engine terminal shows the 500-ton concrete coaling station and the tiny one-stall engine house. Locomotives were serviced here for use on mine shifters on the Coal River lines short of the marshalling yards at Danville and Elk Run Junction, and engines for use as the "Scary Hill pushers." Here K-3a No. 2343 is ready, while K-1 No. 1109 is in the shed. (T. L. Wise photo)

The tender of H-4 2-6-6-2 No. 1466 sticks out of the St. Albans engine house May 31, 1953. (D. Wallace Johnson photo)

C&O's "reclamation plant." This was a shop and yard where C&O sent all its scrap materials for recycling. For example, a bridge girder might no longer be needed at a particular point, and instead of scraping it, the Barboursville reclamation plant would take it, make any repairs necessary, and hold it for future needs. The same held true or everything from tie plates to signal bridges. C&O was very proud of this operation which was said to save huge amounts of money by reusing serviceable or refurbished items. Barboursville shop was also the center for repair of Maintenance-of-Way equipment, including motor cars, spreaders, rail layers, etc. This was important by mid-century as C&O was at the forefront of mechanizing track work.

Huntington is reached just a few miles west of Barboursville with the shop area at MP 502.4 and the passenger station at MP 504. Huntington is one of the cities that has always been prominent in C&O's operations. It was created by C&O president Collis P. Huntington in the early 1870s when he decided on this location as the C&O's western terminal as it was building across West Virginia. He erected a large passenger station and office building here, organized a land company, laid out and sold city plots, and named the city for himself.

Since a major locomotive repair shop was needed for the western end of the road, it was placed here. A private company, the Ensign Car Works opened a business to build railroad cars, first for C&O and then for many other new lines in the area. It was eventually taken over by the American Car and Foundry Company, which produced a huge quantity of cars right up to modern times. Though no cars are actually built there as of this writing, some repair work is carried on. During the mid-century era it was an important industry for the city and shipper for C&O, and, of course, many C&O cars were built there.

The C&O shops at Huntington began on a fairly small scale, but soon grew as the line's operations expanded and locomotives became more numerous, larger, and more complex. By mid-20th Century the Huntington shops were the most important repair facility on the line. All major locomotive rebuilding and major refurbishment was done here, while lighter work was done at Clifton Forge, Virginia (and Grand Rapids, Michigan on the old Pere Marquette Railway after it was merged in 1947). In the early 1920s the shop was completely rebuilt and greatly expanded. By this time much larger locomotives were in service, and the old facilities were no longer adequate. The reconstruction was done while the old shop continued to function, with the new building actually being built over the old one. After this time C&O had a heavy locomotive repair shop complex that was equal to any in the country.

When diesels replaced steam, the Huntington shop was again rebuilt, changing the existing structures into a diesel repair shop for the heaviest repair and rebuilding work for the C&O system. An interesting part of this transition is that the employees and managers of the steam shop designed the new facility themselves and presented the plan to C&O management, which enthusiastically adopted and implemented it. Since less space was needed for the diesel shop work, a portion of the old steam shop was converted for passenger car repair work, which was moved to this point from Richmond. This reshaping of the shop facilities occurred in 1954-55.

At the same time, a new modernistic, two-stall rectangular diesel engine house was built to the west of the shop area, whose sole purpose was as the servicing, inspection, and repair facility for C&O's fleet of E8 passenger diesels. These locomotives were given a cycle on C&O's various passenger trains, and then returned to Huntington for routine inspection and work.

Beside the shop, on its western edge, was the ordinary roundhouse and ready track area, including water and coaling stations, for the Kanawha subdivision's operations. This was needed because many trains originated or terminated at Huntington, even though it was not a divisional end-point terminal (those were Handley and Russell). This facility took care of day-to-day operations for passenger and freight locomotives operating in the region.

Doubleheaded K-4 2-8-4s leave St. Albans after picking up eastbound tonnage about 1954. (Adrian Gwinn photo)

The westbound grade out of St. Albans ascends to Scary at 0.30%, and eastbound the grade is also 0.30%. This required pushers in both directions on coal trains. Here H-5 USRA 2-6-6-2 No. 1538 is pushing an eastbound train that had originated in Logan. The pusher followed the train from Barboursville and coupled on when it stalled at Milton, in February 1951. (Gene Huddleston Photo)

Huntington also had a large yard that was used for coal operations because there were several river terminals in or near the city. C&O hauled its trains from the coal fields, delivered the cars to the Huntington yard where they were transferred to one of these river terminal/barge companies, and the coal was then dumped into barges for further transportation by water. This still occurs as of this writing.

Huntington also grew in size as not only a transportation center but as an industrial city, with numerous large manufacturing plants, requiring a large presence by C&O to handle its inbound and outbound traffic.

In 1913 C&O erected a new red brick three story station building for its passenger operations and to house offices. Appended was a wide platform covered by a shed supported by pairs of columns similar to other important stations on the line of the era. Passenger trains were often switched here to add or remove cars or locomotives, or to make up trains either for the Kentucky mainlines or for branch lines, although most of the mainline train consist adjustment was usually conducted at Ashland, Kentucky, just across the Big Sandy River.

Huntington was also the center for a number of C&O offices, including the coal department and accounting department, and the company had a tall office building emblazoned with its 1930s-era C&O Lines logo well into the 1950s. In 1960 its mechanical department and engineering department moved from Richmond to Huntington and occupied a no longer used General Electric factory which C&O called the "Operating Headquarters" building. It continued to house these departments and their subordinate elements until the CSX merger in the mid-1980s removed them to Jacksonville, Florida.

K-4 Kanawha type No. 2788 has crested the Scary Hill at Teays and is accelerating in May 1949. (Gene Huddleston Photo, C&O Hist. Soc. Coll., Image No. 1197)

The C&O diesel shop continued in its accustomed work until the C&O/B&O affiliation, which took some work on the combined system to Cumberland, Maryland, on the B&O. After the CSX merger, the Huntington shops were kept in operation and made one of major diesel shop facilities on the modern CSX. The 1923-era buildings are still in use as of this writing for this purpose.

C&O connected with B&O at Huntington long before the two lines merged, the B&O line coming in from the north along the Ohio River. C&O connected with Norfolk & Western's east-west main line at Kenova, W. Va., at MP 511.3, six miles west of Huntington depot. A union station was erected here in the early 1900s, and served until the end of C&O passenger service at this point when Amtrak took over. It was a two-level station with ticket office and waiting rooms on the bottom floor opposite the C&O tracks, and an elevated waiting area and platform/canopy on an elevated level which served N&W. N&W crossed over the C&O and thence directly across the Ohio River at this point. The name Kenova was originated by combining letters from the three states that joined each ether near here (Kentucky, Ohio, and West Virginia). Kenova also had a small yard, and B&O interchanged with C&O at this point as well, it being the terminal point of B&O's Ohio River Division. As long as there were passenger trains on this B&O line, they used Kenova Union Station as well, on the C&O level.

About two miles west of Kenova the Kanawha Subdivision mainline crosses the Big Sandy River and enters Kentucky. In Kentucky the line served the medium-sized city of Ashland, where C&O built its largest on-line passenger station and from which passenger trains were dispatched to Cincinnati, Louisville, and Detroit. At mid-century, the era of this book, the Ashland Division also controlled the Ashland-Lexington-Louisville line and the Big Sandy coal branch, though both of these lines actually intersected the Kanawha Subdivision mainline.

At MP 523.9 Russell was the western terminal of the Kanawha Subdivision. The huge yard facility here was, however, not part of the Kanawha Subdivision. At mid-20th century the Russell yard complex was the largest yard in the world owned

Another 2-8-4, No. 2748, powers a train near Ona in 1953. The good alignment here was a result of the complete rebuilding of a great deal of the mainline east of Barboursville in the 1903-1906 era. Ona was the site of a tunnel of 1,316 feet length until it was eliminated in the late 1920s. (C&O Ry. Photo, C&O Hist. Soc. Coll., image No. CSPR-3183)

The old depot at Hurricane is close to the end of its days in this 1962 photo but is still in very good condition. Note the standard C&O fire barrel and bucket (the barrel was filled with sand). This style station was built all along the C&O when it was built in the 1871-1875 era. (TLC Collection)

by a single railroad. It remains today a very important part of CSX's scheme of operations.

Motive Power

In the early era, the Kanawha Subdivision had the usual early light C&O locomotives that were used all over the railway. But by the time that the 4-4-2s and 4-6-2s arrived in 1902 they were used on the Kanawha Subdivision lines on the through passenger trains. As heavier Pacifics arrived, they were put on the name trains, and by the time the F-19 Pacifics came in the mid-1920s they became the largest passenger locomotives in use on the Kanawha lines, because the Mountain types (4-8-2s) of 1911, and the Greenbriers (4-8-4s) of 1935 were kept east of Hinton. In the mid-20th century era of this book the through passenger trains had heavy Pacifics or 4-6-4 Hudsons (which arrived in 1941 and 1948), as well as the streamlined 4-6-4s which were rebuilt at Huntington shops from F-19 Pacifics in 1946-47. Passenger locomotives were generally changed at Hinton and Huntington, though some operated through between Hinton and Cincinnati or Detroit. In the late 1940s 4-4-2s were still occasionally used on branch line passenger trains, and Brill gas-electric motor cars were

These two photos show the passenger and freight stations at Milton in about 1946. The freight station was located in the town proper along the old alignment of the main line, a part of which was left in place to serve as a spur to the freight house. The passenger station was located about ½ mile away on the new mainline alignment and reflects the C&O standard station design of the era. Note the interesting use of awnings, not usual for C&O stations. (TLC Collection)

K-3 2-8-2 No. 1238 with a coal train crosses the massive deck plate girder bridge across the Mud River at Barboursville in 1949. This massive bridge looks like it could hold just about any weight. Note the add-on pier, the lower, older portion holding the deck-truss bridge that is barely seen behind, holding the second track. (T. L. Wise photo)

The Barboursville Reclamation Plant was pride of the C&O in this 1946 photo, which incidentally shows a section gang at work in the foreground. The plant saved the C&O huge amounts of money by refurbishing and reusing materials of all kinds. An early form of recycling! (C&O Ry. Photo)

K-4 Kanawha No. 2754 rolls east with 84 cars of coal past the buildings of the Reclamation Plant at Barboursville on Sept. 22, 1955. It will pick up other loads at some point to fill out its train. (Robert F. Collins Photo)

used on the Coal River and Logan lines in this era.

Consolidation type 2-8-0s, Mikado type 2-8-2s, and compound articulated 2-6-6-2s were employed for local freights, and coal operations on the many branches. Switchers of the 0-8-0 types were found at Handley, Charleston, and Huntington as well as at some coal marshalling yards, and 0-10-0 heavy switchers were operated at Peach Creek on the Logan branch.

The earlier locomotives of the 2-8-0 Consolidation type that were in use in 1900 were supplanted with 2-8-2s in 1911 and as more came in 1920-23, as well as the 2-6-6-2s that came in large numbers in the 1911-1923 era. One seldom found the H-7 simple 2-8-8-2s, which generally were kept east of Hinton, and were largely gone by 1943. In the post-war steam era the 2-6-6-6s generally didn't operate on the Kanawha Subdivision except for trains terminating at Handley to and from Hinton.

Most fast freight and coal trains used the famous K-4 class 2-8-4 "Kanawha" types that arrived between 1943 and 1948 in large quantity [90 by 1948]. Consolidations persisted on some branch line runs, work trains, and occasionally on local freights, though the latter also used 2-8-2s. On rare occasions after the strengthening of the Big Sandy bridge in 1948 the T-1 2-10-4 Texas types would take interdivisional freights between Russell and Hinton, but this was at best an exceptional operation for these big locomotives. Three odd engines that worked at Charleston were 0-6-0 "Fireless" locomotives. These engines had no firebox or boiler, but in the boiler's location was a large high-pressure steam storage tank. This tank was filled with steam and the steam was then used until almost exhausted, at which time the locomotive had to go to a steam source and be recharged. These were kept around even after the coming of diesels for special use in the chemical plant at Blaine Island in the Kanawha River, where the atmosphere was not conducive to open flame or sparks from diesel exhausts. They were finally retired in the early 1960s, a lingering anachronism of the steam era, long after regular steam had disappeared.

After the coming of diesels, the Kanawha Subdivision mainline and branches essentially followed the dieselization pattern on other areas of C&O. Initially, Alco RSD-7s and RSD-12s were used on coal trains from the Logan lines down to the mainline and on into Russell or Handley, and Alco switcher locomotives supplanted the 0-8-0s at the terminal yards. F7s were seen on through manifest freights until they left the C&O in the early 1960s to finish their lives on the B&O. On occasion they would handle coal trains and empties to and from coal marshalling yards of the Kanawha fields.

It was, however, the EMD GP7s and GP9s that dieselized the Kanawha Subdivision main line and branches just as they did in most other areas of the C&O. They were used for all types of trains, and lasted as almost exclusive power into the late 1960s. When new SD18s arrived in 1963 they were at first used on mainline trains between Clifton Forge and Huntington, but finally were relegated to heavy switcher work. Several of them were stationed at Handley into the 1970s. Some odd locomotives also saw service on the line. C&O's only two Alco RS-1s were used in passenger train and other service at the Huntington station and yard. Alco RSD-5s were used on some coal branches at first.

With the coming of the second generation diesels in the early 1960s, the SD35 and SD40 types of EMD began to supplant the GP7s and GP9s.

The impressive C&O passenger station at Huntington was built in 1913 and housed offices in the upper floors. The long covered platform accommodated the heavy trains that regularly visited here. In the track-side photo a westbound mainline name train is arriving, while the consist of the Logan branch train rests at the right in this 1949 view. (C&O Ry. Photo, C&O Hist. Soc. Coll., CSPR-524)

In the street side photo from 1975 the building and its annex remain largely unchanged. Today CSX uses the station as a dispatch center and offices. (T. W. Dixon, Jr. photo)

Further modernization of diesel operations by Chessie System and CSX is beyond the scope of this book.

Traffic

As with other West Virginia lines, the Kanawha Subdivision traffic was heavily coal business. Coal trains were assembled at the branch line marshalling yards and came down to mainline terminals for transport eastbound to Clifton Forge and points east

C&O always had extensive operations in Huntington including accounting, coal department, mechanical, and engineering. This building with its nice C&O sign was easily visible to people passing through on trains at the station. (C&O Ry. Photo, C&O Hist. Soc. Coll., Image No. CSPR-3601)

As with any large town or city, the less-than-carload (LCL) freight business was extensive and occupied a large station, a small yard, and many laborers. Here workers load cylinders of some type into a box car at the Huntington freight station in 1942. (C&O Ry. Photo, C&O Hist. Soc. Coll., Image No. CSPR-57.13)

or to Russell and points west. The system for doing this was fairly complicated and is covered further in other parts of this book. Manifest freight trains passed though, but because of the heavy industrial areas of Huntington and Charleston, they had consist adjustments (set-offs and pick-ups) at these points. Local freights operated in the usual way.

Passenger traffic consisted of the through trains, but they also underwent consist and motive power adjustments at Huntington, and some passenger trains for local work were made up at Huntington. Most of the coal branches had local passenger runs up until 1949, and a few after that time. They will be covered in more details in other parts of this book. The Coal River trains out of St. Albans lasted until the fall of 1954, and were among the last of the branch line passenger operations to be discontinued. However, the last local passenger operation in the region was the Huntington-Logan train on the

Aerial view from 1945 shows the Huntington shop complex at its height. In the foreground are the Kanawha Subdivision roundhouse, water, and coaling stations, but behind it are the large structures that accommodated the main C&O heavy-repair locomotive shop. The Kanawha Subdivision main line runs diagonally on the right. (C&O Ry. Photo, C&O Hist. Soc. Coll., Image No. CSPR-57.334)

Huntington's engine terminal included a roundhouse, water and coaling stations, and ready tracks for locomotives operating to coal branches, along the mainline, and in switching service in and around the city. Behind the engine terminal are the huge buildings of the Huntington Shop, C&O's premier mechanical facility, taken in 1948. (C&O Ry. Photo, C&O Hist. Soc. Coll., Image No. CSPR-1490)

C&O steam locomotives undergoing major repairs in the Huntington shop erecting hall in about 1945. K-1 class 2-8-2 No. 1169 is being positioned on its wheels by a heavy overhead crane, while a giant H-8 2-6-6-6 Allegheny type is stripped down in the background. (C&O Ry. Photo, C&O Hist. Soc. Coll., Image No. CSPR-982)

After dieselization the shop was converted in 1954 to diesel repair work. Here several models of first generation diesels are undergoing major rebuilding in 1956. (C&O Ry. Photo, C&O Hist. Soc. Coll., Image No. CSPR-4826)

Kenova was a junction for C&O with both B&O, and N&W. Here a westbound C&O coal train led by GP9s passes the small B&O engine terminal at Kenova in 1957, where steam still dominates. (Gene Huddleston Photo)

Logan Subdivision, which was not discontinued until April 1959. The principal passenger traffic generating points were Huntington and Charleston, West Virginia's two largest cities, with good quantities of passengers also handled at St. Albans and Montgomery as well. Local passenger trains operated on varying schedules in the earlier period but by 1950 only one set was functioning, and it was gone by 1958. The six mainline trains continued until 1962 when one set was discontinued (No. 6 by that time was only operating east of Huntington), then two more trains (3 & 4) left in 1968, leaving only the night-time Nos. 1 & 2, *The George Washington*, until Amtrak day 1971. Today Amtrak's *Car-*

One of C&O's 1920s-era standard brick signal towers (called Cabins on the C&O) was still in use in this 1970s photo of KV Cabin at Kenova. (T. W. Dixon, Jr. photo)

Kenova's union station served C&O on the bottom level and N&W on the top (accessed by the elevator in the tower). B&O used the bottom level via C&O trackage. (Jim Corbett collection)

dinal operates over the line three days per week.

Statistics (1948)

Distance Terminal-to-Terminal: 95.7 miles
Distance in West Virginia: 84.8 miles
Branches Connecting: 9 (See Chapter 7)
Connections with other Railroads: Virginian (Deepwater), New York Central (Gauley Bridge and Charleston), Baltimore & Ohio (Huntington and Kenova), Winifrede RR (Winifrede Jct.), Norfolk & Western (Kenova)
Coaling Stations: Handley (500-tons), Charleston (automatic, from cars), St. Albans (500-tons), Huntington (300-tons)
Yards: Handley, Charleston, St. Albans, Huntington (Ashland)
Turntables: Handley (115-ft.), Charleston (80-ft.), Huntington (100-ft), (Ashland 73 ft)
Wyes: St. Albans, Barboursville, Huntington, (Ashland)
Stock Pens: Handley, Charleston, Milton, Barboursville, Huntington, (Catlettsburg, Ashland)
Track Scales: Handley (22-tons), Elk (150-tons), Huntington (200-tons and 100- tons), (Ashland 200-tons)
Tunnels: None (in 1948).

The coal preparation plant of the Truax-Traer Company received run-of-the-mine coal from its mines on the C&O, cleaned and prepared the coal here, and then dumped it into Ohio River barges at this Ceredo facility, adjacent to Kenova. N&W also delivered large amounts of coal this river port area. This photo is from the mid-1950s.(C&O Ry. Photo, C&O Hist. Soc. Coll., Image No. CSPR-3382)

K-4 2-8-4 No. 2747 brings a C&O manifest freight train across the Big Sandy Bridge that connected West Virginia and Kentucky, in 1948. This was the westernmost point on the C&O in West Virginia, though the Kanawha Subdivision continued for about another ten miles through Catlettsburg and Ashland, into Russell, Kentucky. (C&O Ry. Photo, C&O Hist. Soc. Coll.)

At Handley the New River Subdivision ended and the Kanawha Subdivision began. Handley itself served as a division point for the changing of crews on most mainline trains, and as the coal collecting or marshalling yard for some branches nearby. It had large facilities including a roundhouse, machine shop, 500-ton concrete coaling station, water station, and ready track facilities for steam. In the diesel era it continued to be important, but is now completely abandoned, with one track besides the mainline present in today's CSX operations. (see page 84ff)

Morris Creek Subdivision

The first branch on the Kanawha Subdivision mainline, which was actually just east of Handley yard, was the Morris Creek Subdivision, which joined at milepost 428.2 It was built about 1890 by C&O and extended in 1915, but was treated as a sidetrack until 1916 when it was designated as a branch (later Subdivision). It ran only 2.81 miles from Morris Creek Junction to a point beyond Morris Creek. At the mid-century era of this book C&O listed no producing mines on this line.

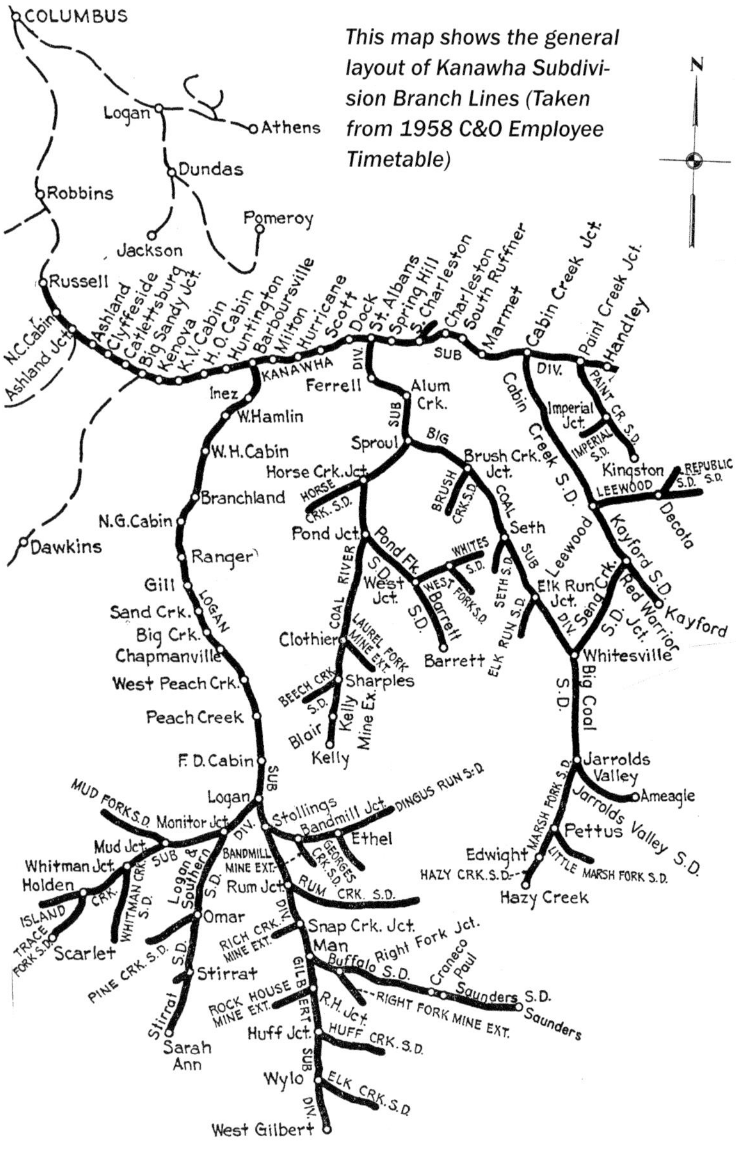

This map shows the general layout of Kanawha Subdivision Branch Lines (Taken from 1958 C&O Employee Timetable)

Paint Creek Branch

The first important coal branch entering the Kanawha Subdivision west of Handley was the Paint Creek Subdivision. It was, in turn fed by the Imperial Subdivision.

The Paint Creek line left the main at Pratt (MP 431.8), and ran 22.12 miles to a point just beyond Kingston. It was built from Pratt to Mahan and extended to Westerly in 1905 by the Kanawha & Pocahontas Railroad. This road built the Imperial Branch from Imperial Junction to the Imperial Mine in 1904. All these lines were sold to C&O in February 1905, and C&O completed the final leg of the line to Kingston in May 1911.

In the mid-century era the Paint Creek line had four large active mines and the Imperial Subdivision one. The mine shifters for this line were operated from Handley, which served as its marshalling yard. In the late steam era the standard 2-6-6-2s were used for the shifters operating on this branch. The line proved to be quite productive over the decades of the first half of the 20th Century. The remains of the right-of-way can be seen today along Interstate-77 (West Virginia Turnpike). It declined when the recoverable coal was worked out and the mines closed.

PAINT CREEK SUB-DIVISION

Dist. from Ft. Monroe	Tel. Calls	Station No.	Code No.	STATIONS
431.8	Booth	431	1672	Pratt..........W Va
433.0		U1½	1673	†Holly Grove...W Va
433.6		U2	1674	Scale Yard....W Va
434.8		U3	1676	Gallagher.....W Va
436.0		U4	1677	†Livingston....W Va
436.9		U6	1679	†Standard......W Va
437.0		U7	1680	††Bedford......W Va
439.2		U8	1681	†Glen Huddy...W Va
441.3		U10	1684	†Nuckolls......W Va
442.3		U11	1685	Whitaker......W Va
443.6		U12	1686	†Green Castle..W Va
444.1		U12¾	1687	②†Imperial Jct.W Va
446.0		U14	1689	††Collinsdale...W Va
446.6		U15	1690	‡Mahan.........W Va
448.2		U15½	1692	Coalfield......W Va
448.6		U16	1693	‡Milburn.......W Va
451.1		U20	1695	Westerly......W Va
452.8		U21	1697	Mossy.........W Va
453.4		U22	1699	Kingston......W Va
444.4		UA1	1702	Burnwell......W Va
445.0		UA2	1703	Imperial No. 2 W Va

Cabin Creek Branch

An even more important coal region was served by the Cabin Creek Subdivision and its three connecting subdivisions. It joined the mainline at Cabin Creek Junction (MP438.1), had 16 active mines in the 1950 *C&O Coal Mine Directory*, and was alive with trains and business. Because it had a large production, a marshalling yard was established at Cane Fork, near Eskdale, about 10 miles, or halfway up the branch. It had a large rectangular frame engine house, a water station, and the smallest coaling station on the C&O, a concrete 50-ton tower of unique design. Track scales (150-ton capacity) were also located at this point for weighing coal loads, as well as a Railroad YMCA to accommodate the many crews working the mine shifter runs.

At Cabin Creek Junction where a number of side tracks, a tower, and a fairly large station to accommodate the interchange with the mainline. The line ended in two legs, creating a wye with the mainline, which facilitated operations east and west from this point. Coal from this line generally moved to Handley for further assembly.

Construction of the line was as follows:

- Cabin Creek to Acme by the Kanawha Railway Company, 1889.
- Purchased by C&O Jan. 31, 1902.

General map of the Paint Creek and Imperial Subdivisions.

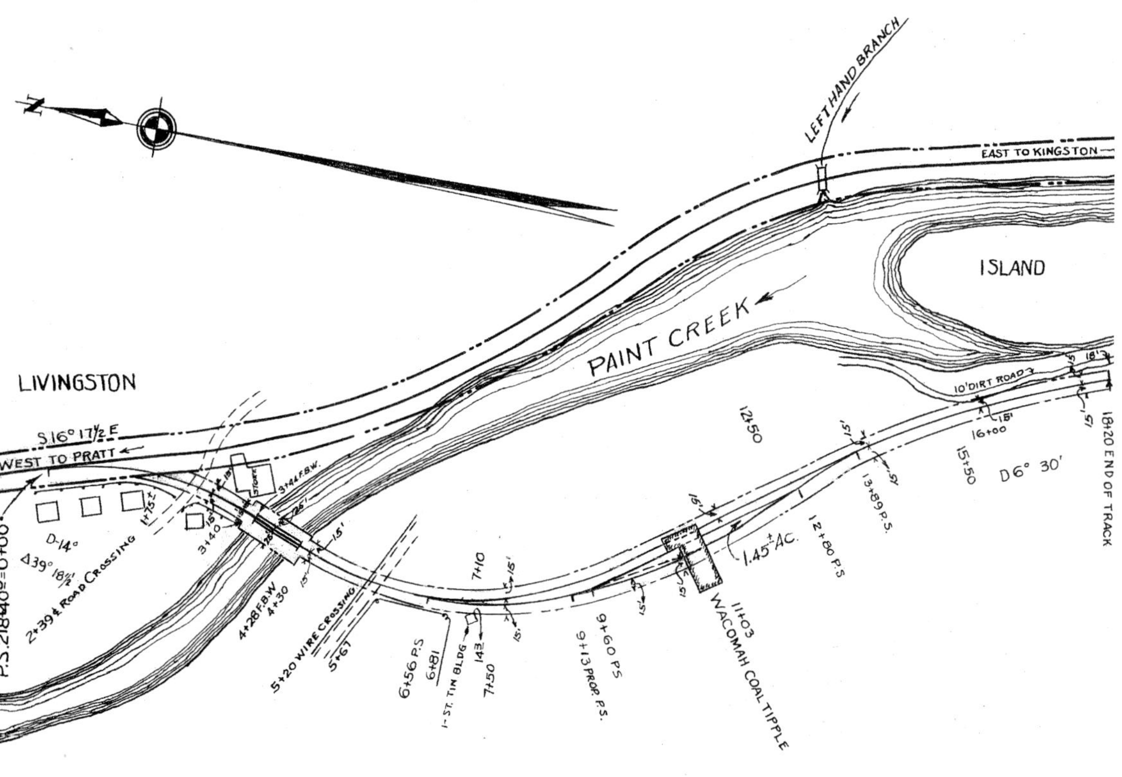

This C&O track map shows the Paint Creek Mining Company's Wacomah Mine at Livingston, about four miles up the Paint Creek Branch. This is included to show the track layout for a typical mine in the region. In this particular case, the mine, located across the creek from the branch's main track, is reached on a stub-end spur. The tipple is relatively small, with three tracks under it. The drawing was made in 1926. It should be remembered that tracks on one side of the tipple would hold empties, and those on the other side loads. (C&O Hist. Soc. Coll. C&O Drawing X-5003A)

Built by C&O:

- Kayford to end-of-line, 1904.
- Leewood to United, 1903.
- Dacota to South Carbon, 1903.
- South Carbon to Republic, 1904.
- Paint Branch line, 1904.
- Cane Fork Branch, 1904.

This was early an important coal-producing area for the C&O and remained so throughout the first half of the 20th Century.

The Kanawha Railroad Company began construction of the first railroad up Cabin Creek in 1889, and was sold to C&O in 1902. C&O quickly expanded the line to reach additional coal seams. In 1905 the Seng Creek tunnel line was opened, which connected the Cabin Creek branch with the upper Coal River basin through Seng Creek Tunnel. It was used to take coal from Coal River to Cane Fork and on to the main line, and with its heavy grades was one of the lines that C&O used its famous big Shay geared locomotives until the early 1920s. After the Coal River lines were fully developed, this operation was discontinued, though the line remained in place until the late 1960s, being mainly used to ferry locomotives between Elk Run Junction and Cane Fork for routine servicing there.

Cane Fork Yard was established as the main marshalling yard for the branch in about 1910 (see above).

The Cabin Creek line was the scene of a famous (or infamous) coal miner's strike or "war," in 1912, and a few years later a disastrous flood ravaged the line, including the railway.

The best description of operations on the Cabin Creek Subdivision appeared as an article by Jeffrey Carson in the November 2003 issue of *Mainline Modeler* magazine. Major portions of that material are reprinted below with permission the publisher:

> The Cabin Creek Subdivision ran all the way to Kayford, where the Traux-Traer Coal Company's large Raccoon and Shamrock #1 mines were located. The Leewood Subdivision branched off at Leewood Junction, running to United. The small Republic Subdivision branched at Decota, running to the Carbon Fuel mines at Republic.
>
> Most of the coal coming off this branch was westbound "Lake" coal, and a much smaller amount heading east

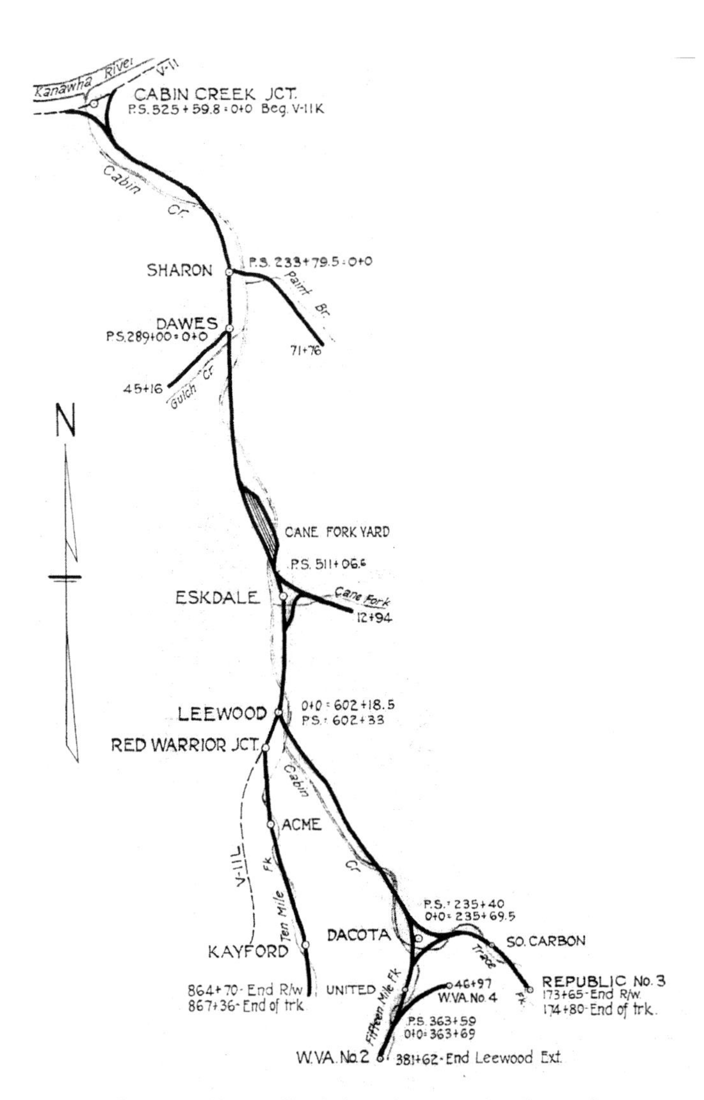

> to "Tidewater." . . . Coal freights on the branch were broken into two types: Mainline and District. Mainline crews ran "west" out of the branch to the terminal at Russell, Ky. District crews shifted the mines as well as taking loads to Handley, W. Va., where they would go east. The District crews would drop loads at Cabin Creek Jct., Winifrede, and Bradford, bringing back empties.
>
> Generally, the mainline crew would bring 160 empties into Cane Fork from Russell. The train would arrive in the evening and the crew would lay over in the YMCA at Cane Fork. They would be called the next morning at around 10:00 am, and return to Russell with between 130 and 145 loads. At times this train would be run out of Handley, or even Handley-Cane Fork-Russell. However, moves coming from Handley did not bring in empties, but were a light engine move that would put a crew on duty for about 50 minutes for the day.
>
> The District crews handled the shifters for the mines above Cane Fork. Usually between five and seven 2-6-6-2s operated out of this facility during the steam era, one of which was used for weighing and yarding loads at Cane Fork. A dispatcher's train sheet for July 27, 1949 showed a train each called for the Kayford, Leewood, and Republic Subdivisions. The first two runs were doubleheaded and each call took

Dist. from Ft. Monroe	Tel. Calls	Station No.	Code No.	STATIONS
438.1	*CA	438	1730	④Cabin Creek Junction W Va
440.0		F2	1732	Dry Branch W Va
441.7		F3	1734	†Ronda W Va
442.3		F4	1736	Sharon W Va
442.9		F5	1738	†Miami W Va
443.5		F6½	1741	Dawes W Va
444.0		F7	1742	†Giles W Va
445.5		F8	1745	†Coal W Va
446.7		F9	1747	†Ohley W Va
447.4	*CJ	F10	1748	Cane Fork W Va
448.5	1L1S1L	F10½	1750	Eskdale W Va
449.4		F12	1752	②Leewood W Va
449.7		F13	1754	Cherokee W Va
450.6		F13¼	1756	②†Red Warrior Junction W Va
450.7		F13½	1757	†Red Warrior W Va
451.2		F14	1758	‡Empire W Va
451.9		F15	1760	‡Acme W Va
453.1		F15	1761	‡Rosecoal W Va
453.6		F18	1762	Kayford W Va
454.1		F18½		End of Line W Va

LEEWOOD SUB-DIVISION

Dist. from Ft. Monroe	Tel. Calls	Station No.	Code No.	STATIONS
449.4		F12	1752	Leewood W Va
450.3		FA½	1775	†Holly W Va
451.6		FA1	1777	†Quarrier W Va
452.1		FA2	1778	†Wake Forest W Va
452.4		FA2½	1779	‡Laing W Va
453.5		FA3½	1781	†Nabob W Va
454.0		FA4	1782	②Decota W Va
455.0		FA5	1784	W. Va. No. 1 W Va
456.0		FA6	1785	United W Va
456.5		FA7	1787	W. Va. No. 2 W Va
457.3		FA8	1790	W. Va. No. 4 W Va

REPUBLIC SUB-DIVISION

Dist. from Ft. Monroe	Tel. Calls	Station No.	Code No.	STATIONS
454.0		FA4	1782	Decota W Va
454.7		FB1	1795	South Carbon W Va
456.6		FB3	1797	Republic No. 2 W Va

SENG CREEK SUB-DIVISION

Dist. from Ft. Monroe	Tel. Calls	Station No.	Code No.	STATIONS
450.6	------	F13¼	1756	†Red Warrior Jct W Va
454.0	1S2L2S	FC3	1800	††Tunnel Siding W Va
455.5	1L4S	FC5	1802	‡High Coal W Va
457.2	4S2L	FC7	1805	‡Ferndale W Va
460.9	2L2S	FC9	1808	Whitesville W Va
451.6	3S	FC11	1810	②Jarrolds Valley W Va
462.1		FC11½	1811	‡Leevale W Va
463.7		FC13	1812	†Rock House W Va
465.6	3L1S	FC15	1813	Dorothy W Va
466.2		FC15½	1814	Sarita W Va
468.2	1L1S	FC17	1816	Colcord W Va
469.2		FC18	1817	‡Ameagle W Va

MARSH FORK SUB-DIVISION

Dist. from Ft. Monroe	Tel. Calls	Station No.	Code No.	STATIONS
461.6	3S	FC11	1810	Jarrolds Valley W Va
462.6	S31L	FD1	1830	②Pettus W Va
463.6		FD2	1833	Eunice W Va
464.6		FD3	1832	‡Birchton W Va
466.6	2S3L1S	FD5	1835	‡Montcoal W Va
467.4		FD6	1836	‡Stickney W Va
468.0		FD7	1834	†Jarro W Va
469.1	3S	FD8	1837	②Edwight W Va

approximately twelve hours, hauling the following:

- Kayford - 62 empties out - 97 loads back
- W. Va. #2 -84 empties out -106 loads back
- Republic #1 -69 empties out -68 loads back.

The C&O also ran local coal trains, known as "Bulldogs," in and out of Cane Fork. These set out and picked up along the line, including eastbound shorts set out at Cabin Creek Junction and the mines between there and Cane Fork. They would usually arrive in Cane Fork around 1:00 or 2:00 in the afternoon, and lay over until the next morning. At times there were two Bulldogs a day. The 1st Bulldog would work the westbound coal out of Cane Fork, and then run to Bradford and Winifrede, further west on the mainline. Bradford was the location of a coal to barge transfer and the shortline Winifrede Railroad provided interchange traffic there. The crew would pull empties and return to Cane Fork. The 2nd Bulldog would work eastbound coal into Handley and return with empties for Cane Fork. In addition, the 2nd would sometimes drop loads at the large Appalachian Power plant at Cabin Creek Junction. All told, between the mainline and district runs, there were sometimes as many as 350 loads per day coming out of Cabin Creek.

Additionally, a local crew was kept at Cabin Creek Junction. This crew worked the local freight for the company stores and mines. Less-than-carload freight was loaded and unloaded as well as company material going to section houses and the scale yard. Three locals ran over the entire subdivision, including branches and occasionally through Seng Creek Tunnel to Whitesville on the Coal River.

The local out of Cabin Creek Junction also handled the tank cars for the Pure Oil Company oil refinery. This refinery was located about a mile up Cabin Creek from the Junction, on a broad bend in the creek. There were several large brick buildings and multiple storage tanks. . . .Oil wells dotted the hillsides for the first several miles up Cabin Creek, as far as Dawes and the Gulch Creek spur. At the peak of production there were between 75 and 100 tank cars per day coming from Pure Oil. The refinery was closed in 1954, but may have been used as a temporary storage facility, with oil being piped in and out, and limited car movements for several more years.

The light engine moves from Coal River continued into the 1950s. These were usually four engines coupled together, both Mallets and Consols. They would make the run through Seng Creek Tunnel into Cane Fork for their federally mandated monthly inspections. It seems odd that these were brought onto the Cabin Creek Sub for servicing, but the railroad did not have a steam engine shop at Elk Run Junction, making Cane Fork the closest shop. . . .

By the fading years of steam, the C&O Class H-4 and H-6 Mallets reigned supreme.... They would handle approximately 65 loads, and double heading was common.

Mainline crews utilized different locomotives, generally K-4 2-8-4 Kanawhas and K-3a 2-8-2 Mikados. The K-4s were the mainline workhorses and averaged well over 100 loads per run. Up until 1952 the occasional K-3 Mike or class N-3 ex-Pere Marquette 2-8-4 would show up.

In 1951 the first diesel to work on Cabin Creek Junction arrived, Alco S-2 #5039. At noon on January 2nd, 1953, RSD-5 #5581 left Cabin Creek with 166 empties, bound for Cane Fork. This was the first diesel to enter the heart of the Sub, taking 45 minutes to make the run. By the fall of 1953 the diesels had arrived. On the mainline runs and the Bulldog, F7A's and B's, with the occasionally FP7, were making their presence known....

[By 1954] Gene Huddleston recounted how he saw most of the shifter chores being handled by Alco RSD-5's in the 5570-5595 series, while steam was still being used for the district crews. However, at the end of 1955, and into the spring of 1956 there was a sudden upturn in traffic that caught the C&O off guard. In addition to the new diesels, H-4 and H-6 Mallets came back to handle the loads. To accompany the steam were the new Baldwin and EMD offerings. In logbooks from April to May 1956 there are over 100 westbound trains departing Cane Fork. Of these, around 70 were steam powered, with Mallets 1361, 1451, 1466, 1473, 1496, and 1506 making regular appearances. EMD [F7s], Baldwin AS-616's, and Alco RSD7 "Dragon Ladies," and a few GP9's handled the remainder of the runs.

By the end of June, the Mallets were to be no more on the shifters above Cane Fork. AS-616's 5526, 5536, 5554, 5555, 5556, 5563, and 5568 handled most of the rest. GP9 6080 managed two runs. At 5:20 pm, on August 26, 1956, the crew was called for #1328 out of Cane Fork. As the H-4 cleared the yard westbound, the age of steam came to an end on the Cabin Creek Subdivision.

GP9s were to rule the Cabin Creek Subdivision for the next twenty years.

Cane Fork Operations

Cane Fork is located 9.5 miles upstream and geographically south of Cabin Creek Junction.... Cabin Creek cuts right through the heart of the engine facilities and by the 1950s there was a series of five double span plate girder bridges each totaling almost 100 feet in length. The rest of the facilities were confined to the narrow valley, on a crescent shaped bend of the creek. The station for Cane Fork was located at Eskdale, the closest actual town. Eskdale was just south of the wye.

The engine house was anchored to the north of the bridges. Actually two engine houses were built at

H-6 2-6-6-2 is running light on the west leg of the wye at Cabin Creek Junction in 1946. (A.R. Hoffman photo, C&O Hist. Soc. Coll., Image No. COHS-16000)

Cane Fork. [The 1908 engine house] was enlarged in 1926. The second house also had two tracks but was long enough to hold a total of four Mallets.

Next to the engine house was a large pump house that also supplied steam and heat for the engine house [and the standard wooden water tank on steel legs. A second steel tank was located beside it].

Incoming coal was weighed on a 150-ton scale next to the coaling tower. The scale house was unusually large, and served as the yard office as well. The north switch for the scale house was actually on the bridge over Cabin Creek. A tall signal mast next to the scales, with a repeating signal on the top of the coaling tower, controlled the scale movements.

The coal dock at Cane Fork was a 50-ton capacity round concrete tower with exposed coal hoist. This dock was built in the mid-1920s. Just south of the coaling tower was a Robertson cinder conveyor. . .. Crews laid over in a red brick YMCA on the west side of the facility. . . . There was a large wye at the south end of the yard for turning locomotives.. . .

The yard was composed of ten tracks, the main, two sidings and RIP tracks for scrap dealer. The yard tracks ran about 2,600 feet each, and because of parallel ladder arrangements, each track was nearly the same length.

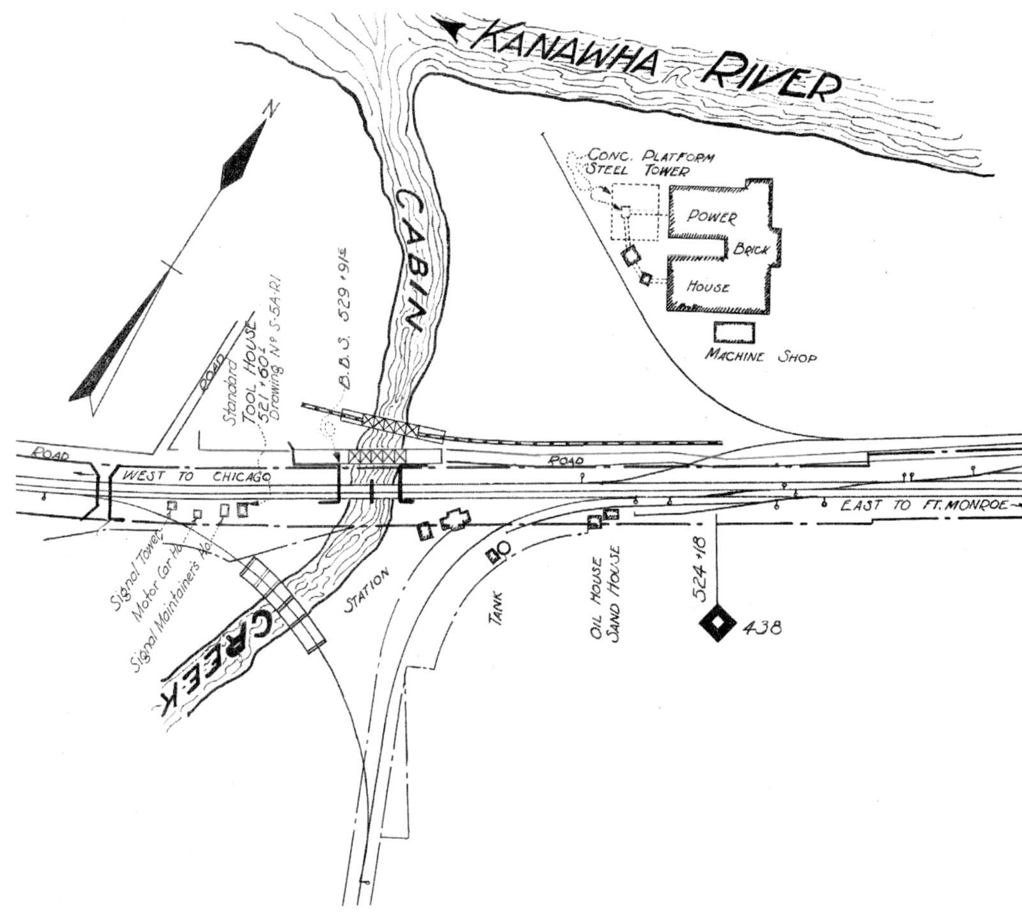

This map shows the layout at Cabin Creek Junction, with the station in the wye, and other facilities. The "Power House" shown across the main line was Appalachian Power Company's generation plant, which used large quantities of C&O coal. (C&O Hist. Soc. Coll., Drawing No. X-5583)

After the arrival of the second batch of F7 diesels in 1952, they began to appear in place of K-4 2-8-4s on coal trains going to and from several of the coal marshalling yards. Here a 2-unit set, headed by 7045, is bringing a coal train out of Cane Fork yard at Ronda, about three miles from Cabin Creek Junction, where it will head either toward Handley or Russell. F7 units were soon replaced by GP9s when they arrived in quantity. (C&O Ry. Photo, C&O Hist. Soc. Coll., Image No, CSPR-3403)

This ca. 1950 photo shows a mine shifter at left and a cut of loads at right at Cane Fork Yard. It looks like the weed-spray train needed to visit this location from the amount of vegetation that was present between the rails. Note that the mine shifter has a box car and tank car in addition to empty hoppers. Local freight to towns and companies along the branches was often handled by the mine shifters. (J. I. Kelly photo, D. Wallace Johnson Collection)

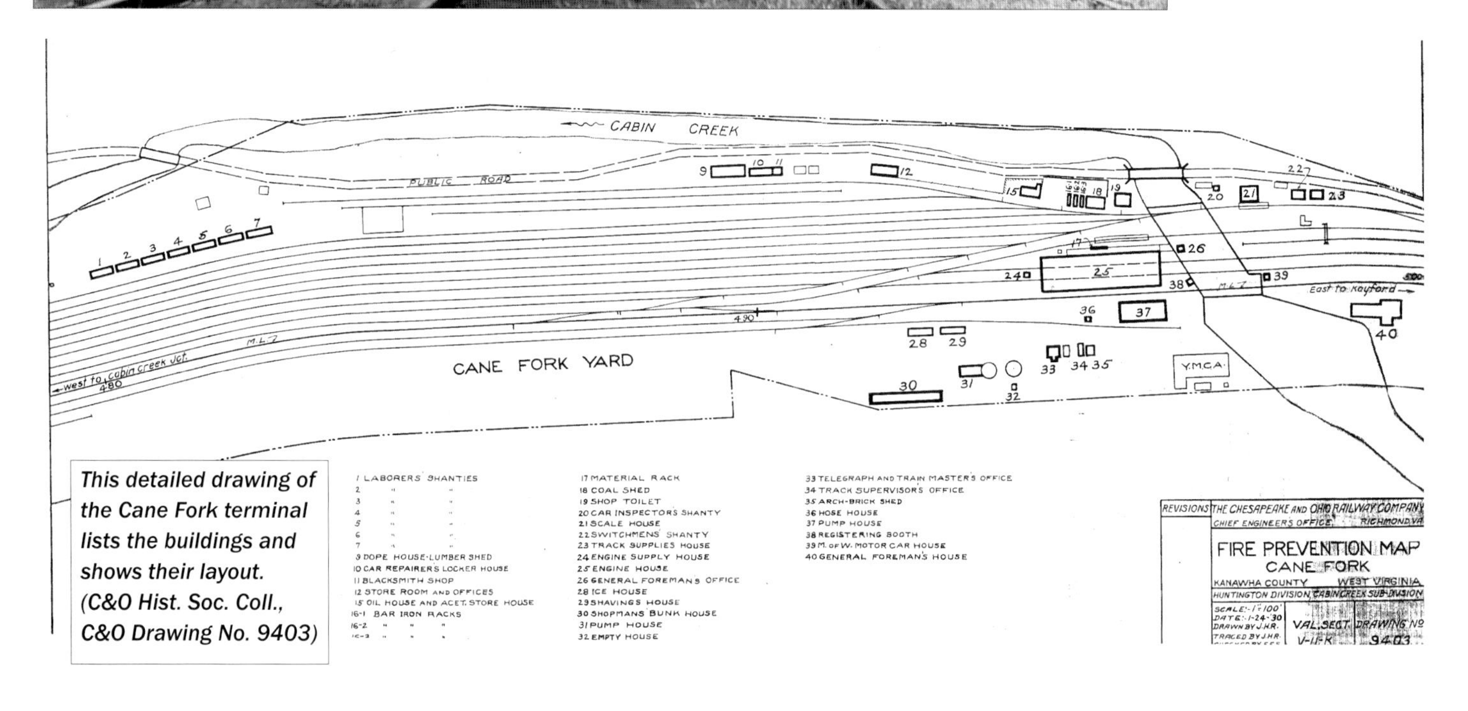

This detailed drawing of the Cane Fork terminal lists the buildings and shows their layout. (C&O Hist. Soc. Coll., C&O Drawing No. 9403)

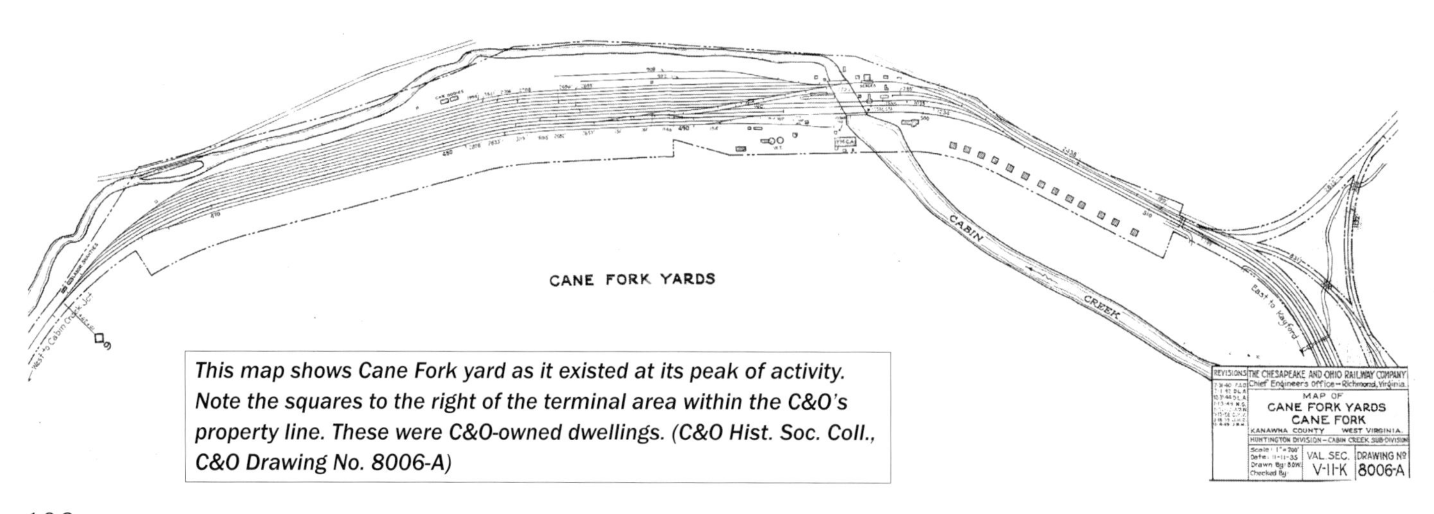

This map shows Cane Fork yard as it existed at its peak of activity. Note the squares to the right of the terminal area within the C&O's property line. These were C&O-owned dwellings. (C&O Hist. Soc. Coll., C&O Drawing No. 8006-A)

This view shows the engine house in full along with the power house behind, which supplied steam for the water pumping station and for the engine house. The lean-to style structure appended to the 2-stall house is for the machine shop. (D. Wallace Johnson photo)

The Cane Fork engine house was busy on May 5, 1953, when this photo was made. H-4 No. 1329 is in one of the stalls, while on the left H-6 No. 1503 is moving a cut of cars. (D. Wallace Johnson photo)

The engine house is seen in the distance here, where the unusual 50-ton coaling station, the smallest on the C&O, is also visible. The cinder conveyor has loaded cinders into cars at left. The building on the right is the combined scale house and yard office. (D. Wallace Johnson photo)

Alco RSD-5 units 5575 and 5591 have a minc run train at Leewood in April 1954. (Gene Huddleston Photo, C&O Hist. Soc. Coll., Image No. COHS-1441)

Up the Leewood Subdivision at Dacota was Carbon Fuel Company Mine No. 3. The 1954 photo is made from the loaded yard. Note the many empties beyond the tipple waiting to pass under and be loaded. (C&O Ry. Photo, C&O Hist. Soc. Coll., Image No. 3411)

On Cabin Creek's Marsh Fork Branch we find an Armco Steel Company mine tipple at Montcoal in June 1954, populated with a variety of C&O hopper cars. A tram from one of three mine drift openings up the hillside runs overhead with a mesh wire screen to catch falling coal. In 2010 this was near the location of a major mine explosion disaster. (C&O Ry. Photo, C&O Hist. Soc. Coll., Image No. 10057.KK11)

The Winifrede Railroad

About two miles west of Cabin Creek Junction, C&O was met by the short line Winifrede Railroad, beginning operation before the War Between the States. This line had been in operation for decades before the C&O arrived in the region, carrying coal on a mule-powered tram road. Its production was used locally by the many salt-brine furnaces making salt from the wells that abounded in the region, or was dumped into barges on the Kanawha River where it was shipped as far as Cincinnati when the river's water level allowed.

After the coming of the C&O in the early 1870s the Winifrede interchanged some of its coal with C&O, and C&O established a station and agent here to handle that business, but it also continued the barge traffic as the river navigation was steadily improved over the decades. It is one coal branch in the region that was never acquired by C&O. Today it still has an active mine, its own motive power and cars, and dumps its production into Kanawha River barges.

Coal River Branches

One of the most productive C&O coal branches of the 20th Century and still a source of a large production at this writing was and is the Coal River Branch which connected with the Kanawha Subdivision mainline at St. Albans (MP 465.5).

This main branch actually had no less than 14 subsidary branches that fed into it, each of which constituted an operational subdivision on the C&O of 1950.

By means of a line (Seng Creek Subdivision) built over steep grades and through a difficult tunnel, this maze of branches was connected with the Cabin Creek line (see section on Cabin Creek), thus allowing coal from the further reaches of each of these lines to be routed a second way.

The Coal River Subdivision connected the Coal River Coal District to the mainline. It had the following smaller branches (each a discrete Subdivision) that fed into it:

- Horse Creek Subdivision (Horse Creek Jct. to end-of-line)
- Pond Fork Subdivisions (Pond Jct. to Barrett)
- West Fork Subdivision (West Jct. To Robinhood and end-of-line)
- Whites Subdivision (Van Jct., to Gordon)
- Laurel Fork Mine Extension (departs Coal River SD at Clothier)
- Beech Creek Subdivision(Sharples to Monclo)
- Big Coal Subdivision (Sproul to Hazy Creek)
- Brush Creek Subdivision (Brushton to Ridgeview)
- Seth Subdivision (Seth to Prenter)
- Elk Run Subdivision (Elk Run Jct., to Blue Pennant)
- Seng Creek Subdivision (Whitesville to Red Warrior Jct.)
- Jerrolds Valley Subdivision (Ameagle to Jarrolds Valley)
- Little Marsh Fork Subdivision (Pettus to Edwight)
- Hazy Creek Subdivision [later Marsh Fork SD] (Edwight to Hazy Creek)

The first attempt at building a line to tap the coal reserves up Coal River was in about 1890, when Michael P. O'Hern of New York, incorporated the St. Albans & Coal River Railway, however little work was

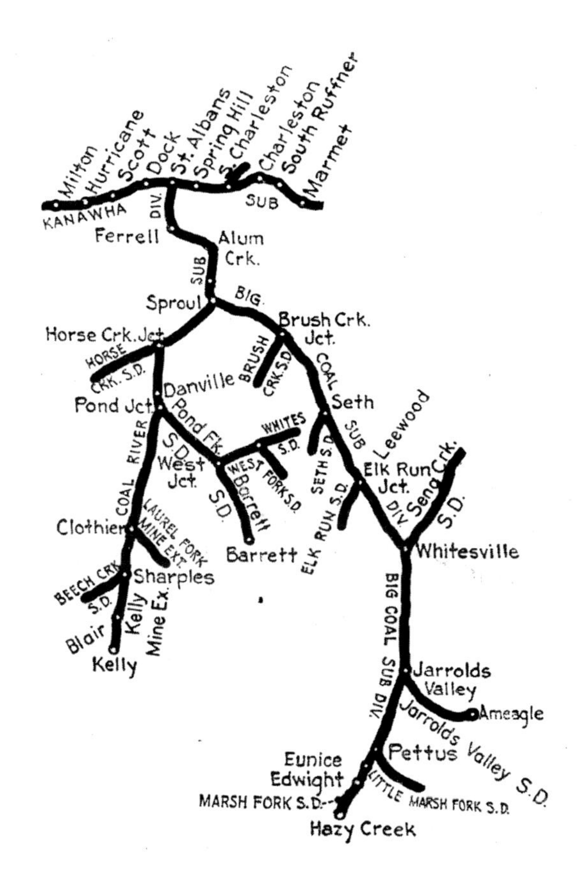

done, and he died in 1897. Although several paper railroads were incorporated and some did some work on the line, it was not until 1901 that J. K. R. Skinner of Ohio and Senator Sproul of Pennsylvania, both of whom had coal land holdings on Coal River, incorporated the Coal River & Western Railway, which actually did the initial construction mentioned above, operating about 20 miles of line. In 1906 C&O purchased the property for $3 million and over the next 13 years extended the line to its final form.

Because of some steep grades encountered on the line south of St. Albans, C&O coal trains in the early era, being powered by 2-8-0 Consolidations, required pushers. Later 2-6-6-2 compound articulateds improved the situation, but C&O decided to build a new route south of St. Albans to further improve operations. The new line joined the main about half a mile to the west of the former junction. The new alignment required the boring of a tunnel and was put into service on January 10, 1923. The new alignment plus the 2-6-6-2s increased train size, an important factor as the Coal River District continued its expansion in the 1920s and 1930s.

Because of the heavy traffic, the length of the line, and the number of branches, marshalling yards were necessary on the branch itself.

The line divided Sproul, with the Coal River Subdivision heading southwesterly, while the Big Coal Subdivision was built

COAL RIVER SUB-DIVISION

Dist. from Ft. Monroe	Tel. Calls	Station No.	Code No.	STATIONS
465.5	*1L4S	465	1925	(4)St. Albans.....W Va
467.5		CR2	1927	Indian.........W Va
468.2		CR3	1928	††Calvert.......W Va
470.6	*2S	CR5	1930	‡Ferrell.........W Va
471.7	1L3S1L	CR6	1931	Upper Falls ....W Va
473.8		CR8	1933	‡Lincoln.........W Va
475.9		CR10	1935	†Fuqua.........W Va
477.7	1L2S	CR12	1937	Alum Creek....W Va
478.8		CR13	1940	Forks of Coal...W Va
480.9	*1L	CR15	1942	(2)Sproul.........W Va
482.1		CR16	1944	Bluetom.........W Va
485.1		CR20	1946	†Dunlapville.....W Va
487.6	4S	CR22	1948	MacCorkle.....W Va
488.6		CR23	1949	†Dice...........W Va
489.7		CR24	1951	†Irene...........W Va
491.7		CR26	1952	††Adams........W Va
492.0	2L	CR27	1953	Altman.........W Va
492.5		CR27½	1954	(2)†Horse Creek Junction.....W Va
493.1		CR28	1955	Julian..........W Va
495.3		CR30	1957	†Lory...........W Va
498.3		CR33	1959	Rock Creek.....W Va
499.4		CR34	1960	†Hopkins........W Va
500.7	*2S1L	CR35	1961	Danville.......W Va
502.6	1L3S	CR37	1962	Madison........W Va
503.0		CR38	2035	(2)Pond Jct......W Va
505.5		CR40	1963	Haddleton......W Va
506.1		CR41	1964	†Low Gap.......W Va
509.7		CR44	1966	Greenview.....W Va
510.7		CR45	1968	†Ramage........W Va
511.8		CR46	1969	†Secoal.........W Va
513.0		CR48	1970	Jeffrey.........W Va
513.5		CR49	1971	Ottawa.........W Va
514.6	4L	CR50	1973	Clothier.......W Va
515.7		CR51	1975	†Mifflin.........W Va
516.3		CR52	1976	†Dobra.........W Va
517.4	1S1L2S	CR53	1977	(2)‡Sharples.....W Va
519.2		CR55	2063	†Five Block....W Va
523.0		CR58	2064	†Spruce Valley..W Va
523.8	1L2S1L	CR59	1982	Blair..........W Va

(4)-Coupon Stations.
*-Day and Night Telegraph Offices.
‡-Private Siding only.
(2)-Junction of Sub-division shown elsewhere.
Telephone Calls: L-Long; S-Short ring.
†-No Siding.
††-Passing Siding only.

WHITES BRANCH SUB-DIVISION

Dist. from Ft. Monroe	Tel. Calls	Station No.	Code No.	STATIONS
15.3		WPF1	2045	†Van Jct.......W Va
15.8		WPW1	2044	‡Gordon........W Va
17.7				End of Line....W Va

BEECH CREEK SUB-DIVISION

Dist. from Ft. Monroe	Tel. Calls	Station No.	Code No.	STATIONS
7.4	1S1L2S	CR53	1977	‡Sharples.......W Va
8.4		CB2	2060	‡Monclo........W Va

BRUSH CREEK SUB-DIVISION

Dist. from Ft. Monroe	Tel. Calls	Station No.	Code No.	STATIONS
491.1		BC10	2208	Brushton......W Va
493.1		BCB2	2305	†Easley........W Va
493.6		BCB3	2302	‡Nellis.........W Va
495.1		BCB4	2304	‡Ridgeview.....W Va

SETH SUB-DIVISION

Dist. from Ft. Monroe	Tel. Calls	Station No.	Code No.	STATIONS
501.8	*3S1L	BC21	2222	Seth...........W Va
504.8		SL3	2234	†Hopkins Fork..W Va
505.7		SL4	2235	†Nelson........W Va
509.0		SL7	2239	Cabot..........W Va
511.1		SL9	2243	‡Prenter.......W Va

†-No Siding.
††-Passing Siding only.
‡-Private Siding only.
(1)-Junction with connecting lines.
(2)-Junction of Sub-division shown elsewhere.
Telephone Calls: L-Long; S-Short ring.

ELK RUN SUB-DIVISION

Dist. from Ft. Monroe	Tel. Calls	Station No.	Code No.	STATIONS
514.4	1S1L1S	BC33	2232	Elk Run Jct....W Va
515.4		ER1	2370	†Janie..........W Va
517.5		ER3	2371	‡Blue Pennant...W Va

HORSE CREEK SUB-DIVISION

Dist. from Ft. Monroe	Tel. Calls	Station No.	Code No.	STATIONS
492.5	2L1S	CR27½	1954	†Horse Creek JctW Va
492.9		HC1	2020	‡Craft..........W Va
494.4		HC2	2022	Woodville......W Va
494.8		HC3	2023	Fork Jct.......W Va
497.4		HC5	2025	†Breece........W Va
498.0		HC6	2026	†Morrisvale....W Va
499.0		HC7	2027	†Dodson Jct....W Va
500.4		HC8	2030	‡Cameo.........W Va

POND FORK SUB-DIVISION

Dist. from Ft. Monroe	Tel. Calls	Station No.	Code No.	STATIONS
503.0		CR38	2035	Pond Jct.......W Va
		PF2	2036	†Foch...........W Va
506.9		PF4	2037	†Uneeda........W Va
507.9		PF5	2038	†Quinland......W Va
508.9		PF6	2039	†Reston........W Va
511.4		PF8	2040	†Lanta.........W Va
512.9		PF10	2041	†Bigson........W Va
514.5	3S	PF12	2042	(2)West Jct.....W Va
515.4		PF13	2068	†Fennimore.....W Va
516.4		PF14	2070	†Bob White....W Va
518.1		PF15	2072	Kohlsaat......W Va
518.8		PF16	2073	†Jackson.......W Va
520.8		PF18	2077	†Bim...........W Va
521.9		PF19	2079	‡Wharton......W Va
522.5		PF20	2080	†Pondco.......W Va
523.4	1S	PF21	2082	Barrett........W Va

WEST FORK SUB-DIVISION

Dist. from Ft. Monroe	Tel. Calls	Station No.	Code No.	STATIONS
514.5	3S	PF12	2042	West Jct.......W Va
514.8		WPF0	2043	Van............W Va
514.9		WPF½	2046	Essex..........W Va
515.3		WPF1	2045	Van Jct........W Va
518.6		WPF4	2049	Marnie.........W Va
523.9		WPF8	2047	Robinhood.....W Va
524.3				End of line....W Va

BIG COAL SUB-DIVISION

Dist. from Ft. Monroe	Tel. Calls	Station No.	Code No.	STATIONS
480.9	*1L	CR15	1942	Sproul.........W Va
482.9	1S2L	BC2	2200	(1)††Brounland...W Va
483.4		BC3	2201	Hollyhurst.....W Va
486.0		BC5	2202	†Emmons.......W Va
487.1		BC6	2203	†Grippe.........W Va
488.3		BC8	2205	Dartmont......W Va
489.8	2L1S	BC9	2206	Ashford........W Va
491.1		BC10	2208	(2)Brushton.....W Va
492.7		BC12	2209	†Johns.........W Va
494.7	1L1S1L	BC14	2210	Peytona.......W Va
496.1		BC15	2213	†Myrtle........W Va
496.5		BC16	2214	Racine.........W Va
498.3		BC17	2216	†Toney's BranchW Va
499.0		BC18	2217	†Sharlow.......W Va
499.7		BC19	2218	†Maxine........W Va
500.4		BC20	2220	Joe Creek.....W Va
501.8	*3L1S	BC21	2222	(2)Seth..........W Va
502.8		BC22	2223	†Kirbyton......W Va
505.2		BC25	2224	Fred...........W Va
507.2		BC26	2225	†Unique........W Va
508.9		BC27	2226	†Orgas.........W Va
509.2		BC28	2228	‡Darby.........W Va
510.2		BC29	2229	†Keith.........W Va
514.4	*1S1L1S	BC33	2232	(2)Elk Run Jct....W Va
460.9	2L2S	FC9	1808	Whitesville....W Va (1.4 miles from Elk Run Jct.)

K-4 Kanawha type No. 2704 with a loaded coal train is coming off Coal River at St. Albans in June 1954, headed for Handley. (Gene Huddleston photo, C&O Hist. Soc. Coll., Image No. 1803)

slightly to the east. Sproul itself was considered as a collecting yard, but eventually two other terminals were established instead. A small wooden coaling station was built here, as well as a turntable for locomotives, and an operator's cabin which controlled the area of the junction. A water station was also built at this point. The turntable was removed at an early date, so by the mid-century era of this book only the small cabin, coaling station and water station remained in use until the end of steam.

On the Coal River Subdivision a major yard and engine facility was built at Danville, about 35 miles, or a little over half way up the line. At mid-century it had numerous yard storage tracks, and a full engine terminal with a 300-ton concrete coaling station, and a 100-foot turntable, and watering facilities. In the late steam era 2-6-6-2s were used as mine shift-

A set of three F7s (ABA) have invaded thc coal country in this June 1953 photo, with a train of empty hoppers headed up Coal River just out of St. Albans. Although the F7s replaced K-4s initially on coal trains to and from some of the marshalling yards, GP9s replaced them as soon as enough were available. (Gene Huddleston Photo, C&O Hist. Soc. Coll., Image No. 1320)

This is how the tiny terminal at Sproul looked in 1929, with turntable, water and coaling station, big hotel/bunkhouse, small depot/operator's office, and an old coach for use as yard office, etc. The Big Coal Subdivision track goes left, while the main Coal River line goes right across the bridge an through a tunnel. (From 1929 C&O Employee Magazine)

Sproul

By Gene Huddleston

There was nothing at Sproul until the C&O decided to construct a line up Big Coal to connect the Cabin Creek branch with the Big Coal River (via Seng Creek Tunnel), near Whitesville [in 1919]. A line already existed up Little Coal River; it had been rebuilt from a winding, narrow gauge lumber road (the Sproul and Blue Tom Tunnels did much to straighten it out). As business grew, a terminal was needed up Coal River. At first Sproul was picked. A turntable and coaling station were built, yard tracks put in, and a bunk house erected. In addition, certain C&O officials bought up land nearby in anticipation of a small real estate boom. This boom never materialized, because C&O decided that Sproul, only 15 miles up Coal River, made too short a division for crews from Russell or Handley. The new terminals were established at Danville and Elk Run Junction, further up Little Coal River and the Big Coal line, respectively. Sproul did remain the headquarters for the dispatcher. The dispatcher's office was a converted wooden coach until CTC was installed in 1947. This installation covered the single track with sidings from St. Albans through Sproul and up Little Coal to McCorkle and up Big Coal to Brounland (the junction with the now long abandoned Kanawha Central shortline).

Sproul was still busy in 1948, though. Usually the local freight up Big Coal had a USRA H-5 2-6-6-2 on it. There were one or two crews out of Russell to Elk Run Junction daily; one of these would go up to Handley with an eastbound with the other going back to Russell with a 'turn.' The same was true for Danville, for there were usually two westbound and an eastbound called out of there daily. All of these loaded trains were generally called between 2 a. m. and 5 a. m., as soon as the yard switchers at Danville and Elk Run could switch the loads that came off mine runs into eastbounds, westbounds, shorts, and river coal for Huntington or Kenova. Besides these trains, with K-3 2-8-2s and K-4 2-8-4s, there were a couple of mine shifters with 2-6-6-2s serving mines and branches on Big Coal and Little Coal short of the terminals at Danville and Elk Run. A daily passenger local from St. Albans to Danville and beyond had an F-15 class light Pacific, and the local passenger run to Whitesville (near Elk Run) had a Brill gas-electric car or 4-4-2 Atlantic steam locomotive.

ers from this point, which was the typical operation, but some 2-8-0s were also present. After the arrival of the K-4 2-8-4s starting in 1943, they were often used to take 150-165 car coal trains from Danville yard to the mainline, and on to Handley or Russell.

After construction of the Big Coal Subdivision and its many branches an engine terminal and yard was built at Elk Run Junction, near the town of Whitesville, as the marshalling yard for coal originated by the several mines on the branches nearby. A large concrete 500-ton coaling station as well as ready tracks, water station, 100-foot turntable, and other facilities were set up here to accommodate trains using this routing. Thus Elk Run Jct. became another terminal for mine shifter runs operating up and down the branches of the Big Coal Subdivision. This yard was variously known on the C&O as either "Elk Run Junction," or "Whitesville yard," from the nearby town.

As on all branches, the Coal River line had local passenger trains. As automobiles, buses, and good roads arrived, these branch trains were gradually eliminated. C&O discontinued most of its branch line passenger service in 1949-50, however the Coal River trains continued to operate several years, being discontinued in 1954. After C&O acquired its Brill gas-electric motor cars, they covered the Coal River trains, although in the later days when these cars weren't always available, the branch passenger trains had ancient 4-4-2 Atlantic types for power on its two-car passenger trains.

Opposite Top: K-4 No. 2755 pauses in July 1947 at Sproul to take on water. Fireman Banks is getting off with a bag of soda ash to dump in the tender when he takes on water. C&O had no water-softening plant located here, so the work had to be done each time the locomotive was watered here. (Gene Huddleston Photo, C&O Hist. Soc. Coll., COHS-1810)

Opposite Center: An F-15 Pacific type brings the branch line local, No. 219 across the Coal River bridge at Sproul en route to St. Albans. (Gene Huddleston Photo, C&O Hist. Soc. Coll., Image No. COHS-1291)

Opposite Bottom: Another K-4, No. 2740, approaches the old wooden coaling station at Sproul on a July morning in 1949. (Gene Huddleston Photo)

CHESAPEAKE & OHIO
C & O
441

A Trip to Danville

By Gene Huddleston

Danville, the terminal near Madison, seat of Boone County, one of West Virginia's leading coal producers, is one of those origin points that made C&O "Blue Chip" for so long. Danville is atypical in that it isn't set in a narrow valley between towering mountains, like most C&O coal assembly points. The valley of the Little Coal River in this area seems much more small farm country in character. The engine terminal especially had 'character,' though not as much as Cane Fork's. There was a 100-foot turntable, with long angle bars supporting the center swivel post. Nearby was a shack for workers and tools, which had a large sycamore tree growing in front of it and overshadowing the tracks–most unusual. A 300-ton cylindrical concrete coaling station completed the layout.

In the forties and fifties, "district" shifter engines that one would find here included two or three 2-6-6-2s, a K-2 2-8-2, and a G-9 2-8-0. These would take mine runs up extensions of two major 'branches' that converged just south of Madison–Pond Fork and Little Coal River Subdivisions. From the other direction–the mainline at St. Albans–would come long trains of empties from either Russell or Handley, usually headed by K-4 2-8-4s Returning trains of loads would usually be called out of Danville early in the morning. In the late Forties, one 11,500-ton coal train went east and two went west. In the Fifties and early Sixties more were run in both directions as the coal field in this area expanded.

For a trip I made in June 1953, I have notes to help my memory. I arrived at Danville and found a 2-8-0, a 2-6-6-2, and a 2-8-2 in the engine terminal. Soon the 2-8-0 left town with one box car and a caboose, and the 2-6-6-2, #1390, prepared to go out. I photographed it on the turntable, with a fifty-pound block of ice on the pilot beam. It was about noon, and I decided to go up to Sharples–the men in the yard office had told me that was where the 2-8-0 (#1037) had gone. They also told me that a shifter was due soon from Barrett. Halfway between Danville and Madison we pictured Mallet #1463 drifting along with 100 loads at about 25 m.p.h. It stopped before entering the yard. Proceeding on to Sharples, I found the one-car train resting near the depot under the shade of a hillside. The crew was in the depot getting bills. Soon the crew backed up to the mine at Monclo. I noted that empties off the main line had arrived while I was gone, and there on the caboose track was my Dad's caboose (he was conductor).

Leaving town I could look down on the engine terminal and see, near the turntable, the K-4 2-8-4 that had brought Dad's train from Russell. There was the possibility that after his rest was up he would be called on an eastbound to Handley, but more likely he would get a westbound to Russell.

In the 1960s the yard was expanded, the old engine facilities eliminated, and later a super highway on a high bridge crossed over the yard about where the engine terminal was, on a high bridge.

A June 1950 overview of the Danville marshalling yard shows a K-4 2-8-4 for use in taking loaded coal trains to the mainline (thence to Russell or Handley) and a 2-6-6-2 for mine shifter work in the engine terminal. The 300-ton coaling station and 100,000-gallon water tank are part of the steam facilities here. The depot/ yard office is in the far left distance. (Gene Huddleston Photo, C&O Hist. Soc. Coll., Image No. COHS-1144)

The 100-foot turntable at Danville yard, with the coaling station in the background on July 31, 1953. (D. Wallace Johnson photo)

H-6 No. 1510 shoves a cut of cars past the Danville station in 1955. (A. C. Phelps photo, P&K Enterprises Collection)

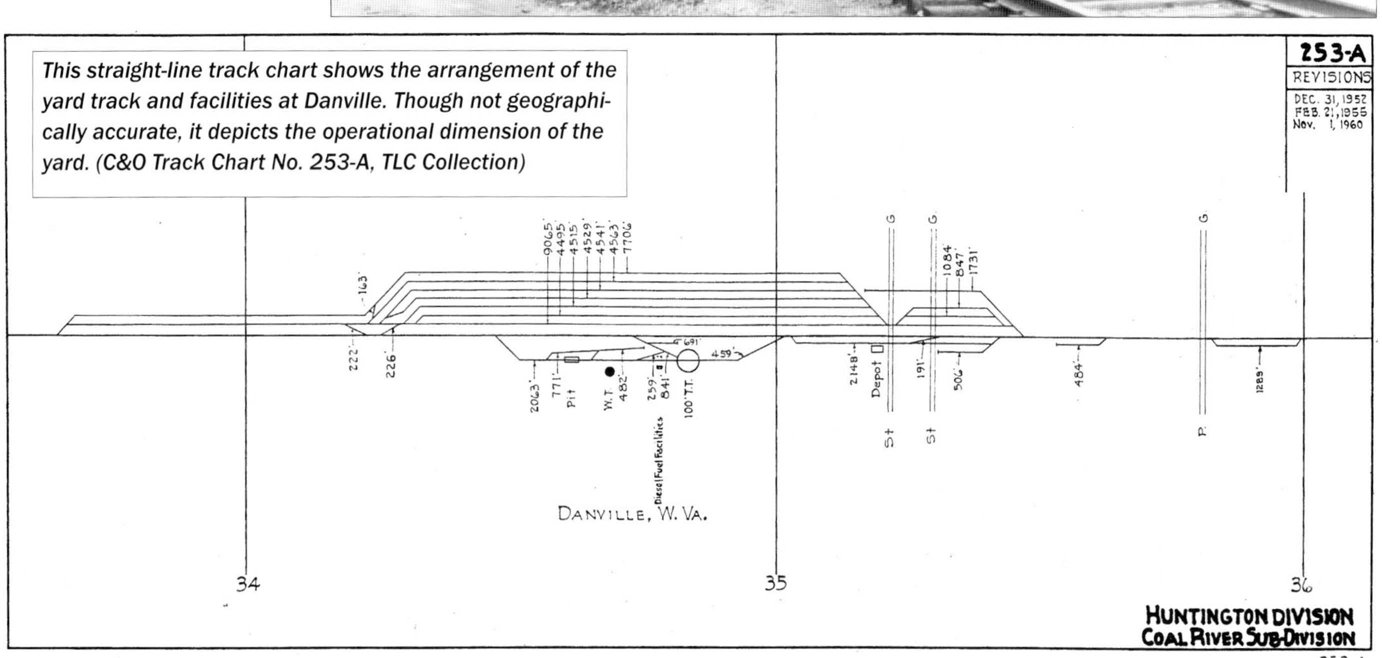

This straight-line track chart shows the arrangement of the yard track and facilities at Danville. Though not geographically accurate, it depicts the operational dimension of the yard. (C&O Track Chart No. 253-A, TLC Collection)

Elk Run Junction

The C&O yard and facilities at Elk Run Junction were established when the line was extended up Big Coal in 1907. The town in the area was known as Jarrolds Valley, but in 1935 it was incorporated as Whitesville, named for E. B. White, an early settler in the area. The Jarrolds Valley Subdivision, Little Marsh Fork Subdivision, and Marsh Fork Subdivisions were branches that connected to the Big Coal Subdivision south of Whitesville. Elk Run Jct. and its yard and engine terminal served as the hub for mines served by these lines.

Elk Run Junction in the Days of Steam

By Gene Huddleston

My first trip to Elk Run Junction, West Virginia, was in June of 1950. There's nothing at Elk Run Junction except the railroad. The highway leading to civilization runs on the opposite bank of the river, but about half a mile east of the yard office, the railroad crosses a deck girder bridge, and after about a mile beyond you are in Whitesville (the only town between Beckley and Marmet). The town of Whitesville is across the river from the railroad.

The shifter crews operating out of Elk Run Junction went up about four branches of the railroad there. The most interesting operational feature around Elk Run was the Seng Creek Subdivision, linking Cabin Creek with the Big Coal via the Seng Creek Tunnel.

For many years until a line was constructed up the big Coal from Seth to Elk Run, about 1918, Shays ran from Cane Fork up to the tunnel and down to Big Coal, to serve mines further up the valley.

When I first visited Elk Run Junction in 1950, there was still a shifter operating on the Seng Creek Subdivision, but it went only from Big Coal Junction to High Coal, near the mouth of the tunnel. The shifter came out of Elk Run yard, went up the river about a mile, the backed through the switch at Big Coal Junction. In fact the 1948 station book didn't even list this as an operational point on the railroad. Since the line started upgrade immediately, there was no chance for a switch to be installed for entering the branch from the west. From Big Coal Junction, the shifter would run upgrade four miles to serve two mines, one at Ferndale, two miles up the narrow hollow, and the other at High Coal, where another depot was located. When I saw the shifter at Ferndale it had two 2-8-0 Consolidations on it, one pushing and one pulling. As it headed up the branch, it shoved its caboose ahead of it, with the engines backing up–much like the Keeney's Creek operation during the same period.

Besides these two 2-8-0s, there would be about six other locomotives at Elk Run Junction, all 2-6-6-2 Mallets. One 2-6-6-2 was used as the three-shift-a-day yard switcher. In 1950 No. 1400 was used in this work. The engine terminal at Elk Run would also include K-3 2-8-2s and K-4 Kanawhas (2-8-4s) from the mainline at St. Albans.

Further up the line at Dorothy, Sanita, and Eunice, the C&O once had its own coal mines to supply its own locomotive fuel, but by 1950, the railroad was no longer getting its fuel from this source. The biggest mine at that time in the Big Coal District was at Montcoal, where the Armco Steel Company had a complex that tapped several different seems.

Elk Run Junction itself was the end of a four mile branch line to Blue Pennant, at that time a big coal producer. From the east throat of the yard this branch continued up the south side of the river a short distance, while the primarily line crossed a deck-girder bridge to get to the north side of the Big Coal River. Beyond the bridge was Big Coal Junction, and beyond that was the town of Whitesville. Whitesville sported a frontier-type business section and very narrow streets.

In 1950, or thereabouts, daily service would see two mainline crews operating from Russell, to pick up the coal from Elk Run. Another crew from Handley would take coal eastbound to the mainline. A Brill gas-electric motor car train served Elk Run from St. Albans, where it connected with mainline passenger trains.

To house these mainline crews, C&O provided a bunkhouse complex at Elk Run. The "district" crews presumably lived in Whitesville or up one of the hollows. Old box cars strung together made up the dining complex, one was a dining room and the other two were quarters and kitchen. There were apparently two other wheel-less box cars for the Handley men to stay in, and a small building for the Russell men to stay in. These structures were approximately 25 car-lengths from the coal dock. Because the main road up the Big Coal valley was on the other side of the river, the only way to drive into this area was over an unpaved company road from the east end of the yard.

On the Big Coal Subdivision, H-5 2-6-6-2 No. 1534 has a mine run train at Brounland in the summer of 1949. At Brounland, about two miles up the Big Coal line from Sproul, the short line Kanawha Central Railroad joined to the Coal River line and shipped its coal via C&O. (Gene Huddleston Photo, C&O Hist. Soc. Coll., Image No. COHS-1812)

The salient feature of Elk Run Junction was the unusually shaped 500-ton concrete coaling station, seen here in August 1953, populated with 2-6-6-2s ready for mine shifter work. (D. Wallace Johnson photo)

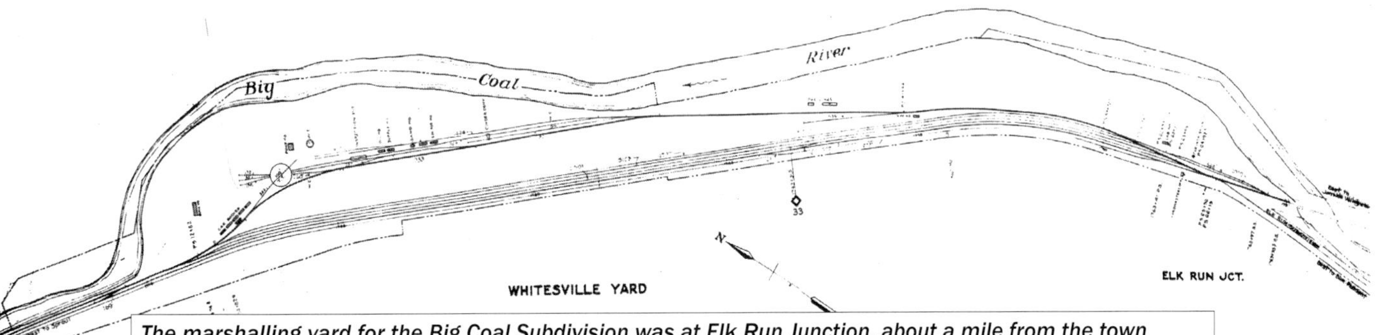

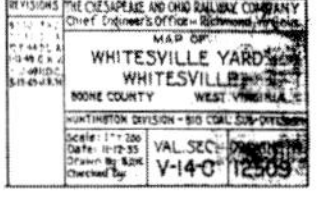

The marshalling yard for the Big Coal Subdivision was at Elk Run Junction, about a mile from the town of Whitesville. This map shows the long yard, turntable, coaling station, water tank, and other facilities located along the Coal River. This map labels it as "Whitesville Yard," though it was almost always known as "Elk Run Junction" on the C&O. (C&O Hist. Soc. Coll., C&O Ry. Drawing No. 12509)

H-2 2-6-6-2 No. 1493 makes a grand show of exhaust as it passes the Whitesville station area and water tank with a mine run in July 1948. Note the old style paddle train order semaphore, long outdated in at most C&O locations by this time. This is on the Seng Creek Subdivision which climbed over the divide to the Cabin Creek line. (John Krause Photo, TLC Collection)

Not all mine shifters were handled by 2-6-6-2s. Here G-9 2-8-0 No. 1037 departs Sharples on a mine shifter run up the short Beech Creek Subdivision to Monclo in June 1953, with two cabooses and a box car. Freight for mining towns and mine companies was often carried on mine shifters when a local freight didn't operate on a particular branch. The two wooden cabooses add color to this operation. Photographer Gene Huddleston recalls "This shifter left Danville light and we chased it to Sharples, where it parked to await all the loads that had been billed at Monclo, then one of the biggest underground mines on the C&O. It brought about 90 loads back to Danville. Later a 2-6-6-2 would supply the mine with empties and would not take any loads." (Gene Huddleston Photo, C&O Hist. Soc. Coll., Image No. COHS-1349)

North American Coal Corporation's Red Parrot Mine is seen here at Prenter in June 1954, on the Seth Subdivision, a 9-mile long branch which left the Big Coal main stem about 12 miles south of Elk Run Junction. (C&O Ry. Photo, C&O Hist. Soc. Coll., Image No. CSPR-10057.KK01)

The large, very modern looking tipple of Eastern Gas and Fuel Associates Wharton #2 mine is seen here at Wharton in June 1954. It was one of two mines that this company operated that were the only operations on the Pond Fork branch at this date. (C&O Ry., C&O Hist. Soc. Coll., Image No. CSPR-10057.Y01)

Logan Branch

At Barboursville C&O's Logan Branch and all its feeder branches joined the main line. The Logan Branch at mid-20th Century consisted of 14 subdivisions that tapped one of the richest and most productive coal areas on the C&O. The Logan Subdivision mainline ran from Barboursville 85.1 miles to West Gilbert. The city of Logan served as the hub of the coal business in this region and C&O's Peach Creek Yard was located just outside the town.

Connection with the Virginian Railway was made south of Gilbert, at the end of the Logan Subdivision, and a good deal of westbound coal from Virginian mines was interchanged with C&O at this point, and from there was sent to Russell to be forwarded to locations west.

The following branch subdivisions fed into the Logan Subdivision:

- Merrill Subdivision (Henlawson to end-of-line) 2.5 miles
- Dingess Run Subdivision (Stollings to end-of-line) 7.19 miles
- Georges Creek Subdivision (Ethel to Hetzel) 5.3 miles
- Rum Creek Subdivision (Rum Jct., to Slagle) 6.61 miles
- Huff Creek Subdivision (Huff Jct., to Huffsville) 2.54 miles
- Elk Creek Subdivision (Wylo to end-of-track) 2.08 miles
- Buffalo Subdivision (Man to Saunders) 15.6 miles
- Mud Fork Subdivision (Mud Jct., to Argonne) 3.1 miles
- Island Creek Subdivision (Logan to Holden) 22.22 miles
- Whitman Creek Subdivision (Whitman Jct., to Mine No. 20) 4.6 miles
- Trace Fork Subdivision (Holden to Mine 21)(extended in 1952) 2.3 miles
- Logan & Southern Subdivision (Monitor Jct., to Sarah Ann) 18.18 miles
- Little Creek Subdivision (Stirrat to end-of-line) 0.03 miles
- Pine Creek Subdivision (Omar to Pine Creek) 5.3 miles

During the 1890s decade not only was coal becoming more important for America's fast-developing heavy industry, but the availability of high quality coal was becoming better known in the southern West Virginia area. In the previous decade C&O's freight traffic had become dominated by coal, and through the 1890s this only increased, and it soon became evident that branch lines off the C&O main would be necessary to reach the coal reserves. As has been shown previously in this book, the 1890s decade was the era when the coal culture of C&O really began, and the branch lines started to tap the rich coal fields south of the mainline through West Virginia.

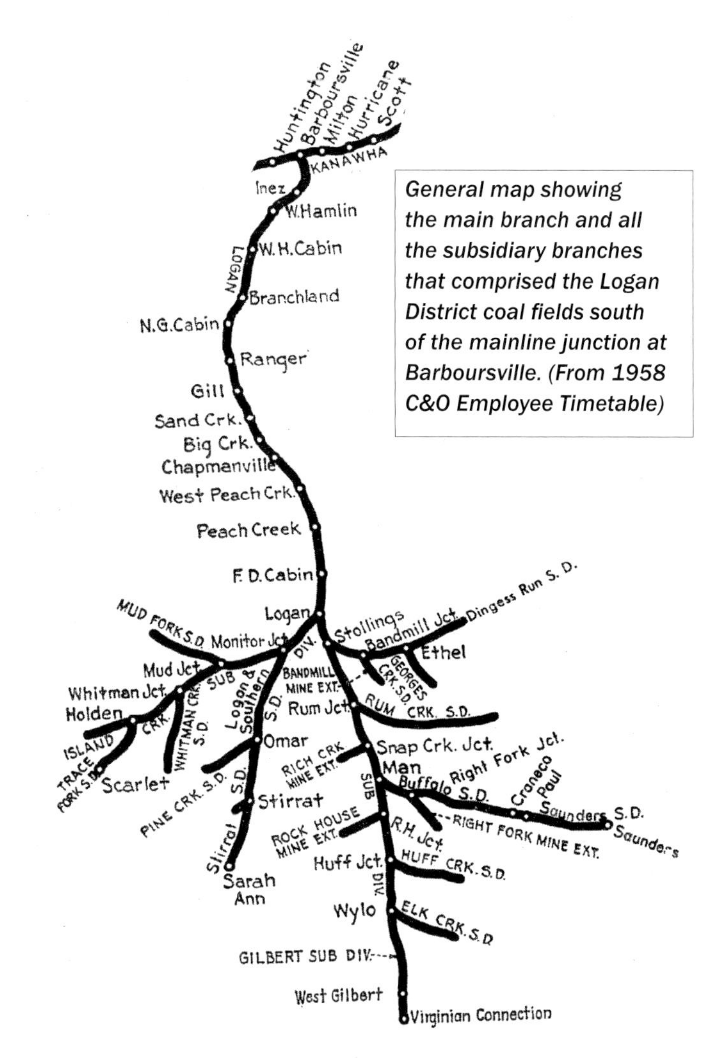

General map showing the main branch and all the subsidiary branches that comprised the Logan District coal fields south of the mainline junction at Barboursville. (From 1958 C&O Employee Timetable)

In 1899 the Guyandot [also spelled Guyandotte] Railway was incorporated with a purpose of building a line from the C&O's Kanawha Subdivision main at Barboursville up the Guyandot River toward coal lands around Logan. The new road was built 27 miles from Barboursville to Midkiff between July 1899 and June 1901, and then ran out of capital. C&O purchased the entire stock of the company and completed the line another 23.2 miles to Big Creek by October 1903. At the end of October, the company was merged into the C&O and became first its Guyandot Valley Branch, and later "Logan Subdivision." The C&O finally reached Logan with the first train arriving on September 9, 1904.

Before the coming of the railway, several coal companies bought land in the area. On Island Creek the United States Coal & Oil Company bought 10,000 acres around Holden. It later became the Island Creek Coal Company. The Mount Fisher Coal Company also had 800 acres at the mouth of Island Creek, about two miles south of Lo-

LOGAN SUB-DIVISION

494.7	*BR	495	2525	Barboursville - W Va
500.1		X5	2531	Martha-------W Va
504.6		X10	2535	Inez----------W Va
505.8		X13	2536	Roach---------W Va
508.8		X14	2538	Salt Rock-----W Va
511.9	WA	X17	2540	West Hamlin--W Va
514.0	*WH	X19		†W. H. Cabin---W Va
515.6		X21	2542	Sheridan------W Va
517.2	BN	X22	2545	Branchland----W Va
518.7		X24	2546	‡Hubball-------W Va
521.1	MF	X26	2548	Midkiff-------W Va
523.1		X28	2549	†Brady---------W Va
524.7		X30		†N. G. Cabin---W Va
526.0	*RG	X31	2551	Ranger--------W Va
529.6		X35	2553	Lattin---------W Va
531.1	GI	X36	2554	Gill-----------W Va
534.8		X40	2557	Sand Creek----W Va
537.1		X42	2559	†Atenville------W Va
538.8		X44	2561	Harts---------W Va
540.0		X46	2562	Ferrellsburg---W Va
541.3		X47	2563	†Fry-----------W Va
543.3		X49	2565	†Toney---------W Va
544.4			2564	†Baber---------W Va
544.9	*BC	X50	2566	Big Creek-----W Va
546.1		X51	2567	†Stone Branch--W Va
546.5		X51½	2568	Kitchen-------W Va
549.1	SA	X54	2570	Chapmanville- W Va
550.7		X56	2571	‡Phico---------W Va
551.9		X57	2572	†Godby--------W Va
553.4		X58	2575	Pecks Mill-----W Va
556.3		X62	2578	②Henlawson---W Va
558.1	*OB	X64	2579	Peach Creek---W Va
559.8	*FD			F. D. Cabin---W Va
560.1		X65	2581	②④**Logan**------W Va
561.9		X67	2583	②‡Stollings----W Va
562.7		X68	2584	†McConnell----W Va
563.6	*SW			S. W. Cabin----W Va
565.5	1L1S1L	X70	2586	②††Rum Jct----W Va

gan. This company later became Gay Coal & Coke Company and developed much additional reserves.

The first car of coal was shipped on Thanksgiving Day 1905 by the Gay Coal & Coke company. It was hauled by wagon from the mine to Logan and transferred to a C&O car, and the Monitor Coal & Coke Company made the second shipment. From that point until the mid-20th Century coal traffic on the Logan line was always in high gear.

U. S. Coal & Oil Company soon built its own railroad to connect its Holden mine with the C&O and began shipping coal at a high level. This railroad was called, appropriately enough, The Island Creek Railroad. It was leased by C&O in 1912 (and finally merged in 1933).

By 1907 C&O had built to Ethel, creating the Dingess Run Subdivision, which was extended to Hetzel in 1910, and additional track beyond in 1912, and from Ethel in a different direction a short distance in 1916, all to reach additional mines. The branch connected with the Logan Subdivision at Stollings, and the total mileage was 5.54 miles from Stollings to end of track on the stem, and 2.24 miles from Ethel to Hetzel.

By 1907 C&O was handling over 500,000 tons of coal of the Logan District, and by 1920 numerous other branches had been built and the whole Logan Coal District was in full bloom. In addition to coal, lumbering played an important part in traffic on the Logan branch in the early decades, with several large band sawmills in operation.

In 1916 shops and repair tracks were moved to Peach Creek just a little over a mile north of the old location in the town of Logan. A five-stall roundhouse was built along with all attendant facilities. During WWI the coal business boomed and in 1921 more tracks were added in both the loaded and empty yards, and five more stalls added to the roundhouse. This hodge-podge of facilities was completely rebuilt and an all new terminal built by C&O in 1923.

In that year there were 148 mines in operation, shipping a huge 12,478,290 tons of coal. This was the highpoint as far as the number of mines in operation in the district, but many of the older, less productive mines closed during the Depression years. In the following years coal traffic from Logan remained one of the most important parts of C&O traffic, much of it headed west. [Initially, most C&O coal was shipped east to its Tidewater terminal at Newport News, but by about 1920 the balance was turning westward, especially after 1917 when a link was made between the C&O mainline west of Russell across the Ohio River and a connection with N&W's line, so that coal could reach Columbus, where it could be taken north to the Lakes traffic or interchanged with other railroads north of Columbus using the C&O-owned Hocking Valley Railway.]

In the mid-century era of this book the *C&O Coal Mine Directory* for the year 1950, listed 61 mines in the District:

Logan Subdivision main line	21
Island Creek SD	2
Mud Fork SD	3
Whitman Creek SD	1
Trace Fork SD	2
Logan & Southern SD	5
Pine creek SD	2
Little Creek SD	1
Dingess Run SD	3

Georges Creek SD	3
Rum Creek SD	5
Buffalo SD	10
Huff Creek SD	1
Elk Creek SD	2
Total	61 mines

As can be imagined, the amount of business handled required a large fleet of locomotives and cars. In the pre-WWI era the 2-8-0 Consolidation types of G-4, G-5, G-6, G-7, and G-9 classes were all present in numbers, in addition to some K-1 2-8-2 Mikados.

By the 1920s the 2-6-6-2 Mallets joined this fleet, as they did on other coal branches and marshalling yards. In the 1930s-1940s most of the smaller locomotives were moved away and the 2-6-6-2s used exclusively out of Peach Creek.

Up until 1919 C&O had few locomotives specifically built for switching work in heavy traffic circumstances. Up to that time its switchers had all been of the 0-6-0 wheel arrangement, which were used in normal yard work. The exception was a set of two 0-8-0s received in 1908 specifically for shifting heavy cuts of coal at Clifton Forge. Switching at the marshalling yards and in other yards where large cuts of coal had to be moved was usually done by the same types as were used on the road. However, in 1919 C&O received the first ten of its eventual fleet of 15 ultra-powerful 0-10-0s, which C&O assigned Class C-12. It was only in 1925 that Lima began to deliver the C-15 class 0-8-0s. Though the 0-8-0 became the C&O standard switcher the 0-10-0s were still used in areas where the heaviest type work was required. The 0-10-0s seemed to concentrate at Peach Creek yard in the later years. From two to five of these big locomotives were assigned to Peach Creek most of the time. At the time of their arrival about 1920 Peach Creek was handling about 2,000 cars per day.

C-16 0-8-0s arrived in 1931 to help out with the switching duties. K-1 Mikados were often used as were the newer K-3s, and by the late 1930s and through the 1940s, many of the coal trains leaving Peach Creek were headed by K-3s and then after 1943 by K-4 2-8-4s, as well as 2-6-6-2s. The H-4, 5, and 6 classes of 2-6-6-2 compound locomotives were used almost exclusively for the coal mine shifter runs, and when needed were doubleheaded. In the 1940s some of the former Hocking Valley H-3 2-6-6-2s were used here as well.

After WWII C&O was still very much committed to steam locomotive power and as a consequence upgraded its fleet. Included in this order for new power was a group of 10 2-6-6-2 compounds for use on coal branches. The entire series, Nos. 1300-1309, which were delivered in 1949, was assigned to Peach Creek to replace some of the old 2-6-6-2s which had been in heavy use since the mid-1920s.

In the late 1940s, on the eve of diesels, the following locomotives were assigned to Peach Creek:

C-12 0-10-0 Switchers: Nos. 137, 141, 142, 143

C-16 0-8-0 Switchers: Nos. 177, 179, 184, 192, 219, 220, 225, 232

G-9 2-8-0: No. 1053

H-4 2-6-6-2: Nos. 1331, 1344, 1365, 1402, 1404, 1421, 1429, 1436, 1437, 1450, 1451, 1465, 1468.

H-6 2-6-6-2: Nos. 1475, 1476, 1492, 1494, 1500, 1508, 1515, 1517, 1518, 1300, 1301, 1305, 1306, 1307, 1308, 1309.

It was also in 1949 that C&O finally decided that it could no longer resist the diesel-electric locomotive and began to replace steam. The last trip by a steam locomotive was No. 1475, which handled a mine run on August 26, 1956. This was historic in that it was also the last run of a steam locomotive anywhere on the C&O.

The first diesel arrived at Peach Creek yard on March 31, 1952 in the form of EMD F7s Nos. 7054-7531-7063 with 150 empties from Russell. From that date onward more and more diesels were used. The F7s were used for the empty trains coming from Russell and loads going back. They were road engines and not suitable for mine shifter work, which was still the domain of the Mallets. Later in 1952 Baldwin AS-616 road switcher No. 5567 arrived with a local freight from Huntington and was used as a yard switcher. Steam was replaced on the last set of remaining passenger trains, Nos. 50 & 51 on Feb. 28, 1951, with Brill gas-electric cars, replacing light Pacifics (F-15s) used up until that time.

A set of F7s was even used on a mine run to Scarlett on June 3, 1952, and this was repeated when available. By November of 1952 several Alco road switchers were on hand for yard work, but were withdrawn and didn't return until January 1954. In August 1954 a serious attempt to dieselize the district was made using GP7s in the 5700-series. From their arrival onward the use of steam steadily declined.

One type of diesel that saw considerable use out of Peach Creek was the Alco RSD-7s Nos. 6800-6811, which, with their three axle trucks and 2,400 horsepower, were considered one-for-one replacements for 2-6-6-2s or 2-8-4s. They often handled coal trains between Peach Creek and Russell as a single unit, as well as mine runs. RSD-12s, with 1,800 hp, were also frequently used on the Logan Subdivision.

The GP9s and GP7s eventually became standard power here by the late 1950s.(*)

(*) Most of the detailed data about operations at Peach Creek was preserved and written down by the late Carl A. Coulter, who was a long-time engineer at Peach Creek. He had a great interest in the history of the region and preserved a multitude of operational details about the area for future use.

The coaling station at West Hamlin, about 19 miles up the Logan Branch from Barboursville was positioned along the branch main with no sidings except to serve the tower itself. The 300-ton concrete tower was used to top off trains traveling between Logan and Huntington or Russell, or eastbound to Handley. Here K-3a 2-8-2 No. 2338 has paused for some coal in 1952 with empty coal train (plus a few box cars up front) . (Gene Huddleston photo, C&O Hist. Soc. Coll., Image No. COHS-1778)

Coal business in the 1950s averaged about 1,200 cars per day, but by the 1960s was down to 900 per day. Some of this was because cars of larger capacity were being used, but also fewer mines were in operation, and by 1965 loadings were about 700 cars daily. BY 1973 the last shop forces were eliminated, and the number of crews handling the diminished traffic had declined precipitously. Today CSX still loads considerable coal from the Logan Branch, but nothing like the great days of 1904-1960.

In May 1957, GP9s have a loaded coal train in tow, passing the station at Ranger, about 30 miles up the Logan Branch, while cars from a "truck mine" sit on the siding. The last of steam operated in the late summer of 1956, and diesels were then supreme. (Gene Huddleston Photo, C&O Hist. Soc. Coll., Image No. COHS-1401)

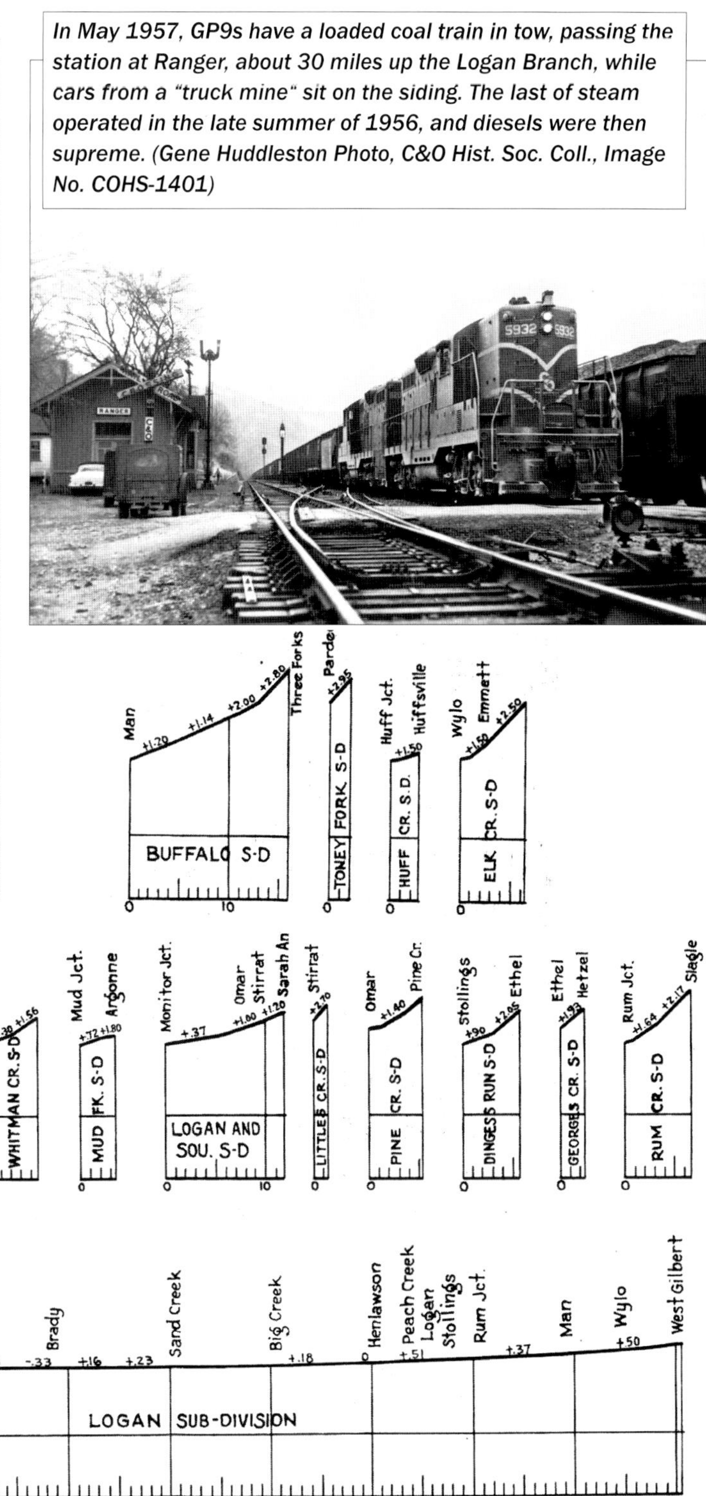

Profiles showing grades on the Logan Subdivision main as well as the many branches that fed it. (From C&O Drawing 13812, C&O Hist. Soc Coll.)

H-6 1308 takes a coal train west past the neat station at Big Creek, about 15 miles out of the Logan yard headed for Russell in 1955, toward the end of steam. No. 1308, one of the last new steam locomotives on the C&O, arrived in June 1949, and today is preserved in a park setting at Huntington. (C&O Ry. Photo, C&O Hist. Soc. Coll., Image no, 10115.1)

The Logan Branch main is seen at right at Chapmanville, about 10 miles north of Logan, where the Winisle Coal Corp. mine is in full production in this June 1954 photo. Several grades of coal are being loaded. (C&O Ry. Photo, C&O Hist. Soc. Coll., Image No. CSPR-10057.AA01)

As diesels arrived they began to be used on coal branches, and by late 1956 had supplanted all steam. Here an ABA set of F7s pulls a heavy coal train along the Logan Subdivision mainline about 15 miles out of Peach Creek, in May 1957. The lead unit is FP7 No. 8077, bought for use in handling extra passenger service, but when not thus employed used in general freight service. Soon the GP9s would supplant the F7s in service on the Logan line. (Gene Huddleston photo, C&O Hist. Soc. Coll., Image No. COHS-1178)

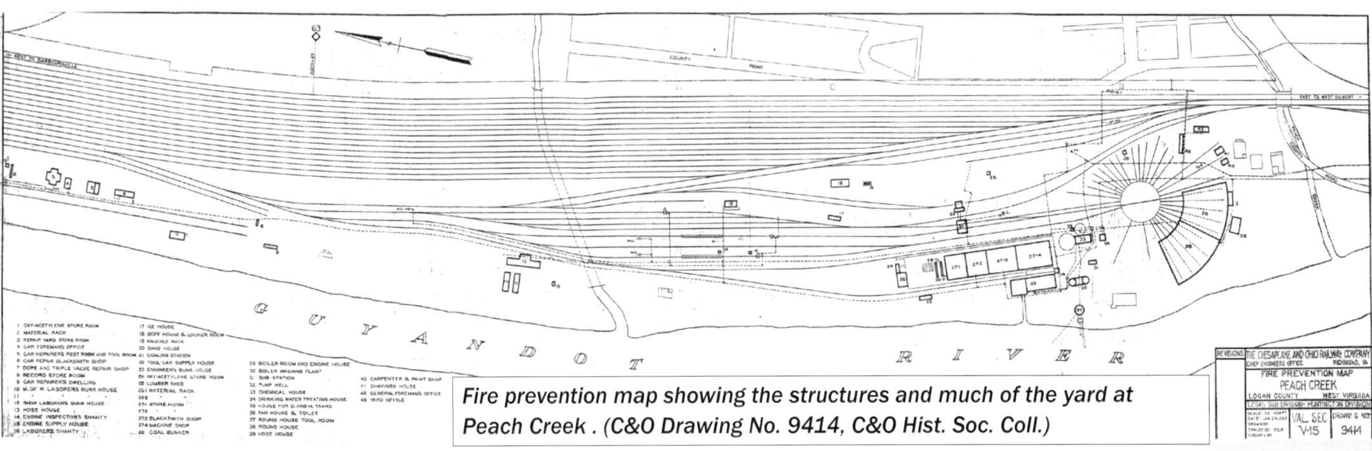

Fire prevention map showing the structures and much of the yard at Peach Creek . (C&O Drawing No. 9414, C&O Hist. Soc. Coll.)

At Pecks Mill, about seven miles north of Peach Creek, H-4 No. 1439 has a mine shifter with loads headed for the yard after having picked up loads between Harts and Peach Creek along the Logan main stem on September 23, 1955. (John Krause photo, TLC Collection)

0-8-0 switchers work the Peach Creek yard in 1946. The coaling station is in the background. (C&O Ry. Photo, C&O Hist. Soc. Coll., Image No CSPR-234)

The huge 0-10-0 switchers were used at Peach Creek because of their ability to move very heavy cuts of loaded cars as they made up trains to head toward the mainline. Here No. 137 has a cut of loads in August 1956, the very last month of steam at Peach Creek and on the C&O. (Gene Huddleston Photo, C&O Hist. Soc. Coll., Image No. COHS-1087)

This interesting photo was taken by the fireman (C. A. Coulter) of an 0-8-0 as K-4 No. 2788 arrived at Peach Creek in the early 1950s. A mine spur is seen at right. (C.A. Coulter Photo, TLC Collection)

Peach Creek Terminal & Shop

When C&O first arrived in Logan in 1904 the shops were at a place called Slabtown, a small settlement just north of the town. A short pit, a shed track with a shed for freight, a wye track, and a small yard with three tracks was installed soon after the building of the line. Later another 3-track yard was built farther to the north of this one and was used to assemble coal trains. It was lengthened and more tracks were added and became the empty yard in the Peach Creek complex.

In about 1916 the full scale Peach Creek shop and yard was established. The name of the location comes from a small cluster of homes at the mouth of the creek by that name. A new town was laid out under the name of West Logan, lying on the west bank of the Guyandot River. The facility consisted of a five-stall roundhouse, an 88-foot turntable (adequate for the 2-8-0s then in common use here), a small machine shop, water station, coaling station, and ready track area.

The modern 500-ton concrete coaling station was erected in 1921 and a 100-foot turntable was installed at the same time to accommodate the 2-6-6-2s which were being used in the district by that time. Car repair tracks were located at the north end of the yard, and often handled over 80 cars per day for running repairs.

In 1923 C&O undertook a complete rebuilding of the facilities at Peach Creek. At that time the WWI flood of traffic had ceased and about 115 mines were producing 900-1,000 cars of coal per day. [This would increase to about 1,800 cars by 1945.]

During the refurbishment and reconstruction the five-stall roundhouse was expanded to ten stalls, and all the older facilities were replaced, except the coaling station. The original five stalls of the roundhouse were 115-feet in length with 90-foot drop pits. The five new ones were 120 feet, with 90-foot pits. A large new power plant was built with Babcock & Wilcox 1500 hp boilers. A machine shop of 272x60 foot dimension was built which also housed the oil house and storehouse all in one building. A 60x75 foot blacksmith shop was located north of the machine shop. The new water station consisted of two steam pumps of 500-gallons-per-minute capacity, supplying a 100,000-gallon steel storage tank.

In the era from the 1916 up thorough the 1930s about 300 men worked at the shops and in the car department. In the early 1930s the number of shop workers was reduced by about 1/3rd as much of the work previously done here was transferred to Huntington. The amount of work needed was also reduced when the very old 2-8-0s were replaced by newer 2-6-6-2s.

H-4 2-6-6-2 No. 1329 sits near the Peach Creek terminal offices, with the coaling station to the right, in about 1950. (C.A. Coulter Photo, TLC Collection)

RSD-7s and RSD-12s were common power at Peach Creek in the early diesel years. Here two of each type of these large units await assignment at Peach Creek in May 1957. (Gene Huddleston photo, C&OHS Collection, Image No. COHS-1859)

August 1956 sees both steam and diesel mine shifter runs passing FD Cabin at Logan. H-6 No. 1506 has empties outbound as does Alco RSD-7 No. 6701, whose crew is about to pick up orders, and which has recently replaced a 2-6-6-2. Steam would be entirely gone by the end of this month, just days after these photos were taken. (Gene Huddleston Photos, C&O Hist. Soc. Coll., Image Nos. COHS-1571 and COHS-1561)

Amherst Coal Company's MacGregor plant at Slagle on the Rum Creek Subdivision is typical of the mines that populated the Logan fields in the early 1950s. (C&O Ry. Photo, C&O Hist. Soc. Coll., Image CSPR-10057.AA08)

This 1948 photo shows the largest tipple/cleaning plant on the C&O in this ear. It is the West Virginia Coal & Coke Company preparation plant on the Logan & Southern Subdivision at Omar. (C&O Ry. Photo, C&O Hist. Soc. Coll., Image CSPR-2107)

Doubleheaded H-6s, Nos. 1309 and 1300 are getting loads under way near Island Creek Mine No. 21 on the Trace Fork Subdivision in August 1952. The very steep grade on the extension to the Trace Fork line which reached as Island Creek Coal Co. mine in Mingo County necessitated two 2-6-6-2s, sometimes doubleheaded and sometimes one on each end. (Gene Huddleston Photo, C&O Hist. Soc. Coll., Image COHS-1296)

This chapter gives some general material about passenger trains operated by C&O through and in West Virginia.

Although passenger trains accounted for only a small part of C&O's traffic and thus its income, people have a large interest in them because they were the part of railroading that touched the daily lives of almost everyone, and are today remembered very fondly. Rather than try to treat the service C&O offered to West Virginia points as part of each line's history, it was thought better to consider the service as a more integrated whole in this separate chapter.

There were, of course, two aspects to C&O passenger service in West Virginia. The first deals with the through mainline trains that originated and terminated outside the state. The second is branch line and local trains that operated entirely within the confines of the state to offer service to local communities not touched by the mainline or mainline towns at which the more important through trains didn't stop.

We must first look at C&O's passenger service in its larger context. The road's mainline name trains operated mainly between Washington, D. C. and Cincinnati, Ohio. However, sections were also operated in Virginia between Newport News and Charlottesville (there joining with the Washington-Cincinnati consists), and in Kentucky between Louisville and Ashland (there joining the Washington-Cincinnati consists). In this arrangement, the trains were the largest in number of cars carried while passing through West Virginia, because cars from the Virginia and Kentucky sections were carried in addition to the Washington-Cincinnati ones.

These trains also carried through cars that operated beyond each of the end-points to carry sleeping car passengers to such points as Indianapolis, Chicago, St. Louis, and Cleveland in the west and New York in the east.

These trains provided the principal service on the main line. From 1932 until 1962 there were three sets of C&O name trains passing through West Virginia:

Nos. 1 & 2 - *The George Washington*

Nos. 3 & 6 - *The Fast Flying Virginian (FFV)*

Nos. 4 & 5 - *The Sportsman (*)*

Additional mainline local passenger trains consisted of:

Westbound:

No. 13 - Charlottesville to Huntington

No. 15 - Hinton to Cincinnati

Eastbound:

No. 14 - Huntington to Hinton

No. 16 - Cincinnati to Hinton

No. 104 - Huntington to Charlottesville

The following picture of C&O passenger service in West Virginia will reflect mid-year 1949. Many of the branch line trains were discontinued later that year. The reasons for the wholesale discontinuance were multi-fold. First, there had been a general decline in ridership with the coming of autos, buses, and better roads after about 1920 and this became precipitous after the end of the war. Second, C&O was not willing to subsidize losing operations after the severe financial problems that it suffered in 1949 attendant on a major coal strike and other issues. Thirdly, by this time the socio-economic make-up of towns and stations along the branch lines was changing, with the populations becoming less dependent on railroad service overall.

Although C&O trains connected major Eastern and Midwestern cities, a great deal of its traffic on the through trains was to and from stations in West Virginia rather than through traffic terminal-to-terminal.

Of particular note was the traffic generated by

(*) The *Sportsman* was the exception to the way that the mainline trains operated, in that it carried no Kentucky connecting train. Rather, some of its cars traveled between Ashland and Detroit via Columbus and Toledo. Specifically eastbound No. 4 was the Cincinnati to Washington section, No. 46 was the Detroit to Newport News section. Similarly, wesbound No. 5 was the Washington to Cincinnati section and No. 47 was the Newport News to Detroit section. In the late 1948 date that we will examine in this work, Nos. 5 and 47, the westbound Sportsman, were actually separated at Hinton westbound and operated through West Virginia from that point as separate trains, one section ultimately headed to Cincinnati and the other to Detroit. The eastbound counterparts, Nos. 4 and 46 joined at Ashland, Ky. and ran as a combined train through West Virginia, known on the railroad as Train 4/46. It was not until late 1949 that the separation of the westbound trains was made at Ashland again. This was part of a major rearrangement of service that brought it back to levels before WWII for mainline operations.

This is mainline local train No. 13 at Tuckahoe, just after it crossed over from Virginia into West Virginia on its westbound trek in 1948. It has 4-8-4 Greenbrier No. 612 for power and a consist of four express cars, a combination mail and express car with a 30-foot RPO section, a storage mail car, a coach, a sleeper and some other cars that aren't visible behind the bluff. The local trains sometimes carried sleeping cars that were being taken from one point to another before or after their use on through trains. (B. F. Cutler Photo, C&O Hist. Soc. Coll.)

the Greenbrier Hotel at White Sulphur Springs (as mentioned before in this book). In the later decades of service, most C&O mainline passenger service was operated so as to best serve this location and its traffic. This was both because the resort hotel was highly popular in the era and was not reachable by good roads or airports, but also because it had been a wholly owned subsidiary of C&O since 1910.

As an example, train service at **Hinton** a typical day in June 1949 would have been as follows:

Westbound:

No. 1 - *The George Washington* - lv. 1:45 am

No. 15 - Local - lv. 5:30 am (originates here)

No. 3 - *The FFV* - lv. 6:40 am

No. 13 - Local - lv. 1:20 pm

No. 47 - *The Sportsman* - lv. 8:00 pm

No. 5 - *The Sportsman* - lv. 8:25 pm

Eastbound:

No. 2 - *The George Washington* - lv. 12:55 am

No. 4 - *The Sportsman* - lv. 6:10 am

No. 104 - Local - lv. 9:15 am

No. 14 - Local - ar. 1:10 pm (terminated at Hinton)

No. 16 - Local - ar. 6:40 pm (terminated at Hinton)

No. 6 - *The FFV* - lv. 7:45 pm

As can be seen, the whole day was fairly well covered by available trains, giving passengers a choice of several different trains to desired locations east or west. All trains stopped at Hinton, of course, because it was a division point at which crews were changed and locomotives serviced or changed. In the steam era all passenger trains exchanged locomotives at Hinton. Coming from the east, heavier locomotives used over the mountains were taken off and lighter engines added for the trip west, and conversely eastbound.

In 1948, locomotives used between Clifton Forge and Hinton were usually of the 4-8-4 Greenbrier type on the through trains, with occasional 4-8-2 Mountain types also used. The local trains were handled by F-15, F-16, F-17 class Pacific (4-6-2) types, J-1 and J-2 Mountain (4-8-2) types, K-4 Kanawha (2-8-4) types, and occasionally a J-3 or J-3a Greenbrier (4-8-4). If lighter engines were used or the train was particularly heavy, two locomotives, double-headed, would be assigned. This was especially dependent on the mail and express business being handled on these trains, which was seasonally heavy at certain times of the year, especially before Christmas as people received packages. In addition to the regular local passenger trains, dedicated mail and express trains No. 103 and No. 104 were run, but were not shown in passenger timetables. However, in a postwar money saving move, local passenger No. 14 was combined with No. 104 (see Hinton schedule above), although No. 103 continued to operate exclusively for mail and express. This arrangement stopped in 1958 when Nos. 13 and 104 were discontinued. This eliminated the last local passenger trains on the C&O mainline in West Virginia.

Of the three sets of through trains, Nos. 1 and 2, *The George Washington*, had the fewest stops in West Virginia because these trains operated through the state at late night hours. No. 1 arrived White Sulphur at 12:38 am and Huntington at 4:52 am, while No. 2 arrived Huntington at 9:45 pm and White Sulphur at 1:55 am.

At White Sulphur Springs, travelers arriving at the resort from the eastern cities most frequently used No. 3 - The westbound *FFV*. It arrived at 5:30 am, but it dropped sleeping cars from New York that could be occupied until 8:30, thus the passengers could sleep until a normal hour before taking the hotel's limousine from the station to the grounds of the palatial resort just across the road. People using the service would have boarded the White Sulphur Springs sleeper at New York City at 6:25 pm the previous evening, allowing an overnight trip. C&O sleepers were handled between New York and Washington via the Pennsylvania Railroad.

Returning to the east, patrons at the Greenbrier could spend the day at the hotel and then board their sleeper on No. 6, the eastbound *FFV*, at 9:00 pm, with arrival in New York's Pennsylvania Station at 9:15 am the next morning, in time for a full day of work after a restful overnight trip.

Although *The George Washington* was the premier train on the C&O, its westbound arrival of 12:35 am and eastbound arrival at 1:50 am made it less desirable to Greenbrier patrons.

From the west, patrons headed for the Greenbrier most often traveled on the eastbound *Sportsman*, No. 4/46. In 1948 it was carrying a sleeper from Cleveland to White Sulphur Springs. Because of the arrival at 7:20 am, it was not dropped at White Sulphur, but after discharging passengers there, it was carried on through to the terminal at Clifton Forge. Another West Virginia-bound car came from Chicago via Toledo and terminated at Hinton. The exact reason for this particular car is unclear since it didn't serve the springs and the arrival time at Hinton was fairly early at 6:10 am, and even earlier at Huntington and Charleston.

A few miles west of the border was the important passenger facility at White Sulphur Springs. Here 4-8-2 No. 540 brings a westbound train through White Sulphur Tunnel, located just east of the station, in July 1947. Note the little boy holding his ears as the train roars by. (J. I. Kelly photo, C&O Hist. Soc. Coll.)

No. 5, the westbound *Sportsman* called at White Sulphur at 6:00 pm. Anyone wanting to use it to White Sulphur from New York would have to have left the city at 6:00 am that morning for a daytime trip. It was, however, more convenient for westbound traffic, and carried the returning sleepers to Chicago via Toledo, to Cleveland, and one to Detroit. It offered good overnight travel for people returning to the west from the Springs.

Sleeping cars originating at terminating at West Virginia points in mid-1948 were as follows:

Chicago via Toledo to Hinton (No. 47/5)

New York to Huntington (No. 3)

New York to White Sulphur Springs (No. 3)

Huntington to New York (No. 6)

Hinton to Richmond (No. 6)

White Sulphur Springs to New York (No. 6)

Reproduced on the back endsheets are extracts from the June 28, 1948 C&O public timetable which show branch line passenger trains in operation at that date. The longest runs of any of the West Virginia branch passenger trains were between Huntington and Logan on the Logan Branch, 100 miles, and on the Greenbrier Branch, operating between Ronceverte and Durbin, 96 miles. The shortest was between Quinnimont and Hemlock Hollow, on the Laurel Creek Branch, which was only 5 miles, and took a bit less than 30 minutes to make a one-way trip.

On numerous lines the same set of equipment was used on many subdivisions, going back and forth up the various short coal branches. A single locomotive and consist of a couple of cars could change train numbers as it went from one branch line run to the next and might represent as many as 6 or 8 different trains in the timetables.

In 1930 C&O acquired gas-electric motor cars for use in secondary service from the Brill Company. By the late 1940s and 1950s several of these were regularly used on the trains operating between Huntington and Logan on the Logan Subdivision, on the Coal River trains, and on the Greenbrier Branch. In most cases the longer runs also required that the motor car carry a "trailer," usually specially constructed versions of standard combines or coaches whose lighter weight allowed the motor car to pull them, although a heavyweight combination car of some type could be carried if the grades were low. These would provide additional passenger space, but more importantly additional mail and express space. In fact it was the mail and express business that was vitally important in keeping passenger trains in the black or cutting down on losses.

Mountain type (4-8-2) No. 541 is stopped at the White Sulphur Springs platform, with its elegant white canopy, with what is probably No. 5, the westbound Sportsman, in about 1943. The full 60-foot Railway Post Office behind the tender indicates that it is not a local train, as these usually carried the mail & express cars with the shorter 30-foot RPO space. (C&O Ry. Photo, C&O Hist. Soc. Coll.)

Branch line runs not covered by the gas-electrics usually had a small steam locomotive and one or two cars. The locomotives used included old A-16 4-4-2 Atlantic types, some F-15 light Pacific types, and 2-8-0 Consolidations equipped for passenger service.

Dieselization came to most C&O passenger trains in late 1951 and early 1952 when the road acquired EMD E8 model passenger units. These were not used for branch line runs, but only on the mainline through trains in West Virginia. Huntington was chosen as the central location for routine inspection and running repairs for these locomotives and a special engine house and attendant facilities were erected just west of the main shop complex. The E8s were given a special cycle of activity whereby they were used on numerous trains across the C&O system, but ended their run at Huntington after a 12-day cycle, where they were inspected, given necessary repairs and servicing and then put back in service.

By 1952, when the E8s dieselized C&O's mainline trains, the few remaining branch line runs were being handled mainly by gas-electric motor cars. Some of these had been converted, by this time, to diesel power since the old gasoline prime movers were worn out and dangerous.

In 1949 C&O was suffering though one of the most protected coal mine strikes in its history, and as a result its financial position, normally the bluest of the blue chips, was threatened. This caused management to take steps to address the "passenger problem." The passenger problem became a byword in the railroad operating community starting in the 1920s when buses, autos, and better highways began to cause a diminution of the number of passengers, especially those patronizing branch line and local passenger trains. This was exacerbated by the years of the 1930s depression, and was only reversed by the coming of the ultra-modern streamliners on many railroads and ultimately by World War II and the huge glut of passengers that occurred during America's participation in that conflict. In 1943 C&O was so overcome with passenger business that it instituted second sections of most of its mainline name trains. This carried on after the war until the troops were home and things settled down. By the 1948-era that we are examining in this book, the second sections had been discontinued, and overall service was about back to the pre-war pattern. C&O had not been involved in the pre-war streamliner craze in the mid-late 1930s, so it was burdened with a fleet of older heavyweight passenger cars.

During the war, plans were made to re-equip all C&O trains after the war, but because of backlogs and problems with the commercial passenger car builders, C&O's order for cars didn't arrive until 1950. It was not until mid-1950 the C&O could boast of having good, modern, state-of-the-art lightweight streamlined passenger cars, and even at that its new equipment consisted only of coaches and sleepers. Old heavyweight diners were modernized and continued to be used. All the old mail, baggage, and express

No. 104, the eastbound local and mail/express train serving West Virginia pauses at White Sulphur on April 26, 1948, with doubleheaded 4-8-2 and 4-8-4 and a long string of mail and express cars as well as a coach or two. When double heading, the lighter locomotive was in the lead. (John Krause, TLC Collection)

car fleet (built in the 1911-1930 era) was continued in use with new colors to match the new lightweight cars and the E8 diesels that pulled the trains.

In the two decades from 1950 until the end of C&O passenger service on Amtrak Day May 1, 1971, West Virginia continued to be probably the most important source of traffic for C&O mainline trains. By 1958 mainline locals were gone and all branch line service in the state had been discontinued, so from that date forward the state was served by the three sets of name trains coursing over the mainline. This changed in late October 1962 when Trains 5 and 6 were discontinued, leaving only Nos. 1 & 2, *The George Washington*; No. 3 the eastbound *FFV*, and No. 4 the westbound *Sportsman*. Nos. 3 and 4 were discontinued May 12, 1968, leaving only Nos. 1 and 2, which traversed West Virginia in the late night hours.

Over the 20+ years from 1950 to 1971 passenger traffic on C&O had declined to only a tiny fraction of its former size, the same as had occurred nationwide because of the rise of highways, autos, and airlines. It is interesting to note that Nos. 3 and 4 probably lasted as long as they did because of their good West Virginia traffic.

Branch line Passenger Trains as of June 28, 1948:

Greenbrier SD - Ronceverte-Durbin

Nos. 142/143 - 19 stations served - 96 miles

Piney Creek SD - Quinnimont - Beckley - Lester

Nos. 155/156 [Quinnimont-Lester]- 11 stations served - 29 miles

Nos. 157/158 [Quinnimont-Mabscott]- 7 stations served - 19 miles

Laurel Creek SD - Quinnimont - Hemlock Hollow

Nos. 153/154- 4 stations served - 5 miles
(this train shared equipment with trains 155/156 and 157/158 on the Piney Creek Branch.)

Paint Creek SD - Pratt - Kingston

Nos. 170/171- 8 stations served - 22 miles

Cabin Creek SD - Cabin Creek to several terminals -

Nos. 113/114- 21 stations served -
(This is a region where the same trains served numerous branches.)

Coal River SD - St. Albans - Sharples

Nos. 214/215-15 stations served

Big Coal SD - St. Albans - Whitesville - Blue Pennant

Nos. 218/219-10 stations served
(These trains also served several branches under the same numbers.)

Logan SD - Huntington - Lorado:

Nos. 50/51- 17 stations served -100 miles

Logan SD- Man - West Gilbert

Nos. 54/55 - 5 stations served

See the full timetables reprinted on the back endsheets.

Behind the White Sulphur station were several "park tracks" where Pullmans could be set out for passengers to disembark at a later time or for them to board for later pickup. Here a set of E8s is arranging a "Resort Special" by picking up four Pennsylvania Railroad sleepers from one of the park tracks May 19, 1965. (James EuDaly Photo)

The neat colonial revival White Sulphur station is at center and the mainline with its platform and canopy is at right. Several sleepers are parked on the track to the rear of the station, while the additional park tracks are seen in the background. (Frank Schaeffer Photo, TLC Collection)

Train No. 4, The eastbound Sportsman pauses at Ronceverte station on a foggy morning in October 1956 with a long consist including a full RPO just behind the locomotives. (C&O Ry. Photo, C&O Hist. Soc. Coll., Image No. CSPR-10393.127)

In 1956, the single motor car that made up the Greenbrier Branch local passenger train is loading mail before leaving Ronceverte station for its 4 mile run over the mainline to Whitcomb, where it will make its 92 mile run up the Greenbrier Branch to Durbin and return. (C&O Ry. Photo, C&O Hist. Soc. Coll., Image No. CSPR-3891)

Gas-Electric car No. 9055 with trailer combine car No. 550 is shown at the Durbin depot June 11, 1953, at the end of its run up the Greenbrier Branch. This car was still in the pre-1950 green paint scheme. It will soon make the trip back to Ronceverte after connecting with the Western Maryland train that served Durbin from Elkins, W. Va. (Stan Kister photo, C&O Hist. Soc. Coll.)

Typical of mainline passenger trains of the diesel era from 1952 to about 1967, No. 3, the westbound FFV is doing station work at Alderson at about 7:00 am on a summer morning in 1967. The three E8 diesels were used for power between Charlottesville and Ashland, where the trains were the heaviest. (T. W. Dixon, Jr. Photo)

Late in its life in 1967, but not much changed from the way it was in 1953, No. 4, The Sportsman, is roaring by the station at Ft. Spring, just out of Mann's Tunnel and about to enter Ft. Spring Tunnel. (T. W. Dixon, Jr. Photo)

Similar in consist to No. 3, No. 4, The Sportsman, pauses at Alderson with its three E8s and 16 cars on a day in 1967. (T. W. Dixon, Jr. Photo)

In 1947 local No. 13, exiting Little Bend Tunnel westbound with 4-8-2 No. 541 for power and a mail & express car with the 30-foot RPO behind it. (Gene Huddleston Photo, TLC Collection)

In July 1948 J-3 class 4-8-4 Greenbrier No. 600 powers No. 4, The Sportsman, out of Hinton with a heavy consist including a deadhead coach behind the engine. Greenbriers were standard power for most trains on the Alleghany Subdivision at this time. (Gene Huddleston Photo, TLC Collection)

F-19 Pacific type No. 491 has just brought local No. 8 into Hinton in June 1947. At that time this train was operating through West Virginia between Ashland, Ky. and Hinton. It was gone by 1948. (Gene Huddleston photo, C&O Hist. Soc. Coll., Image No. COHS-1173)

This is the Piney Creek Branch passenger train which normally took passengers from Beckley to meet C&O mainline trains at Prince, but here in June 1947 is swollen with a large excursion group of school children probably on their way for a trip to Washington, requiring the assignment of F-17 Pacific No. 475, which was normally to be found on the mainline trains. The normal train on this line would have 3-4 cars and was important in getting people from the great coal city of Beckley to the C&O mainline, but was discontinued in 1949. (Robert G. Lewis Photo, TLC Collection)

More typical of a branch line passenger run is this train at Glen Jean, W.Va. on July 14, 1948, pulled by G-7 2-8-0 No. 876. The coach is an old wooden side – steel underfame car dating back to the early part of the century, and the express/mail combine fills out the short train. (Courtesy of Bob's Photos)

Somewhere deep in the New River Gorge is this passenger train, powered by K-4 2729 in 1947. Normally considered a freight locomotive, all of the 90 K-4 class 2-8-4s were equipped for passenger service and frequently used on passenger trains. (C&O Railway photo, C&OHS Collection, Image No. CSPR-1036)

Deep in the New River gorge at Hawks Nest, local No. 13, with heavy Pacific type No. 483 crosses the bridge to the south side of the New River, in 1947. Mainline locals still had a good deal of business in this region, not only in passengers but also in mail and express. (C&O Ry. Photo, C&O Hist. Soc. Coll., Image No. CSPR-1008)

Right and Below: In September 1959, three E8s lead No. 3, The FFV, into Cotton Hill with a heavy consist of mail and express cars followed by lightweight coaches. No. 3 was heavily trafficked in West Virginia because of its morning schedule west of Hinton. The station at Cotton Hill served the town of Fayetteville, a few miles distant. (C&O Ry. Photo, C&O Hist. Soc. Coll., Image Nos. 4551, 4538)

West Virginia's capital city of Charleston always generated considerable passenger traffic for C&O. The large C&O station (seen in the background here) was on the south side of the river, away from the main part of the city but was accessed by the bridge that is visible above the locomotive. Here No. 3, the FFV, is pausing westbound with Hudson type (4-6-4) No. 300 for power. The 4-6-4s were common power for the name trains west of Hinton. (A. A. Thieme photo, TLC Collection)

E8 No. 4916 is at the head of No. 3 working the station at St. Albans in 1961. (TLC Collection)

On July 2, 1947 ancient 4-4-2 Atlantic type No. 277 has the two-car Coal River branch passenger train on the mainline at St. Albans. One of the longest-lived C&O branch runs, it used gas-electric motor cars as well as steam power in the late 1940s and into the 1950s. (TLC Collection)

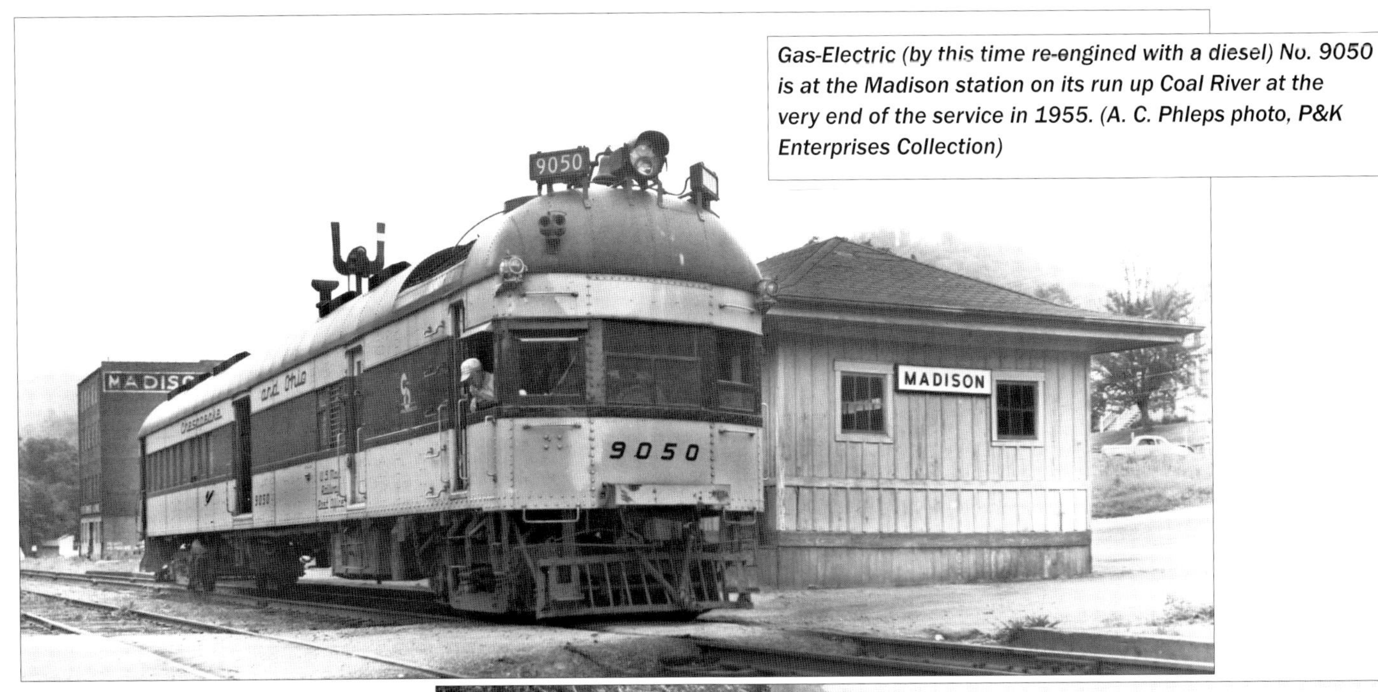

Gas-Electric (by this time re-engined with a diesel) No. 9050 is at the Madison station on its run up Coal River at the very end of the service in 1955. (A. C. Phleps photo, P&K Enterprises Collection)

This July 14, 1948 photo shows the Big Coal motor-train with No. 9051 in the old green paint scheme at Whitesville, near Seng Creek Junction, with the pick-up truck backing up to receive mail from the RPO section. (C. A. Brown Photo, TLC Collection)

Before the early 1950s, the passenger local between Huntington and Logan, Nos. 50/51 was usually assigned a light F-15 class 4-6-2 as seen her in June 1950. No. 441 with its four-car consist is parked next to the impressive two-story brick station at Logan with its long covered platform. (Gene Huddleston Photo, C&O Hist. Soc. Coll. Image No. COHS-1047)

A later photo of the Logan Branch passenger train shows it downgraded to a gas-electric car with a trailing mail and express car with a 30-foot RPO section. It is obvious that mail and express business was the driving force in keeping the train on. This photo was taken in April 1957 shortly before the train was finally discontinued. (Gene Huddleston Photo, C&O Hist. Soc. Coll., Image No. COHS-1072)

In an unusual move, big Hudson type No. 300 is powering the three-car local No. 16 crossing the Mud River bridge at Barboursville in April 1951. The occasion was that the Hudson had just been shopped at Huntington and was being broken in on the local before going on to the big trains. No. 16 was an all-West Virginia local, running from Huntington to Hinton. (Gene Huddleston Photo, C&O Hist. Soc. Coll., Image No,. COHS-1162)

A superb night photo taken in the Huntington yard shows No. 1, The George Washington, resplendent with its new E8 diesels, headed out into the night in December 1952. (C&O Ry. Photo, C&O Hist. Soc. Coll., Image No. 2808)

F-17 Class 4-6-2 No. 472 pauses with a westbound train as the large C&O Huntington depot/office building looms in the background in about 1948. (TLC Collection)

No. 3 is shown with its long 16-18 car consist is making the station stop at Huntington in 1963. (Larry Fellure photo)

C&O's official photographer snapped No. 3 arriving at the Huntington station in about 1953, soon after the trains had been dieselized. The station is now used by CSX as an office building minus the platform shed, while Amtrak now uses a small station on the other side of the yard. (C&O Ry. Photo, C&O Hist. Soc. Coll., Image No. 3630)

The last station stop for westbound trains in West Virginia was the two-level Kenova Union Station which served C&O and B&O (Ohio River Division locals) on the bottom and N&W on the top level. F-15 Pacific No. 440 is power for the four-car local No. 7 in this September 1947 photo. No. 7 operated between Hinton and Cincinnati and was discontinued shortly after this photo was taken. (Gene Huddleston Photo, C&O Hist. Soc. Coll., Image No. COHS-1609)

Washington • Norfolk • Richmond Cincinnati • Detroit • Louisville

TABLE 13

Miles	Eastern Time	The Sportsman 47 Daily	The Sportsman 5/47 Daily	The George Washington 1/41 Daily	The F. F. V. 3/43 Daily	15 Ex. Sun.	
290	Lv Covington	5.45	5.45	12.03	4.55		10.30
307	" Alleghany, Va.						f 11.00
312	" **White Sulphur Springs, W. Va.**	6.30	6.30	12.38	5.30		11.15
323	" Ronceverte Lewisburg	6.55	6.55		5.45		11.45
329	" Fort Spring						11.56
336	" Alderson	7.15	7.15		6.03		12.15
344	" Pence Springs						f 12.27
347	Lv Talcott						12.35
357	Ar **Hinton**	7.50	7.50	1.40	6.35	AM	1.00
357	Lv **Hinton**	8.00	8.25	1.45	6.40	5.30	1.20
370	" Meadow Creek		f 8.47		6.57	5.55	1.48
379	" Quinnimont		f 9.02			6.27	2.16
380	" **Prince (Beckley)**	8.29	9.05		7.13	6.32	2.21
383	" McKendree		f 9.10			f 6.38	f 2.27
391	" **Thurmond** Mt. Hope-Oak Hill	8.46	9.36	C 2.28	7.30	7.02	2.59
398	" Sewell		f 9.50			7.20	3.19
405	" Fayette		f 10.02			7.34	3.35
409	" Hawk's Nest		f			f	3.40
411	" **Cotton Hill** Fayetteville	C 9.15	f 10.14		8.00	7.49	3.51
415	" Gauley					7.57	4.01
421	" Deepwater		f 10.28			8.14	4.16
428	" Montgomery	9.40	10.45		8.25	8.37	4.33
430	" Handley		f 10.50			8.45	4.41
432	" Pratt		f			8.50	4.45
438	" Cabin Creek Jct		f 11.01		C 8.40	9.08	5.00
454	" **Charleston**	10.20	11.40	3.54	9.00	9.42	5.56
457	" So. Charleston		f			f 9.46	f 5.58
466	" St. Albans		12.11		9.18	10.04	6.30
479	" Hurricane		f 12.29			10.29	6.54
486	" Milton		f 12.37			10.40	7.06
495	Lv Barboursville		f 12.45			10.54	f 7.24
504	Ar **Huntington**	11.17	1.00	4.49	10.05	11.07	7.45
504	Lv **Huntington**	11.32	1.45	4.54	10.15	1.40	PM
511	" Kenova, W. Va.		[illegible]		10.29	[illegible]	
514	Lv Catlettsburg, Ky.		f 2.18		10.35	2.01	
520	Ar **Ashland, Ky.** East. Time	11.57	2.30	5.20	10.45	2.12	

Cincinnati • Detroit • Louisville Washington • Richmond • Norfolk

TABLE 14

Miles	Eastern Time	The F. F. V. 6 Daily	The George Washington 2/42 Daily	The Sportsman 4 / 4/46 Daily	104 Daily	16 Ex. Sun.	14 Daily
146	Lv **Ashland, Ky.** East. Time	3.20	9.05	E 1.55		12.21	
152	" Catlettsburg, Ky.	3.31				12.33	
154	" Kenova, W. Va.	3.41				12.44	
162	Ar **Huntington, W. Va.**	3.55	9.30	2.20	AM	1.00	AM
162	Lv **Huntington, W. Va.**	4.05	9.35	2.30	3.35	1.20	7.00
172	Ar Barboursville					1.38	f 7.15
180	" Milton					1.52	7.33
187	" Hurricane					2.03	7.47
201	" St. Albans	4.51			4.35	2.28	8.15
209	" So. Charleston					2.42	f 8.29
213	" **Charleston**	5.15	10.35	3.35	5.10	2.56	8.45
228	" Cabin Creek, Jct.					3.25	9.24
234	" Pratt					3.44	9.51
236	" Handley					3.49	9.56
239	" Montgomery	5.50	11.12	C 4.13	6.21	3.54	10.03
245	" Deepwater					f 4.07	10.18
251	" Gauley					f 4.16	10.32
255	" **Cotton Hill** Fayetteville	6.14			6.51	4.25	10.43
261	" South Fayette					4.37	11.00
268	" Sewell					4.59	11.22
275	" **Thurmond** Mt. Hope-Oak Hill	6.45	12.01	C 5.06	7.33	5.21	11.42
283	" McKendree					f 5.39	f 12.01
286	" **Prince (Beckley)**	7.01		5.23	f 7.50	5.47	12.10
287	" Quinnimont				8.12	5.58	12.21
297	" Meadow Creek				8.42	6.15	12.43
309	Ar **Hinton**	7.35	12.45	6.00	9.05	6.40	1.10
309	Lv **Hinton, W. Va.**	7.45	12.55	6.10	9.15	PM	PM
319	" Talcott				9.20		
323	" Pence Springs				9.36		
330	" Alderson	8.14		6.38	9.55		
337	" Fort Spring			C	10.03		
343	" Ronceverte Lewisburg	8.38		7.00	10.20		
354	" **White Sulphur Springs, W. Va.**	9.00	1.50	7.20	10.40		
359	" Alleghany, Va.				f 10.50		
376	Ar Covington	9.32		7.52	11.25		

TABLE 23

Quinnimont • Beckley • Lester

Miles	Eastern Time	155 Daily	157 Ex. Sun.
		AM	PM
0	Lv **Quinnimont, W. Va.**	7.35	2.45
1	" Prince	A 7.40	2.50
3	" McCreary	f 7.46	f 2.55
7	" Stanaford	f 7.57	f 3.07
15	" Raleigh	8.25	3.31
17	Ar **Beckley Jct.**	8.36	3.40
19	Ar Beckley	8.43	3.45
19	Lv Beckley	9.00	
17	Lv **Beckley Jct.**	9.06	4.16
18	" Mabscott	9.09	4.18
23	" Admiralty	f 9.23	
27	" Surveyor	9.38	
29	Ar **Lester, W. Va.**	9.45	

Eastern Time	156 Daily	15[cut off] Ex. [cut off]
	AM	P[cut off]
Lv **Lester, W. Va.**	9.55	
" Surveyor	10.03	
" Admiralty	f 10.19	
" Mabscott	10.35	4.[cut off]
Ar **Beckley Jct.**	10.38	4.[cut off]
Ar Beckley	10.44	
Lv Beckley	10.49	
Lv **Beckley Jct.**	10.55	4.[cut off]
" Raleigh	11.05	4.[cut off]
" Stanaford	f 11.26	f 4.[cut off]
" McCreary	f 11.38	f 5.[cut off]
" Prince	11.50	5.[cut off]
Ar **Quinnimont, W. Va.**	11.55	5.[cut off]

TABLE 24

Quinnimont • Hemlock Hollow

Miles	Eastern Time	154 Daily
		PM
0	Lv **Quinnimont, W. Va.**	12.25
4	" Laurel	f12.42
5	" Brownwood	f12.50
5	Ar **Hemlock Hollow, W. Va.**	12.52

Eastern Time	15[cut off] Da[cut off]
	P[cut off]
Lv **Hemlock Hollow, W. Va.**	12.[cut off]
" Brownwood	f12.[cut off]
" Laurel	f 1.[cut off]
Ar **Quinnimont, W. Va.**	1.[cut off]

TABLE 26

Ronceverte Durbin

Miles	Eastern Time	142 Ex. Sun. Motor
		AM
......	Lv **Ronceverte, W. Va.**	9.05
0	" Whitcomb	f 9.10
2	" North Caldwell	9.14
9	" Loopemount	f 9.27
11	" Kelster	f 9.32
14	" Anthony	f 9.42
22	" Spring Creek	9.58
25	" Renick	10.08
38	" Beard	f 10.40
39	" Denmar	f 10.42
46	" Seebert	10.58
52	" Buckeye	f 11.10
56	" Marlinton	11.23
62	" Clawson	f 11.38
71	" Clover Lick	f 11.59
77	" Sitlington	f12.12
81	" Cass	12.23
88	" Hosterman	f12.42
96	Ar **Durbin, W. Va.**	1.15

Eastern Time	143 Ex. Sun. Motor
	PM
Lv **Durbin, W. Va.**	1.40
" Hosterman	f 1.53
" Cass	2.10
" Sitlington	f 2.27
" Clover Lick	2.30
" Clawson	f 2.48
" Marlinton	3.03
" Buckeye	f 3.18
" Seebert	3.27
" Denmar	f 3.40
" Beard	f 3.42
" Renick	4.10
" Spring Creek	f 4.16
" Anthony	f 4.32
" Keister	f 4.43
" Loopemount	f 4.47
" North Caldwell	f 4.56
" Whitcomb	f 5.00
Ar **Ronceverte, W. Va.**	5.15

REFERENCE NOTES

A—Held maximum of 30 minutes for train No. 43, 3 and 15 when passengers reported.

f—Stops on signal to receive or discharge passengers.